PECULIAR EDITIONS

Peculiar Pages presents new editions of vital Mormon texts alongside overdue critical analysis. These carefully edited volumes bring deserving artistic works back to public attention.

FOR MORE INFORMATION, CONTACT
PECULIAREDITIONS@PECULIARPAGES.COM.

SERIES EDITOR
ERIC W JEPSON

VOLUME EDITOR
Dorian
ERIC W JEPSON

DORIAN

NEPHI ANDERSON

A PECULIAR EDITION WITH ANNOTATED TEXT & SCHOLARSHIP

EDITED BY

ERIC W JEPSON

2015

DORIAN: A Peculiar Edition with Annotated Text & Scholarship
Nephi Anderson, 1921
Criticism and annotations © 2015
>   Mason Allred
>   Jacob Bender
>   Scott Hales
>   Blair Dee Hodges
>   Eric W Jepson
>   Sarah C. Reed
>   A. Arwen Taylor

ISBN: 978-0-9911892-2-9 (hardcover)
ISBN: 978-0-9911892-3-6 (paperback)
ISBN: 978-0-9911892-4-3 (ebook, all formats)
Library of Congress Control Number: 2014904517

Editor: Eric W Jepson
Footnotes: Tyler Gardner
Hand-letterer (cover): Billy Ola Hutchinson
Cover design: Lynsey Jepson
Copyediting, book design, digitization: Elizabeth Beeton

Published By:
PECULIAR PAGES
115 Ramona Avenue
El Cerrito, CA 94530
PeculiarPages.com

in collaboration with

B10 Mediaworx
PO Box 1233
Liberty, MO 64069-1233
b10mediaworx.com

Dedicated to the memory of

RICHARD CRACROFT

(1936 – 2012)

as great an advocate for Mormon literature as anyone this last hundred years and the first non-contemporary Anderson scholar to recognize his place in our literary pantheon, with gratitude for his willingness to help this project even in the waning months of his life.

CONTENTS

ANDERSON CAPS HIS LITERARY career with *Dorian* (1921), probably his best, and certainly his boldest novel ... The novel is real: in the foreground are serious human dilemmas and problems ... [which] suggest a maturity and wisdom in Anderson's final novel which makes it the success it generally is. Dorian recalls Thomas Hardy's *Tess of the D'Urbervilles* ... Carlia is real: she pouts, frets, grows angry, despairs. Dorian is real: he becomes angry, fights, swears, and irritates the reader in his short-sightedness regarding Carlia's plight. All this tempers Dorian's superior intellectual powers and gentles him to believability. His triumph comes in his struggle to harmonize his knowledge of science and Mormonism and in his forgiving relationship with Carlia.

Dorian ... underscores a maturity not only in Anderson, but in his readers—or at least in Anderson's respect for his readers—and fosters hope for a more sophisticated LDS Home Literature ...

His accomplishments should be instructive to modern Mormon writers ... He attempted to deal with [Mormon] themes in a way which is at once artistic and orthodox ... Unable to separate Mormonism out from the fibers of his art, Nephi Anderson tried very hard to turn his positive Mormon experience into significant art ... [and] lessons to be learned by modern Mormon readers, critics, and a whole new generation of writers.

—Richard H. Cracroft,
1985, from his essay
"Nephi, Seer of Modern Times: The Home
Literature Novels of Nephi Anderson,"
published in *BYU Studies*

EDITOR'S NOTE

IN HIS PRIME, NO ONE was more respected in Mormon letters than Nephi Anderson. A large fanship born and carried along the massive popularity of his flawed but astonishingly ambitious first novel *Added Upon* —and sustained by a slew of articles, stories, poetry, and novels, some of which were emphatically excellent—mourned his too-young passing at age 57. Following his death, the flaws of his best-remembered and most-read work gradually overwhelmed his reputation—this, simultaneous to Mormon culture becoming both more fully assimilated into mainstream America and becoming grossly leery of anything failing to sugarcoat the Mormon experience. And so the Home Literature whose banner Anderson had so long waved collapsed into a perception of pabulum, while more aesthetically centered writers such as Virginia Sorensen and Maurine Whipple felt rejected by their own people. *Added Upon* remained widely read and celebrated for decades while Anderson's more nuanced works such as *A Daughter of the North*, *Piney Ridge Cottage*, or, especially, *Dorian*, fell out of print, disappeared, were forgotten.

The growth Anderson had catalyzed in himself as a writer and within the culture more broadly seemed lost for decades, each new generation of fictionists feeling the need to reinvent what he had already begun. And to be sure—great work has come from Mormon writers and artists, but often without an understanding of the man who first treated the genre with seriousness and care.

Today is an era in which Mormon Studies programs are becoming established on university campuses across Europe and the United States. To date, their focus has been primarily historical and sociological, but recognition of Mormon literature as a valid and worthy topic of consideration is arriving. But, like any minority literature, appreciation is beginning small and within the community it was meant to serve.

Upon Anderson's death, the editor of the magazine that had carried much of his work, wrote in an obituary that Anderson was "a gifted writer of fiction … [u]nassuming, useful, a diligent worker, faithful, and true to the principles of the gospel, he passed away, a genuine Latter-day Saint." This description is still true, and a reasonable position for his people—and their observers—to begin their reassessment.

Thus, a fresh consideration of the grandfather of Mormon literature—and his best work, 1921's *Dorian*—seems the correct choice for this inaugural volume of Peculiar Editions. Reprinting this quasi-lost novel alongside serious critical consideration gives Anderson—and by association—Mormon literature the respect it deserves and has so often been denied.

Anderson's oeuvre is in the midst of a reappraisal and I am pleased to take my stand beside him—and to learn from him—and to declare that *Dorian* is worthy of your careful consideration. Read it. Write about it. Remember it.

Then let's go forth and do as he did.

Let's declare with him as readers, scholars, critics, and writers, "What a field is here for the pen of the novelist!"

—Eric W Jepson
El Cerrito, California
November 20, 2013

NOTE ON THE TEXT

THIS PECULIAR EDITION of *Dorian* matches the original 1921 publication, including errata, as accomplished through the careful eyes of Adam Lang, Austin Wansick, Arian Gashi, and Julia Mason.

Original page numbers are noted marginally for consistency of citation. When a page began midsentence, the page number appears on that line. (The original page numbers are cited by the critical essays and interpretations included in this volume.)

Scans of Nephi Anderson's original manuscript and typescript of *Dorian* are available for comparison at *dorian.peculiarpages.com* through the researches of Scott Hales and Blair Dee Hodges.

DORIAN

NEPHI ANDERSON

*The keys of the holy priesthood unlock the door of knowledge
and let you look into the palace of truth.*

BRIGHAM YOUNG

I.

DORIAN TRENT WAS GOING to town to buy himself a ³ pair of shoes. He had some other errands to perform for himself and his mother, but the reason for his going to town was the imperative need of shoes. It was Friday afternoon. The coming Sunday he must appear decently shod, so his mother had told him, at the same time hinting at some other than the Sunday reason. He now had the money, three big, jingling silver dollars in his pocket.

Dorian whistled cheerfully as he trudged along the road. It was a scant three miles to town, and he would rather walk that short distance than to be bothered with a horse. When he took Old Nig, he had to keep to the main-traveled road straight into town, then tie him to a post—and worry about him all the time; but afoot and alone, he could move along as easily as he pleased, linger on the canal bank or cut cross-lots through the fields to the river, cross it on the footbridge, then go on to town by the lower meadows.

The road was dusty that afternoon, and the sun was hot. It would ⁴ be cooler under the willows by the river. At Cottonwood Corners, Dorian left the road and took the cut-off path. The river sparkled cool and clear under the overhanging willows. He saw a good-sized trout playing in the pool, but as he had no fishing tackle with him, the boy could only watch the fish in its graceful gliding in and out of sunshine and shadow. A robin overhead was making a noisy demonstration as if in alarm about a nest. Dorian sat on the bank to look and listen for a few moments, then he got up again.

Crossing the river, he took the cool foot-path under the willows. He cut down one of the smoothest, sappiest branches with which to make whistles. Dorian was a great maker of whistles, which he freely gave away to the smaller boys and girls whom he met. Just as it is more fun to catch fish than to eat them, so Dorian found more pleasure in giving away his whistles than to stuff them in his own pockets. However, that afternoon, he had to hurry on to town, so he caught no fish, and made only one whistle which he found no opportunity to give away. In the city, he attended to his mother's errands first. He purchased the few notions which the store in his home town of Greenstreet did not have, checking each item off on a slip of paper with a stub of a pencil. Then, there were his shoes.

5   Should he get lace or button, black or tan? Were there any bargains in shoes that afternoon? He would look about to see. He found nothing in the way of footwear on Main street which appealed to him. He lingered at the window of the book store, looking with envious eyes at the display of new books. He was well known by the bookseller, for he was a frequent visitor, and, once in a while, he made a purchase; however, to day he must not spend too much time "browsing" among books. He would, however, just slip around to Twenty-fifth street and take a look at the secondhand store there. Not to buy shoes, of course, but sometimes there were other interesting things there, especially books.

Ah, look here! Spread out on a table on the sidewalk in front of this second-hand store was a lot of books, a hundred or more—books of all kind—school books, history, fiction, all of them in good condition, some only a little shopworn, others just like new. Dorian Trent eagerly looked them over. Here were books he had read about, but had not read—and the prices! Dickens' "David Copperfield", "Tale of Two Cities", "Dombey and Son", large well-printed books, only a little shopworn, for thirty-five cents; Thackeray's "Vanity

Fair", twenty-five cents; books by Mrs. Humphrey Ward and Margaret Deland; "Robinson Crusoe", a big book with fine pictures. Dorian had, of course, read "Robinson Crusoe" but he had always wanted to own a copy. Ah, what's this? Prescott's "Conquest of Peru", two volumes, new, fifty cents each! Dorian turned the leaves. A man stepped up and also began handling the books. Yes, here were bargains, surely. He stacked a number together as if he desired to secure them. Dorian becoming fearful, slipped the other volume of the Conquest under his arm and made as if to gather a number of other books under his protection. He must have some of these before they were all taken by others. The salesman now came up to him and asked:

"Find something you want?"

"O, yes, a lot of things I like" replied Dorian.

"They're bargains."

Dorian needed not to be told that.

"They're going fast, too."

"Yes, I suppose so."

His heart fell as he said it, for he realized that he had no money to buy books. He had come to town to buy shoes, which he badly needed. He glanced down at his old shoes. They were nearly falling to pieces, but they might last a little longer. If he bought the "Conquest of Peru" he would still have two dollars left. Could he buy a pair of shoes for that amount? Very likely but not the kind his mother had told him to get, the kind that were not too heavy or "stogy" looking, but would be "nice" for Sundays. He held tightly on to the two books, while Dickens and Thackeray were still protectingly within his reach. What could he do?

Down there in Peru there had been a wonderful people whom Pizarro, the bad, bold Spaniard had conquered and abused. Dorian knew about it all vaguely as a dim fairy tale; and here was the whole story, beautifully and minutely told. He must have these books. This bargain might never come again to him. But what would his mother say? She herself had added the last half dollar to his amount to make sure that he could get the nicer kind.

"Well, sir, how many of these will you have?" asked the salesman.

"I'll—I'll take these two, anyway" —meaning Prescott's Conquest— "and let me see", he looked hungrily over the titles— "And this one 'David Copperfield'." It was hard to select from so many tempting ones. Here was one he had missed: "Ben Hur"—, a fine new copy in blue and gold. He had read the Chariot Race, and if the whole story was as interesting as that, he must have it. He handed the volume to the salesman. Then his hand touched lovingly a number of other books, but he resisted the temptation, and said: "That's all—this time."

The clerk wrapped the purchase in a newspaper and handed the package to Dorian who paid for them with his two silver dollars, receiving some small silver in change. Then, with his package under his arm, the boy walked on down the street.

Well, what now? He was a little afraid of what he had done. How could he face his mother? How could he go home without shoes? Books might be useful for the head, but they would not clothe the feet. He jingled the coins in his pocket as he walked on down to the end of the business section of the city. He could not buy any kind of shoes to fit his big feet for a dollar and twenty cents. There was nothing more to do but to go home, and "face the music", so he walked on in a sort of fearsome elation. At a corner he discovered a new candy store. Next to books, Dorian liked candy. He might as well buy some candy for the twenty cents. He went into the store and took his time looking at the tempting display, finally buying ten cents worth of chocolates for himself and ten cents worth of peppermint lozenges for his mother.

You see, Dorian Trent, though sixteen years old, was very much a child; he did many childish things, and yet in some ways, he was quite a man; the child in him and the man in him did not seem to merge into the boy, but were somewhat "separate and apart," as the people of Greenstreet would say.

Dorian again took the less frequented road home. The sun was still high when he reached the river. He was not expected home for some time yet, so there was no need for hurry. He crossed the footbridge, noticing neither birds nor fish. Instead of following the main path, he struck off into a by-trail which led him to a tiny grass plat in the shade of a tree by the river. He sat down here, took off his hat, and pushed back from a freckled, sweating forehead a mop of wavy, rusty-colored hair. Then he untied his package of books and spread his treasures before him as a miser would his gold. He opened "David Copperfield", looked at the frontispiece which depicted a fat man making a very emphatic speech against someone by the name of Heep. It must all be very interesting, but it was altogether too big a book for him to begin to read now. "Ben Hur" looked solid and substantial; it would keep until next winter when he would have more time to read. Then he picked up the "Conquest", volume one. He backed up against the tree, settled himself into a comfortable position, took from his paper bag a chocolate at which he nibbled contentedly, and then away he went with Prescott to the land of the Inca and the glories of a vanished race!

For an hour he read. Then, reluctantly, he closed his book, wrapped up his package again, and went on his homeward way.

The new canal for which the farmers of Greenstreet had worked and waited so long had just been completed. The big ditch, now full of running water, was a source of delight to the children as well as to the more practical adults. The boys and girls played on its banks, and waded and sported in the cool stream. Near the village of Greenstreet was a big headgate, from which the canal branched into two divisions. As Dorian walked along the canal bank that afternoon, he saw a group of children at play near the headgate. They were making a lot of robust noise, and Dorian stopped to watch them. He was always interested in the children, being more of a favorite among them than among the boys of his own age.

"There's Dorian," shouted one of the boys. "Who are you going to marry?"

What in the world were the youngsters talking about, thought the young man, as the chattering children surrounded him.

"What's all this?" asked Dorian, "a party?"

"Yes; it's Carlia's birthday; we're just taking a walk by the canal to see the water; my, but it's nice!"

"What, the party or the water?"

"Why, the water."

"Both" added another.

"We've all told who we're going to marry," remarked a little rosy-faced miss, "all but Carlia, an' she won't tell."

"Well, but perhaps Carlia don't know. You wouldn't have her tell a fib, would you?"

"Oh, shucks, she knows as well as us."

"She's just stubborn."

She who was receiving these criticisms seemed to be somewhat older and larger than her companions. Just now, not deigning to notice the accusation of her friends, she was throwing sticks into the running water and watching them go over the falls at the headgate and dance on the rapids below. Her white party dress was as yet spotless. She swung her straw hat by the string. Her brown-black hair was crowned by an unusually large bow of red ribbon. She was not the least discomposed by the teasing of the other children, neither by Dorian's presence. This was her party, and why should not she do and say what she pleased.

Carlia now led the way along the canal bank until she came to where a pole spanned the stream. She stopped, looked at the somewhat insecure footbridge, then turning to her companions, said:

"I can back you out."

"How? Doin' what?" they asked.

"Crossing the canal on the pole."

"Shucks, you can't back me out," declared one of the boys, at which he darted across the swaying pole, and with a jump, landed safely across. Another boy went at it gingerly, and with the antics of a tight-rope walker, he managed to get to the other side. The other boys held back; none of the girls ventured.

"All right, Carlia," shouted the boys on the other bank.

The girl stood looking at the frail pole.

"Come on, it's easy," they encouraged.

Carlia placed her foot on the pole as if testing it. The other girls protested. She would fall in and drown.

"You dared us; now who's the coward," cried the boys.

Carlia took a step forward, balanced herself, and took another. The children stood in spell-bound silence. The girl advanced slowly along the frail bridge until she reached the middle where the pole swayed dangerously.

"Balance yourself," suggested the second boy.

"Run," said the first.

But Carlia could neither balance nor run. She stood for a moment on the oscillating span, then threw up her hands, and with a scream she plunged into the waters of the canal.

No thought of danger had entered Dorian's mind as he stood watching the capers of the children. If any of them fell in, he thought, they would only get a good wetting. But as Carlie fell, he sprang forward. The water at this point was quite deep and running swiftly. He saw that Carlia fell on her side and went completely under. The children screamed. Dorian, startled out of his apathy, suddenly ran to the canal and jumped in. It was done so impulsively that he still held on to his package of books. With one hand he lifted the girl out of the water, but in her struggles, she knocked the bundle from his hand, and the precious books splashed into the canal and floated down the stream. Dorian made an effort to rescue them, but Carlia clung so to his arms that he could do nothing but stand and see the package glide over the falls at the headgate and then go dancing over the rapids, even as Carlia's sticks had done. For a moment the young man's thoughts were with his books, and it seemed that he

12

13

stood there in the canal for quite a while in a sort of daze, with the water rushing by his legs. Then mechanically he carried the girl to the bank and would have set her down again with her companions, but she clung to him so closely and with such terror in her eyes that he lifted her into his arms and talked reassuringly to her:

"There, now," he said, "you're only a bit wet. Don't cry."

"Take me home. I—I want to go home," sobbed the girl.

"Sure," said Dorian. "Come on everybody."

He led the way, and the rest of the children followed.

"I suppose the party's about over, anyway," suggested he.

"I—I guess so."

They walked on in silence for a time; then Carlia said:

"I guess I'm heavy."

"Not at all", lied the young man bravely, for she was heavier than he had supposed; but she made no offer to walk. By the time they reached the gate, Carlia was herself again, and inclined to look upon her wetting and escape as quite an adventure.

"There," said Dorian as he seated the girl on the broad top of the gate post; "I'll leave you there to dry. It won't take long."

14   He looked at his own wet clothes, and then at his ragged, mud-laden shoes. He might as well carry the girl up the path to her home, but then, that was not necessary. The day was warm, there was no danger of colds, and she could run up the path in a few minutes.

"Well, I'll go now. Goodby," he said.

"Wait a minute—Say, I'm glad you saved me, but I'm sorry you lost your package. What was in it?"

"Only books."

"I'll get you some more, when I get the money, yes I will. Come here and lift me down before you go."

He obeyed. She put a wet arm about his neck and cuddled her dark, damp curls against his russet mop. He lifted her lightly down, and then he slipped a chocolate secretly into her hand.

"Oh girls," exclaimed one of the party, "I know now."

"Know what?" asked Carlia.

"I know who you are going to marry."

"Who?"

"You're going to marry Dorian."

2.

THE DISPOSITION TO LIE or evade never remained long with Dorian Trent; but that evening as he turned into the lane which led up to the house, he was sorely tempted. Once or twice only, as nearly as he could remember, had he told an untruth to his mother with results which he would never forget. He must tell her the truth now.

But he would put off the ordeal as long as possible. There could be no harm in that. Everything was quiet about the house, as his mother was away. He hurriedly divested himself of his best clothes and put on his overalls. He took the milk pail and hung it on the fence until he brought the cows from the pasture. After milking, he did his other chores. There were no signs of mother. The dusk turned to darkness, yet no light appeared in the house. Dorian went in and lighted the lamp and proceeded to get supper.

The mother came presently, carrying a bag of wool. "A big herd of sheep went by this afternoon," she explained, "and they left a lot of fine wool on the barbed-wire fences. See, I have gathered enough for a pair of stockings." She seated herself.

"You're tired," said Dorian.

"Yes."

"Well, you sit and rest; I'll soon have the supper on the table." This was no difficult task, as the evening meal was usually a very simple one, and Dorian had frequently prepared it. This evening as the mother sat there quietly she looked at her son with admiring eyes. What a big boy he was getting to be! He had always been big, it seemed to her. He had been a big baby and a big little boy, and now he was a big young man. He had a big head and big feet, big hands. His nose and mouth were big, and big freckles dotted his face—yes, and a big heart, as his mother very well knew. Along with his bigness of limb and body there was a certain awkwardness. He never could run as fast as the other boys, and he always fumbled the ball in their games though he could beat them swimming. So far in his youthful career he had not learned to dance. The one time he had tried, his girl partner had made fun of his awkwardness, so that ended his dancing. But Dorian was not clumsy about his mother's home and table. He handled the dishes as daintily as a girl, and the table was set and the food served in a very proper manner.

"Did you get your shoes, Dorian?"

17 Dorian burned his fingers on a dish which was not at all hot.

"Mother, sit up; supper is ready."

They both drew up their chairs. Dorian asked the blessing, then became unusually solicitous in helping his mother, continually talking as he did so.

"That little Duke girl was nearly drowned in the canal, this afternoon," he told her, going on with the details. "She's a plucky little thing. Ten minutes after I had her out of the canal, she was as lively as ever."

The mother liked to hear him talk, so she did not interrupt him. After they had eaten, he forced her to take her rocking-chair while he cleared the table and washed the few dishes. She asked no more questions about shoes, but leaned back in her chair with half-closed eyes. Dorian thought to give her the mint lozenges, but fearing that it might lead to more questions, he did not.

Mrs. Trent was not old in years, but hard work had bent her back and roughened her hands. Her face was pleasant to look upon, even if there were some wrinkles now, and the hair was white at the temples. She closed her eyes as if she were going to sleep.

"Now, mother, you're going to bed", said Dorian. "You have tired yourself out with this wool picking. I thought I told you before that I would gather what wool there was."

"But you weren't here, and I could not stand to see the wind blowing it away. See, what a fine lot I got." She opened her bundle and displayed her fleece.

"Well, put it away. You can't card and spin and knit it tonight."

"It will have to be washed first, you foolish boy."

Dorian got his mother to bed without further reference to shoes. He went to his own room with a conscience not altogether easy. He lighted his lamp, which was a good one, for he did a lot of reading by it. The electric wires had not yet reached Greenstreet. Dorian stood looking about his room. It was not a very large one, and somewhat sparsely furnished. The bed seemed selfishly to take up most of the space. Against one wall was set some home-made shelving containing books. He had quite a library. There were books of various kinds, gathered with no particular plan or purpose, but as means and opportunity afforded. In one corner stood a scroll saw, now not very often used. Pictures of a full-rigged sailing vessel and a big modern steamer hung on the wall above his books. On another wall were three small prints, landscapes where there were great distances with much light and warmth. Over his bed hung an artist's conception of "Lorna Doone," a beautiful face, framed in a mass of auburn hair, with smiling lips, and a dreamy look in her eyes.

"That's my girl," Dorian sometimes said, pointing to this picture. "No one can take her from me; we never quarrel; and she never scolds or frowns."

On another wall hung a portrait of his father, who had been dead nine years. His father had been a teacher with a longing to be a farmer. Eventually, this longing had been realized in the purchase of the twenty acres in Greenstreet, at that time a village with not one street which

18

19

could be called green, and without a sure water supply for irrigation, at least on the land which would grow corn and potatoes and wheat. To be sure, there was water enough of its kind down on the lower slopes, besides saleratus and salt grass and cattails and the tang of marshlands in the air. Schoolmaster Trent's operations in farming had not been very successful, and when he died, the result of his failure was a part of the legacy which descended to his wife and son.

Dorian took a book from the shelf as if to read; but visions intruded of some beautiful volumes, now somewhere down the canal, a mass of water-soaked paper. He could not read. He finished his last chocolate, said his prayers, and went to bed.

Saturday was always a busy day with Dorian and his mother; but that morning Mrs. Trent was up earlier than usual. The white muslin curtains were already in the wash when Dorian looked at his mother in the summer kitchen.

20   "What, washing today!" he asked in surprise. Monday was washday.

"The curtains were black; they must be clean for tomorrow."

"You can see dirt where I can't see it."

"I've been looking for it longer, my boy. And, say, fix up the line you broke the other day."

"Sure, mother."

The morning was clear and cool. He did his chores, then went out to his ten-acre field of wheat and lucerne. The grain was heading beautifully; and there were prospects of three cuttings of hay; the potatoes were doing fine, also the corn and the squash and the melons. The young farmer's heart was made glad to see the coming harvest, all the work of his own hands.

For this was the first real crop they had raised. For years they had struggled and pinched. Sometimes Dorian was for giving up and moving to the city; but the mother saw brighter prospects when the new canal should be finished. And then her boy would be better off working for himself on the farm than drudging for others in the town; besides, she had a desire to remain on the spot made dear by her husband's work; and so they struggled along, making their payments on the land and later on the canal stock. The summit of their difficulties seemed now to have passed, and better times were ahead. Dorian looked down at his ragged shoes and laughed to himself good-naturedly. Shucks, in a few months he would have plenty of money to buy shoes, perhaps also a Sunday suit for himself, and everything his mother needed. And if there should happen to be more book bargains, he might venture in that direction again.

Breakfast passed without the mention of shoes. What was his mother thinking about! She seemed uncommonly busy with cleaning an uncommonly clean house. When Dorian came home from irrigating at noon, he kicked off his muddy shoes by the shanty door, so as not to soil her cleanly scrubbed floor or to stain the neat home-made rug. There seemed to be even more than the extra cooking in preparation for Sunday.

The mother looked at Dorian coming so noiselessly in his stocking feet.

"You didn't show me your new shoes last night," she said.

"Say, mother, what's all this extra cleaning and cooking about?"

"We're going to have company tomorrow."

"Company? Who?"

"I'll tell you about it at the table."

"Do you remember," began the mother when they were seated, "a lady and her little girl who visited us some two years ago?"

Yes, he had some recollection of them. He remembered the girl, specially, spindle-legged, with round eyes, pale cheeks, and an uncommonly long braid of yellow hair hanging down her back.

"Well, they're coming to see us tomorrow. Mrs. Brown is an old-time friend of mine, and Mildred is an only child. The girl is not strong, and so I invited them to come here and get some good country air."

"To stay with us, mother?" asked the boy in alarm.

21

22

"Just to visit. It's terribly hot in the city. We have plenty of fresh eggs and good milk, which, I am sure is just what the child needs. Mrs. Brown cannot stay more than the day, so she says, but I am going to ask that Mildred visits with us for a week anyway. I think I can bring some color into her cheeks."

"Oh, gee, mother!" he remonstrated.

"Now, Dorian, be reasonable. She's such a simple, quiet girl. She will not be in the way in the least. I want you to treat her nicely."

Dorian had finished his dinner and was gazing out of the window. There was an odd look on his face. The idea of a girl living right here with them in the same house startled and troubled him. His mother had called her a little girl, but he remembered her as being only a year or two younger than he. Gee!

"That's why I wanted you to get a pair of decent shoes for tomorrow," said the mother, "and I told you to get a nice pair. I have brushed and pressed your clothes, but you must get a new suit as soon as possible. Where are your shoes? I couldn't find them."

"I—didn't get any shoes, mother."

"Didn't get any? Why not?"

"Well, you see—I didn't know about these visitors coming, mother, and so I—bought some books for most of my money, and so; but mother, don't get mad—I—"

"Books? What books? Where are they?"

And then Dorian told her plainly the whole miserable story. At first the mother was angry, but when she saw the troubled face of her boy, she relented, not wishing to add to his misery. She even smiled at the calamitous ending of those books.

"My boy, I see that you have been sorely tempted, and I am sorry that you lost your books. The wetting that Carlia gave you did no harm … but you must have some shoes by tomorrow. Wait."

The mother went to the bureau drawer, opened the lid of a little box, drew from the box a purse, and took from the purse two silver dollars. She handed them to Dorian.

"Go to town again this afternoon and get some shoes."

"But, mother, I hate to take your money. I think I can black my old ones so that they will not look so bad."

"Blacking will not fill the holes. Now, you do as I say. Jump on Nig and go right away."

Dorian put the money in his pocket, then went out to the yard and slipped a bridle on his horse, mounted, and was back to the house.

"Now, Dorian, remember what I say. Get you a nice pair, a nice Sunday pair." 24

"All right, mother, I will."

He rode off at a gallop. He lingered not by creeks or byways, but went directly to the best shoe store in the city, where he made his purchase. He stopped neither at book store or candy shops. His horse was sweating when he rode in at the home yard. His mother hearing him, came out.

"You made quick time," she said.

"Yes; just to buy a pair of shoes doesn't take long."

"You got the right kind?"

"Sure. Here, look at 'em." He handed her the package.

"I can't look at them now. Say, Dorian—" she came out nearer to him— "They are here."

"Who, mother?"

"Mrs. Brown and her daughter. They got a chance to ride out this afternoon, so they did not wait until tomorrow. Lucky I cleaned up this morning. Mildred is not a bit well, and she is lying down now. Don't make any more noise than you can help."

"Gee—but, mother, gosh!" He was very much disturbed.

"They are dear, good people. They know we are simple farmers. Just you wash yourself and take off those dirty overalls before you come in. And then you just behave yourself. We're going to have something nice for supper. Now, don't be too long with your hoe- 25 ing or with your chores, for supper will be early this evening."

Dorian hoed only ten rows that afternoon for the reason that he sat down to rest and to think at the end of each row. Then he dallied so with his chores that his mother had to call him twice. At last he could find no more excuses between him and the strange company. He went in with much fear and some invisible trembling.

3.

ABOUT SIX O'CLOCK in the afternoon, Mildred Brown
went down through the fields to the lower pasture. She wore a gingham apron which covered her from neck to high-topped boots. She
carried in one hand an easel and stool and in the other hand a box of
colors. Mildred came each day to a particular spot in this lower pasture and set up her easel and stool in the shade of a black willow
bush to paint a particular scene. She did her work as nearly as possible at the same time each afternoon to get the same effect of light
and shade and the same stretch of reflected sunlight on the open water spaces in the marshland.

And the scene before her was worthy of a master hand, which, of
course, Mildred Brown was not as yet. From her position in the
shade of the willow, she looked out over the flat marshlands toward
the west. Nearby, at the edge of the firmer pasture lands, the rushes
grew luxuriously, now crowned with large, glossy-brown "cat-tails."
The flats to the left were spotted by beds of white and black saleratus
and bunches of course salt grass. Openings of sluggish water lay hot
in the sun, winding in and out among reeds, and at this hour every
clear afternoon, shining with the undimmed reflection of the burning sun. The air was laden with salty odors of the marshes. A light
afternoon haze hung over the distance. Frogs were lazily croaking,
and the killdeer's shrill cry came plaintively to the ear. A number of

cows stood knee-deep in mud and water, round as barrels, and breathing hard, with tails unceasingly switching away the flies.

Dorian was in the field turning the water on his lucerne patch when he saw Mildred coming as usual down the path. He had not expected her that afternoon as he thought the picture which she had been working on was finished; but after adjusting the flow of water, he joined her, relieving her of stool and easel. They then walked on together, the big farm boy in overalls and the tall graceful girl in the enveloping gingham.

Mildred's visit had now extended to ten days, by which time Dorian had about gotten over his timidity in her presence. In fact, that had not been difficult. The girl was not a bit "stuck up," and she entered easily and naturally into the home life on the farm. She had changed considerably since Dorian had last seen her, some two years ago. Her face was still pale, although it seemed that a little pink was now creeping into her cheeks; her eyes were still big and round and blue; her hair was now done up in thick shining braids. She talked freely to Dorian and his mother, and at last Dorian had to some extent been able to find his tongue in the presence of a girl nearly his own age.

The two stopped in the shade of the willow. He set up the easel and opened the stool, while she got out her colors and brushes.

"Thank you," she said to him. "Did you get through with your work in the field?"

"I was just turning the water on the lucerne. I got through shocking the wheat some time ago."

"Is there a good crop? I don't know much about such things, but I want to learn." She smiled up into his ruddy face.

"The wheat is fine. The heads are well developed. I wouldn't be surprised if it went fifty bushels to the acre."

"Fifty bushels?" She began to squeeze the tubes of colors on to the palette.

Dorian explained; and as he talked, she seated herself, placed the canvas on the easel, and began mixing the colors.

"I thought you finished that picture yesterday," he said.

"I was not satisfied with it, and so I thought I would put in another hour on it. The setting sun promises to be unusually fine today, and I want to put a little more of its beauty into my picture, if I can."

The young man seated himself on the grass well toward the rear where he could see her at work. He thought it wonderful to be able thus to make a beautiful picture out of such a commonplace thing as a saleratus swamp. But then, he was beginning to think that this girl was capable of endless wonders. He had met no other girl just like her, so young and so beautiful, and yet so talented and so well-informed; so rich, and yet so simple in manner of her life; so high born and bred, and yet so companionable with those of humbler station.

The painter squeezed a daub of brilliant red on to her palette. She gazed for a moment at the western sky, then turning to Dorian, she asked:

"Do you think I dare put a little more red in my picture?"

"Dare?" he repeated.

The young man followed the pointing finger of the girl into the flaming depths of the sky, then came and leaned carefully over the painting.

"Tell me which is redder, the real or the picture?" she asked.

Dorian looked critically back and forth. "The sky is redder," be decided.

"And yet if I make my picture as red as the sky naturally is, many people would say that it is too red to be true. I'll risk it anyway." Then she carefully laid on a little more color. "Nature itself, our teacher told us, is always more intense than any representation of nature."

She worked on in silence for a few moments, then without looking from her canvas, she asked: "Do you like being a farmer?"

"Oh, I guess so," he replied somewhat indefinitely. "I've lived on a farm all my life, and I don't know anything else. I used to think I would like to get away, but mother always wanted to stay. There's been a lot of hard work for both of us, but now things are coming more our way, and I like it better. Anyway, I couldn't live in the city now."

"Why?"

"Well, I don't seem able to breathe in the city, with its smoke and its noise and its crowding together of houses and people."

"You ought to go to Chicago or New York or Boston," she replied. "Then you would see some crowds and hear some noises."

"Have you been there?"

"I studied drawing and painting in Boston. Next to farming, what would you like to do?"

He thought for a moment— "When I was a little fellow—"

"Which you are not," she interrupted as she changed brushes.

"I thought that if I ever could attain to the position of standing behind a counter in a store where I could take a piece of candy whenever I wanted it, I should have attained to the heights of happiness. But, now, of course—"

31   "Well, and now?"

"I believe I'd like to be a school teacher."

"Why a teacher?"

"Because I'd then have the chance to read a lot of books."

"You like to read, don't you? and you like candy, and you like pictures."

"Especially, when someone else paints them."

Mildred arose, stepped back to get the distance for examination. "I don't think I had better use more color," she commented, "but those cat-tails in the corner need touching up a bit."

"I suppose you have been to school a lot?" he asked.

"No; just completed the high school; then, not being very strong, mother thought it best not to send me to the University; but she lets me dabble a little in painting and in music."

Dorian could not keep his eyes off this girl who had already completed the high school course which he had not yet begun; besides, she had learned a lot of other things which would be beyond him to ever reach. Even though he were an ignoramus, he could bask in the light of her greater learning. She did not resent that.

"What do you study in High School?" he asked.

"Oh, a lot of things—don't you know?" She again looked up at him.

"Not exactly."

"We studied algebra and mathematics and English and English literature, and French, and a lot of other things." 32

"What's algebra like?"

"Oh dear, do you want me to draw it?"

"Can you draw it?"

"About as well as I can tell it in words. Algebra is higher mathematics; yes, that's it."

"And what's the difference between English and English literature?"

"English is grammar and how sentences are or should be made. English literature is made up mostly of the reading of the great authors, such as Milton and Shakespeare,"

"Gee!" exclaimed Dorian, "that would be great fun."

"Fun? just you try it. Nobody reads these writers now only in school, where they have to. But say, Dorian"—she arose to inspect her work again. "Have I too much purple in that bunch of salt-grass on the left? What do you think?"

"I don't see any purple at all in the real grass," he said.

"There is purple there, however; but of course, you, not being an artist, cannot see it." She laughed a little for fear he might think her pronouncement harsh.

"What—what is an artist?"

"An artist is one who has learned to see more than other people can in the common things about them."

The definition was not quite clear to him. He had proved that he 33 could see farther and clearer than she could when looking at trees or chipmunks. He looked critically again at the picture.

"I mean, of course," she added, as she noted his puzzled look, "that an artist is one who sees in nature the beauty in form, in light and shade, and in color."

"You haven't put that tree in the right place," he objected! "and you have left out that house altogether."

"This is not a photograph," she answered. "I put in my picture only that which I want there. The tree isn't in the right place, so I moved it. The house has no business in the picture because I want it to represent a scene of wild, open lonesomeness. I want to make the people who look at it feel so lonesome that they want to cry!"

She was an odd girl!

"Oh, don't you understand. I want them only to feel like it. When you saw that charcoal drawing I made the other day, you laughed."

"Well, it was funny."

"That's just it. An artist wants to be able to make people feel like laughing or crying, for then he knows he has reached their soul."

"I've got to look after the water for a few minutes, then I'll come back and help you carry your things," he said. "You're about through, aren't you?"

34 "Thank you; I'll be ready now in a few minutes. Go see to your water. I'll wait for you. How beautiful the west is now!"

They stood silently for a few moments side by side, looking at the glory of the setting sun through banks of clouds and then down behind the purple mountain. Then Dorian, with shovel on shoulder, hastened to his irrigating. The blossoming field of lucerne was usually a common enough sight, but now it was a stretch of sweet-scented waves of green and purple.

Mildred looked at the farmer boy until he disappeared behind the willow fence, then she began to pack up her things. Presently, she heard some low bellowing, and, looking up, she saw a number of cows, with tails erect, galloping across the fields. They had broken the fence, and were now having a gay frolic on forbidden grounds.

Mildred saw that they were making directly for the corner of the pasture where she was. She was afraid of cows, even when they were within the quiet enclosure of the yard, and here was a wild lot apparently coming upon her to destroy her. She crouched, terror stricken, as if to take shelter behind the frail bulwark of her easel.

Then she saw a horse leap through the gap in the fence and come galloping after the cows. On the horse was a girl, not a large girl, but she was riding fearlessly, bare-back, and urging the horse to greater strides. Her black hair was trailing in the wind as she waved a willow switch and shouted lustily at the cows. She managed to head the cows off before they had reached Mildred, rounding them up sharply and driving them back through the breach into the road which they followed quietly homeward. The rider then galloped back to the frightened girl.

"Did the cows scare you?" she asked.

"Yes," panted Mildred. "I'm so frightened of cows, and these were so wild."

"They were just playing. They wouldn't hurt you; but they did look fierce."

"Whose cows were they?"

"They're ours. I have to get them up every day. Sometimes when the flies are bad they get a little mad, but I'm not afraid of them. They know me, you bet. I can milk the kickiest one of the lot."

"Do you milk the cows?"

"Sure—but what is that?" The rider had caught sight of the picture. "Did you make that?"

"Yes; I painted it."

"My!" She dismounted, and with arm through bridle, she and the horse came up for a closer view of the picture. The girl looked at it mutely for a moment. "It's pretty" she said; "I wish I could make a picture like that."

Mildred smiled at her. She was such a round, rosy girl, so full of health and life and color. Not such a little girl either, now a nearer view was obtained. She was only a year or two younger than Mildred herself.

36   "I wish I could do what you can," said the painter of pictures.

"I—what? I can't do anything like that."

"No; but you can ride a horse, and stop runaway cows. You can do a lot of things that I cannot do because you are stronger than I am. I wish I had some of that rosy red in your cheeks."

"You can have some of mine," laughed the other, "for I have more than enough; but you wouldn't like the freckles."

"I wouldn't mind them, I'm sure; but let me thank you for what you did, and let's get acquainted." Mildred held out her hand, which the other took somewhat shyly. "Don't you have to go home with your cows?"

"Yes, I guess so."

"Then we'll go back together." She gathered her material and they walked on up the path, Mildred ahead, for she was timid of the horse which the other led by the bridle rein. At the bars in the corner of the upper pasture the horse was turned loose into his own feeding ground, and the girls went on together.

"You live near here, don't you?" inquired Mildred.

"Yes, just over there."

"Oh, are you Carlia Duke?"

"Yes; how did you know?"

"Dorian has told me about you."

37   "Has he? We're neighbors; an' you're the girl that's visiting with the Trent's?"

"Yes."

"Well, I'm glad to meet you. Dorian has told me about you, too."

Thus these two, meeting for the first time, went on chatting together; and thus Dorian saw them. He had missed Mildred at the lower pasture, and so, with shovel again on shoulder, he had followed up the homeward path. The girls were some distance ahead, so he did not try to overtake them. In fact, he slackened his pace a little, so as not to get too close to them to disturb them; but he saw them plainly walk close together up the road in the twilight of the summer evening, the tall, light-haired Mildred, and the shorter, dark-haired Carlia; and the child in Dorian seemed to vanish, and the man in him asserted himself in thought and feelings which it would have been hard for him to describe in words.

4.

INDIAN SUMMER LAY drowsily over the land. It had come
late that season, but its rare beauty compensated for its tardiness. Its
golden mellowness permeating the hazy air, had also, it seems, crept
into the heart of Dorian Trent. The light coating of frost which each
morning lay on the grass, had by noon vanished, and now the earth
was warm and dry.

Dorian was plowing, and he was in no great haste with his work.
He did not urge his horses, for they also seemed imbued with the
languidness of the season. He let them rest frequently, especially at
the end of the furrow where there was a grassy bank on which the
plowman could lie prone on his back and look into the dreamy distances of the hills or up into the veiling clouds.

Dorian could afford to take it a little easy that afternoon, so he
thought. The summer's work was practically over: the wheat had
been thrashed; the hay was in the stacks; the potatoes were in the pit;
the corn stood in Indian wigwam bunches in the yard; the fruit and
vegetables, mostly of the mother's raising, had been sufficient for
their simple needs. They were well provided for the winter; and so
Dorian was happy and contented as everyone in like condition
should be on such an Indian summer afternoon.

Mildred Brown's visit to the farm had ended some weeks ago; but
only yesterday his mother had received a note from Mrs. Brown,

asking if her daughter might not come again. Her former visit had done her so much good, and now the beautiful weather was calling her out into the country. It was a shame, Mildred had said, that Indian summer should "waste its sweetness on the desert air of the city."

"What do you say?" Mrs. Trent had asked Dorian.

"Why—why—of course, mother, if she doesn't make too much work for you."

And so Mildred had received the invitation that she was very welcome to come to Greenstreet and stay as long as she desired. Very likely, she would be with them in a day or two, thought Dorian. She would draw and paint, and then in the soft evening dusk she would play some of those exquisite melodies on her violin. Mildred did not like people to speak of her beloved instrument as a fiddle, and he remembered how she had chastised him on one occasion for so doing. Yes, she would again enter into their daily life. Her ladylike ways, her sweet smile, her golden beauty would again glorify their humble home. Why, if she came often enough and remained long enough, she might yet learn how to milk a cow, as she had threatened to do. At the thought, the boy on the grass by the nodding horses, laughed up into the sky. Dorian was happy; but whether he preferred the somewhat nervous happiness of Mildred's presence or the quiet longing happiness of her absence, he could not tell.

The plain truth of the matter was, that Dorian had fallen deeply in love with Mildred. This statement may be scoffed at by some people whose eyes have been dimmed by age so that they cannot see back into that time of youth when they also were "trailing clouds of glory" from their heavenly home. There is nothing more wholesomely sweet than this first boy and girl affection. It is clean and pure and undefiled by the many worldly elements which often enter into the more mature lovemaking.

Perhaps Mildred Brown's entrance into Dorian's life did not differ from like incidents in many lives, but to him it was something holy. Dorian at this time never admitted to himself that he was in love with the girl. He sensed very well that she was far above him in every way. The thought that she might ever become his wife never obtained foothold in him more than for a fleeting moment: that was impossible, then why think of it. But there could be no harm in loving her as he loved his mother, or as he loved the flowers, the clear-flowing water, the warm sun and the blue sky. He could at least cast adoring eyes up to her as he did to the stars at night. He could also strive to rise to her level, if that were possible. He was going to the High school the coming winter, then perhaps to the University. He could get to know as much of school learning as she, anyway. He never would become a painter of pictures or a musician, but surely there were other things which he could learn which would be worth while.

There came to Dorian that afternoon as he still lay on the grass, his one-time effort to ask a girl to a dance. He recalled what care he had taken in washing and combing and dressing, how he had finally cut cross-lots to the girl's home for fear of being seen, for surely he had thought, everybody must know what he was up to!—how he had lingered about the back door, and had at last, when the door opened, scudded back home as fast as his legs could carry him! And now, the finest girl he had ever seen was chumming with him, and he was not afraid, that is, not very much afraid.

When Mildred had packed up to go home on the occasion of her former visit she had invited Mrs. Trent to take her pick of her drawings for her own.

"All but this," Mildred had said. "This which I call 'Sunset in the Marshland' I am going to give to Dorian."

The mother had looked over the pile of sketches. There was a panel in crayon which the artist said was the big cottonwood down by the Corners. Mrs. Trent remarked that she never would have known it, but then, she added apologetically, she never had an eye for art. There was a winter scene where the houses were so sunk into the earth that only the roofs were visible. (Mrs. Trent had often wondered why the big slanting roofs were the only artistic thing about a house). Another picture showed a high, camel-backed bridge, impossible to cross by anything more real than the artist's fancy. Mrs. Trent had chosen the bridge because of its pretty colors.

"Where shall we hang Dorian's picture?" Mildred had asked.

They had gone into his room. Mildred had looked about.

"The only good light is on that wall." She had pointed to the space occupied by Dorian's "best girl."

And so Lorna Doone had come down and Mildred's study of the marshlands glowed with its warmer colors in its place.

The plowboy arose from the grass. "Get up there," he said to his horses. "We must be going, or there'll be very little plowing today."

CARLIA DUKE WAS the first person to greet Mildred as she alighted at the Trent gate. Carlia knew of her coming and was wait-
43 ing. Mildred put her arm about her friend and kissed her, somewhat to the younger girl's confused pleasure. The two girls went up the path to the house where Mrs. Trent met them.

"Where's your baggage?" asked the mother of the arrival, seeing she carried only a small bag and her violin case.

"This is all. I'm not going to paint this time—just going to rest, mother said, so I do not need a lot of baggage."

"Well, come in Honey; and you too, Carlia. Dinner is about ready, an' you'll stay."

By a little urging Carlia remained, and pretty soon, Dorian came stamping in to be surprised.

"Yes; we're all here," announced Carlia, as she tossed her black curls and laughed at his confusion.

"I see you are," he replied ,as he shook hands with Mildred. After which ceremony, it did not just look right to slight the other girl, so he shook hands with her also, much to her amusement.

"How do you do, Mr. Trent" she said.

"Carlia is such a tease," explained the mother.

"For which I like her," added Mildred.

"We all do. Even Dorian here, who is usually afraid of girls, makes quite a chum of her."

"Well, we're neighbors," justified the girl.

After dinner Carlia took Mildred home with her. It was not far, just around the low ridge which hid the house from view. There Mildred met Pa Duke, Ma Duke and Will Duke, Carlia's older brother. Pa Duke was a hard-working farmer, Ma Duke was likewise a hard-working farmer's wife, and Will Duke should have been a hard-working farmer's boy, but he was somewhat a failure, especially regarding the hard work part. Carlia, though so young, was already a hardworking farmer girl, with no chance of escape, as far as she could see, from the hard-working part. The Duke house, though clean and roomy, lacked the dainty home touches which mean so much. There were no porch, no lawn, no trees. The home was bare inside and out.

In deference to the "company" Carlia was permitted to "visit" with her friend that afternoon. Apparently, these two girls had very little in common, but when left to themselves they found many mutual interests.

Toward the close of the afternoon, Dorian appeared. He found the girls out in the yard, Carlia seated on the topmost pole of the corral fence, and Mildred standing beside her.

"Hello girls," Dorian greeted. "I've come to give you an invitation."

"What, a party!" exclaimed Carlia, jumping down from her perch.

"Not a dancing party, you little goose—just a surprise party."

"On who?"

"On Uncle Zed."

"Uncle Zed. O, shucks!"

"Well, of course, you do not have to go," said Dorian.

"I think you're mean. I do want to go if Mildred is going."

"I don't know Uncle Zed," said Mildred, "but if Mrs. Trent and Dorian wish me to go, I shall be pleased; and of course, you will go with us."

"She's invited," repeated Dorian. "It's Uncle Zed's seventy-fifth birthday. Mother keeps track of them, the only one who does, I guess, for he doesn't do it himself. We're just going down to visit with him this evening. He's a very fine old man, is Uncle Zed," this last to Mildred.

"Is he your uncle?"

"Oh, no; he's just uncle to everybody and no one in particular. He's all by himself, and has no folks?"

Just before the dusk of the evening, the little party set out for the home of Zedekiah Manning, generally and lovingly known as Uncle Zed. He lived about half a mile down the road in a two-roomed log house which had a big adobe chimney on one side. His front yard was abloom with the autumn flowers. The path leading to his door was neatly edged by small cobble stones. Autumn tinted ivy embowered his front door and climbed over the wall nearly to the low roof.

Uncle Zed met the visitors at the door. "Well, well," he exclaimed, "come right in. I'll light the lamp." Then he assisted them to find seats.

46   Mildred looked keenly at Uncle Zed, whom she found to be a little frail old man with clean white hair and beard, and kindly, smiling face. He sat down with his company and rubbed his hands in a way which implied: "And what does all this mean?" Mildred noted that the wall, back of his own chair, was nearly covered with books, and a number of volumes lay on the table. The room was furnished for the simple needs of the lone occupant. A fire smouldered in the open grate.

"Now, Uncle Zed, have you forgotten again?" inquired Mrs. Trent.

"Forgotten what? I suppose I have, for my memory is not so good as it used to be."

"Your memory never was good regarding the day of the year you were born."

"Day when I was born? What, has my birthday come around again? Well, sure; but I had quite forgotten. How these birthdays do pile up on one."

"How old are you today?" asked Dorian.

"How old? Let me see. I declare, I must be seventy-five."

"Isn't he a funny man," whispered Carlia to Mildred, who appeared not to hear the comment, so interested was she in the old man.

"And so you've come to celebrate," went on Uncle Zed, "come to congratulate me that I am one year nearer the grave."

"Now, Uncle Zed, you know—"

"Yes; I know; forgive me for teasing; I know why you come to wish me well. It is that I have kept the faith one year more, and that I am twelve months nearer my heavenly reward. That's it, isn't it?"

Uncle Zed pushed his glasses up on his forehead to better see his company, especially Mildred. Mrs. Trent made the proper introduction, then lifted the picnic basket from the table to a corner.

"We're just going to spend an hour or so with you," explained Mrs. Trent. "We want you to talk, Mildred to play, and then we'll have a bite to eat. We'll just sit about your grate, and look into the glow of the fire while you talk." However, Dorian and Mildred were scanning the books.

"What's this set?" the young girl asked.

Dorian bent down to read the dim titles. "The Millennial Star" he said.

"And here's another set."

"The Journal of Discourses" he replied.

"My, all sermons? they must be dry reading."

Uncle Zed heard their conversation, and stepped over to them. "Are you also interested in books?" he asked. "Dorian and I are regular book-worms, you know."

Oh, yes, she was interested in books.

"But there are books and books, you know," went on Uncle Zed. "You like story books, no doubt. So do I. There's nothing better than a rattling good love story, eh, young lady?"

48 Mildred hardly knew just how to take this remark, so she did not reply.

"Here's the most wonderful love story ever written." He took from the shelf a very ordinary looking volume, called the "Doctrine and Covenants." Carlia and Mrs. Trent now joined the other three. They also were interested.

"You wouldn't be looking in the 'Doctrine and Covenants' for love stories, would you; but here in the revelation on the eternity of the marriage covenant we find that men and women, under the proper conditions and by the proper authority, may be united as husbands and wives, not only for time, but for eternity. Most love stories end when the lovers are married; but think of the endlessness of life and love under this new and everlasting covenant of marriage—but I mustn't preach so early in the evening."

"But we like to hear it, Uncle Zed," said Dorian.

"Indeed, we do," added Mildred. "Tell us more about your books."

"Here is one of my precious volumes—Orson Pratt's works. When I get hungry for the solid, soul-satisfying doctrines of the kingdom, I read Orson Pratt. Parley Pratt also is good. Here is a book which is nearly forgotten, but which contains beautiful presentations of the gospel, 'Spencer's Letters'. Dorian, look here." He handed the young man a small, ancient-looking, leather bound book.

49 "I found it in a secondhand store and paid fifteen cents for it. Yes, it's a second edition of the 'Doctrine and Covenants,' printed by John Taylor in Nauvoo in 1844. The rest of my collection is familiar to you, I am sure. Here is a complete set of the 'Contributor' and this is my 'Era' shelf, and here are most of the more modern church works. Let us now go back to the fire."

After they were again seated, Mildred asked him if he had known Brigham Young. She always liked to hear the pioneers talk of their experiences.

"No" replied Uncle Zed, "I never met President Young, but I believe I know him as well as many who had that pleasure. I have read everything that I could get in print which Brigham Young ever said. I have read all his discourses in those volumes. He was not a polished speaker, I understand, and he did not often follow a theme; but mixed with the more commonplace subjects of irrigation, Indian troubles, etc., which, in his particular day had to be spoken of, are some of the most profound gospel truths in any language. Gems of thought shine from every page of his discourses."

Carlia was nodding in a warm corner. Uncle Zed rambled on reminiscently until Mrs. Trent suddenly arose, spoke sharply to Carlia, and lifted the basket of picnic on to the table.

"We'll have our refreshments now," she said, "and then we must   50
be going. Uncle Zed goes early to bed, and so should we."

The table was spread: roast chicken, brought by Carlia; dainty sandwiches, made by Mildred; apple pie from Mrs. Trent's cupboard; a jar of apricot preserves, suggested by Dorian. Uncle Zed asked a blessing not only on the food, but on the kind hands which had provided it. Then they ate heartily, and yet leaving a generous part to be left in Uncle Zed's own cupboard.

Then Dorian had a presentation to make. He took from the basket a small package, unwrapped it, and handed a book to the man who was seventy-five years old.

"I couldn't do much by way of the eats," said Dorian, "so my present is this."

"'Drummond's Natural Law in the Spiritual World'" read Uncle Zed. "Why, Dorian, this is fine of you. How could you guess my wishes so nicely. For a long time, this is just the book I have wanted."

"I'm glad. I thought you'd like it."

"Fine, fine," said the old man, fondling the volume as he would some dear object, as indeed, every good book was to him.

Then Mildred got out her violin, and after the proper tuning of the strings, she placed it under her shapely chin. She played without music some of the simple heart melodies, and then some of the Sunday School songs which the company softly accompanied by words.

51   Carlia poked the log in the grate into a blaze, then slyly turned the lamp wick down. When detected and asked why she did that she replied:

"I wanted to make it appear more like a picnic party around a camp fire in the hills."

5.

DORIAN'S HIGH SCHOOL days in the city began that ⁵² fall, a little late because he had so many things to set right at home; but he soon made up the lost time, for he was a student not afraid of hard work. He walked back and forth the three miles. Mrs. Brown offered him a room at her large city residence, but he could not accept it because of his daily home chores. However, he occasionally called on the Brown's who tried to make him feel as much at home as they did at Greenstreet.

Never before were days so perfect to Dorian, never before had he so enjoyed the fleeting hours. For the first week or two, he was a little shy, but the meeting each morning with boys and girls of his own age and mingling with them in their studies and their recreations, soon taught him that they were all very much alike, just happy, carefree young people, most of them trying to get an education. He soon learned, also, that he could easily hold his own in the class work with the brightest of them. The teachers, and students also, soon learned ⁵³ to know this. Boys came to him for help in problems, and the younger girls chattered about him with laughing eyes and tossing curls. What a wonder it was! He the simple, plainly-dressed country boy, big and awkward and ugly as he thought himself to be, becoming a person of some importance. And so the days went all too swiftly by. Contrary to his younger boyhood's experience, the closing hour came too soon, when it was time to go home to mother and chores and lessons.

And the mother shared the boy's happiness, for she could see the added joy of living and working which had come into his life by the added opportunities and new environment. He frequently discussed with his mother his lessons. She was not well posted in the knowledge derived from books, and sometimes she mildly resented this newer learning which he brought into the home and seemed to intrude on her old-established ideas. For instance, when the cold winter nights came, and Dorian kept open his bedroom window, the mother protested that he would "catch his death of cold." Night air and drafts are very dangerous, especially if let into one's bedroom, she held.

"But, mother, I must have air to breathe," said Dorian, "and what other kind of air can I have at night? I might store a little day-air in my room, but I would soon exhaust its life-giving qualities at night. You know, mother," he went on in the assurance of his newly acquired knowledge, "I guess the Lord knew what He was about when He enveloped the earth with air which presses down nearly fifteen pounds to the square inch so that it might permeate every possible nook and corner of the globe." Then he went on to explain the wonderful process of blood purification in the lungs, and demonstrated to her that the breath is continually throwing off foul matter. He did this by breathing into a fruit jar, screwing on the lid for a little while, and then having the nose make the test.

"Some bed rooms I've gone into smell just like that," he said.

"Here, mother is a clipping from a magazine. Listen:

"'Of all the marvels of God's workmanship, none is more wondrous than the air. Think of our all being bathed in a substance so delicate as to be itself unperceived, yet so dense as to be the carriage to our senses of messages from the world about us! It is never in our way; it does not ask notice; we only know it is there by the good it does us. And this exquisitely soft, pure, yielding, unseen being, like a beautiful and beneficent fairy, brings us blessings from all around. It has the skill to wash our blood clean from all foulness. Its weight keeps us from tumbling to pieces. It is a reservoir where the waters lie stored, until they fall and gladden the earth. It is a great-coat that softens to us the heat of the day, and the cold of the night. It carries sounds to our ears and smells to our nostrils. Its movements fill Nature with ceaseless change; and without their aid in wafting ships over the sea, commerce and civilization would have been scarce possible. It is of all wonders the most wonderful.'"

At another time when Dorian had a cold, and consequently, a loss of appetite, his mother urged him to eat more, saying that he must have strength to throw off his cold.

"What is a cold?" he smilingly asked.

"Why, a cold is—a cold, of course, you silly boy."

"What does it do to the activities of the body?"

"I'm not a doctor; how can I tell."

"All mothers are doctors and nurses; they do a lot of good, and some things that are not so good. For instance, why should I eat more when I have a cold?" She did not reply, and so he went on: "The body is very much like a stove or a furnace; it is burning material all the time. Sometimes the clinkers accumulate and stop the draft, both in the human as well as the iron stove. When that happens, the sensible thing to do is not to throw in more fuel but to clean out the clinkers first."

"Where did you get all that wisdom, Dorian?"

"I got it from my text book on hygiene, and I think it's true because it seems so reasonable."

"Well, last night's talk led me to believe that you would become a philosopher; now, the trend is more toward the doctor; tomorrow I'll think you are studying law."

"Oh, but we are, mother; you ought to hear us in our civil government class. We have organized into a Congress of the United States, and we are going to make laws."

"You'll be elected President, I suppose."

"I'm one of the candidates."

"Well, my boy" she smiled happily at him, "I hope you will be elected to every good thing, and that you will fill every post with honor; and now, I would like you to read to me from the 'Lady of the Lake' while I darn your stockings. Your father used to read the story to me a long, long time ago, and your voice is very much like his when you read."

And thus with school and home and ward duties the winter passed. Spring called him again to the fields to which he went with new zeal, for life was opening to him in a way which life is in the habit of doing to the young of his age. Mildred Brown and her mother were in California. He heard from her occasionally by way of postcards, and once she sent him one of her sketches of the ocean. Carlia Duke also was not forgotten by Mildred. Dorian and Carlia met frequently as neighbors will do, and they often spoke of their mutual friend. The harvest was again good that fall, and Dorian once more took up his studies at the high school in the city. Carlia finished the grades as Dorian completed his second year, and the following year Carlia walked with Dorian to the high school. That was no great task for the girl, now nearly grown to young womanhood, and it was company for both of them. During these walks Carlia had many questions to ask about her lessons, and Dorian was always pleased to help her.

"I am such a dunce," she would say, "I wish I was as smart as you."

"You must say 'were' when you wish. I were as smart as you," he corrected.

"O, yes: I forgot. My, but grammar is hard, especially to a girl which—"

"No—a girl who; which refers to objects and animals, who to persons."

Carlia laughed and swung her books by the strap. Dorian was not carrying them that day. Sometimes he was absentminded regarding the little courtesies.

The snow lay hard packed in the road and it creaked under their feet. Carlia's cheeks glowed redder than ever in contact with the keen winter air. They walked on in silence for a time.

"Say, Dorian, why do you not go and see Mildred?" asked Carlia, not looking at him, but rather at the eastern mountains.

"Why? Is she not well?"

"She is never well now. She looks bad to me."

"When did you see her?"

"Last Saturday. I called at the house, and she asked about you— Poor girl!" 58

"What do you mean by that?"

"You are very smart in some things, but are a stupid dunce in other things. Mildred is like an angel both in looks and—everything. I wish I was—were half as good."

"But how am I such a dunce, Carlia?"

"In not seeing how much Mildred thinks of you."

"Thinks of me? Mildred?"

"She just loves you."

Carlia still looked straight ahead as though fearful to see the agitation she had brought to the young man; but he looked at her, with cheeks still aflame. He did not understand Carlia. Why had she said that? Was she just teasing him? But she did not look as if she were teasing. Silently they walked on to the school house door.

But Dorian could not forget what Carlia had said. All day it intruded into his lessons. "She said she loves me" he whispered to his heart only. Could it be possible? Even if she did, what final good would come of it? The distance between them was still too great, for he was only a poor farmer boy. Dear Mildred—his heart did not chide him for thinking that—so frail, so weak, so beautiful. What if she—should die! Dorian was in a strange state of mind for a number of days. He longed to visit the Brown home, yet he could not find excuse to go. He could not talk to anybody about what was in his mind and heart, not even to his 59 mother with whom he always shared his most hidden thoughts.

One evening he visited Uncle Zed, ostensibly, to talk about a book. Uncle Zed was deep in the study of "Natural Law in the Spiritual

World" and would have launched into a discussion of what he had found, but Dorian did not respond; he had other thoughts in mind.

"Uncle Zed," he said, "how can I become something else than a farmer?"

The old man looked questioningly at his young friend. "What's the matter with being a farmer?" he asked.

"Well, a farmer doesn't usually amount to much, I mean in the eyes of the world. Farmers seem to be in a different class from merchants, for example, or from bankers or other more genteel workers."

"Listen to me, Dorian Trent." Uncle Zed laid down his book as if he had a serious task before him. "Let me tell you something. If you haven't done so before, begin now and thank the Lord that you began life on this globe of ours as a farmer's child and boy. Whatever you do or become in the future, you have made a good beginning. You have already laid away in the way of concepts, we may say, a generous store of nature's riches, for you have been in close touch with the earth, and the life which teems in soil and air and the waters. Pity the man whose childish eyes looked out on nothing but paved streets and brick walls or whose young ears heard nothing but the harsh rumble of the city, for his early conceptions from which to interpret his later life is artificial and therefore largely untrue."

Uncle Zed smiled up into the boy's face as if to ask, Do you get that? Dorian would have to have time to assimilate the idea; meanwhile, he had another question:

"Uncle Zed, why are there classes among members of our Church?"

"Classes? What do you mean?"

"Well, the rich do not associate with the poor nor the learned with the unlearned. I know, of course, that this is the general rule in the world, but I think it should be different in the Church."

"Yes; it ought to be and is different. There are no classes such as you have in mind in the Church, even though a few unthinking members seem to imply it by their actions; but there is no real class distinction in the Church of Jesus Christ of Latter-day Saints, only such that are based on the doing of the right and the wrong. Character alone is the standard of classification."

"Yes, I see that that should be true."

"It is true. Let me illustrate: The presiding authority in the Church is not handed down from father to son, thus fostering an aristocratic tendency; also this authority is so wide-spread that anything like a "ruling family" would be impossible. In a town where I once lived, the owner of the bank and the town blacksmith were called on missions. They both were assigned to the same field, and the blacksmith was appointed to preside over the banker. The banker submitted willingly to be directed in his missionary labors by one who, judged by worldly standards, was far beneath him in the social scale. I know a shoemaker in the city who is a teacher in the theological class of his ward, whose membership consists of merchants, lawyers, doctors, and the like. Although he is poor and earns his living by mending shoes, he is greatly respected for his goodness and his knowledge of Scriptural subjects and doctrine."

"So you think—that a young fellow might—that it would not be wrong—or foolish for a poor man to think a lot of—of a rich girl, for instance."

Uncle Zed peered at Dorian over his glasses. The old man took him gently by the shoulders. Ah, that's what's back of all this, he thought; but what he said was:

"My boy, Emerson said, 'Hitch your wagon to a star,' and I will add, never let go, although the rocks in the road may bump you badly. Why, there's nothing impossible for a young man like you. You may be rich, if you want to; I expect to see you learned; and the Priesthood which you have is your assurance, through your diligence and faithfulness, to any heights. Yes, my boy; go ahead—love Mildred Brown all you want to; she's fine, but not a bit finer than you."

"Oh, Uncle Zed," Dorian somewhat protested; but, nevertheless, he went home that evening with his heart singing.

6.

SOME DAYS LATER word came to Mrs. Trent that Mildred was very ill. "Call on them after school," she said to Dorian, "to see just how she is, and ask Mrs. Brown if I can do anything for her."

Dorian did as he was directed. He went around to the back door for fear he might disturb the sick girl. Mrs. Brown herself, seeing him coming, met him and let him in.

Yes, Mildred was very ill. Mrs. Brown was plainly worried. Could he or his mother do anything to help? No; only to lend their faith and prayers. Would he come into the sick room to see her for a few minutes? Yes, if she desired it.

Dorian followed the mother into the sick room. Mildred lay well propped up by pillows in a bed white as snow. She was thinner and paler than ever, eyes bigger, hair heavier and more golden. When she saw Dorian, she smiled and reached out her hand, letting it lie in the big strong one.

"How are you?" she said, very low.

"Well and fine, and how are you?"

She simply shook her head gently and closed her eyes, seeming content to touch the strong young manhood beside her. The mother went quietly from the room, and all became quite still. Speech was difficult for the sick girl, and equally hard for the young man. But he looked freely at the angel-like face on the pillow without rebuke from the closed eyes. He glanced about the room, beautifully clean and airy. All her books and her working material had been carried away as if she were through with them for good. In a corner on an easel stood an unfinished copy of "Sunset in Marshland." Dorian's eyes rested for a moment on the picture, and as he again looked at the girl, he saw a smile pass over the marble-like face.

That was all. Presently, he left the room, and without many words, the house.

Each day after that Dorian managed to learn of the girl's condition, though he did not go into the sick chamber. On the sixth day word came to Dorian at school that Mildred was dying. He looked about for Carlia to tell her, but she was nowhere to be found. Dorian could not go home. Mildred was dying! The one girl—yes, the only one in all the world who had looked at him with her heart in the look, was leaving the world, and him. Why could she not live, if only for his sake? He sat in the school room until all had gone, and he was alone with the janitor. His open book was still before him, but he saw not the printed page. Then the short winter day closed. Dusk came on. The janitor had finished sweeping the room and was ready to leave. Dorian gathered up his books, put on his overcoat, and went out. Mildred was dying! Perhaps she was about to begin that great journey into the unknown. Would she be afraid? Would she not need a strong hand to help her? "Mildred," he whispered.

He walked on slowly up the street toward the Brown's. Darkness came on. The light gleamed softly through the closed blinds of the house. Everything was very still. He did not try to be admitted, but paced back and forth on the other side of the street. Back and forth he went for a long time, it seemed. Then the front door opened, and the doctor passed out. Mildred must either be better or beyond all help. He wanted to ask the doctor, but he could not bring himself to intercept him. The house remained quiet. Some of the lights were extinguished. Dorian crossed the street. He must find out something. He stood by the gate, not knowing what to do. The door opened

65

again, and a woman, evidently a neighbor, came out. She saw the young man and stopped.

"Pardon me," said Dorian, "but tell me how Mildred—Miss Brown is?"

"She just died."

"Thank you."

66

The woman went into a nearby house. Dorian moved away, benumbed with the despair which sank into his heart at the final setting of his sun. Dead! Mildred was dead! He felt the night wind blow cold down the street, and he saw the storm clouds scudding along the distant sky. In the deep blue directly above him a star shone brightly, but it only reminded him of what Uncle Zed had said about hitching to a star; yes, but what if the star had suddenly been taken from the sky!

A form of a girl darted across the street toward him. He stopped and saw that it was Carlia.

"Dorian" she cried, "how is she?"

"She has just died."

"Dead! O, dear," she wailed.

They stood there under the street light, the girl looking with great pity into the face of the young man. She was only a girl, and not a very wise girl, but she saw how he suffered, and her heart went out to his heart. She took his hand and held it firmly within her warmer grasp; and by that simple thing the young man seemed again to get within the reach of human sympathy. Then they walked on without speaking, and she led him along the streets and on to the road which led to Greenstreet.

"Come on, Dorian, let's go home," she said.

"Yes; let's go home, Carlia."

7.

THE DEATH OF Mildred Brown affected Dorian Trent most profoundly. Not that he displayed any marked outward signs of his feelings, but his very soul was moved to its depths, sometimes as of despair, sometimes as of resentment. Why, he asked himself, should God send—he put it this way—send to him this beautiful creature who filled his heart so completely, why hold her out to him as if inviting him to take her, and then suddenly snatch her away out of his life—out of the life of the world!

For many days Dorian went about as if in a pained stupor. His mother, knowing her boy, tried in a wise way to comfort him; but it was not altogether a success. His studies were neglected, and he had thoughts of quitting school altogether; but he did not do this. He dragged through the few remaining days until spring, when he eagerly went to work on the open reaches of the farm, where he was more away from human beings and nearer to that something in his heart. He worked long and hard and faithfully that spring.

On the upper bank of the canal, where the sagebrush stood untouched, Dorian that summer found the first sego blossoms. He had never observed them so closely before nor seen their real beauty. How like Mildred they were! He gathered a bouquet of them that Saturday afternoon as he went home, placed them in a glass of water, and then Sunday afternoon he wrapped them in a damp newspaper and took the bouquet with him to town. His Sunday trips to the city were usually for the purpose of visiting Mildred's grave. The sun shone warm that day from a blue sky as Dorian came slowly and reverently to the plot where lay all that was earthly of one whom he loved so well. The new headstone gleamed in white marble and the young grass stood tender and green. Against the stone lay a bunch of withered wild roses. Someone had been there before him that day. Whom could it be? Her mother was not in the city, and who else would remember the visit af the angel-being who had returned to her eternal home? A pang shot through his heart, and he was half tempted to turn without placing his own tribute on the grave, then immediately he knew the thought was foolish. He took off the wrapping and placed his fresher flowers near the more withered ones. Later that summer, he learned only incidently that it had been Carlia who had been before him that afternoon.

69   During those days, Carlia kept out of Dorian's way as much as possible. She even avoided walking to and from school with him. He was so absentminded even with her that she in time came to resent it in her feelings. She could not understand that a big, very-much-alive boy should have his mind so fixed on a dead girl that he should altogether forget there were living ones about, especially one, Carlia Duke.

One evening Dorian met Uncle Zed driving his cow home from the pasture, and the old man invited the younger man to walk along with him. Dorian always found Uncle Zed's company acceptable.

"Why haven't you come to me with your trouble?" abruptly asked Uncle Zed.

Dorian started, then hung his head.

"We never have any unshared secrets, you know, and I may have been able to help you."

"I couldn't talk to anybody."

"No; I suppose not."

The cow was placed in the corral, and then Uncle Zed and Dorian sat down on a grassy bank. The sun was painting just such a picture of the marshlands as Dorian knew so well.

"But I can talk to you" continued the old man as if there had been no break in his sentences. "Death, I know, is a strange and terrible thing, for youth; when you get as old as I, I hope you will look on death as nothing more than a release from mortality, a moving from one sphere to another, a step along the eternal line of progress. I suppose that it is just as necessary that we pass out of the world by death as that we enter it by birth; and I further suppose that the terror with which death is vested is for the purpose of helping us to cling to this earth-life until our mission here is completed."

Dorian did not speak; his eyes were on the marshlands.

"Imagine, Dorian, this world, just as it is, with all its sin and misery and without any death. What would happen? We would all, I fear, become so self-centered, so hardened in selfishness that it would be difficult for the gentle power of love to reach us; but now there is hardly a family that has not one or more of its members on the other side. And these absent loved ones are anchors to our souls, tied to us by the never-ending cords of love and affection. You, yourself, my boy, never have had until now many interests other than those of this life; now your interests are broadened to another world, and that's something worth while ... Now, come and see me often." They arose, each to go to his home.

"I will, Uncle Zed. Thank you for what you have said."

Dorian completed his four years high school. Going to the University might come later, but now he was moved by a spirit of activity to do bigger things with his farm, and to enlarge it, if possible. About this time, dry-farming had taken the attention of the farmers in his locality, and many of them had procured lands on the sloping foothills. Dorian, with a number of other young men had gone up the nearby canyon to the low hills of the valley beyond and had taken up lands. That first summer Dorian spent much of his time in breaking up the land. As timber was not far away, he built himself a one-roomed log house and some corrals and outhouses. A mountain stream rushed by the lower corner of his farm, and its wild music sang him to sleep when he spent the night in the hills. He furnished his "summer residence" with a few simple necessities so that he could live there a number of days at a time. He minded not the solitude. The wild odorous verdure of the hills, the cool breezes, the song of the distant streams, the call of the birds, all seemed to harmonize with his own feelings at that time. He had a good kerosene lamp, and at nights when he was not too tired, he read. On his visits to the city he usually had an eye for book bargains, and thus his board shelving came to be quite a little library. He had no method in his collecting, no course of connected study. At one time he would leisurely read one of Howell's easy-going novels, at another time he would be kept wide-eyed until midnight with "Lorna Doone" or with "Ben Hur."

72

Dorian had heard of Darwin, of Huxley, of Ingersol and of Tom Payne, but he had never read anything but selections from these writers. Now he obtained a copy of the "Origin of Species" and a book by Ingersol. These he read carefully. Darwin's book was rather heavy, but by close application, the young student thought he learned what the scientist was "driving at." This book disturbed him somewhat. There seemed to be much truth in it, but also some things which did not agree with what he had been taught to be true. In this he realized his lack of knowledge. More knowledge must clear up any seeming contradiction, he reasoned. Ingersol was more readable, snappy, witty, hitting the Bible in a fearless way. Dorian had no doubt that all of Ingersol's points could be answered, as he himself could refute many of them.

One day as Dorian was browsing as usual in a book store he came across a cheap copy of Drummond's "Natural Law in the Spiritual World," the book which he had given Uncle Zed. As he wanted a copy himself, he purchased this one and took it with him to his cabin in the hills. Immediately he was interested in the book, and he filled its pages with copious notes and marks of emphasis.

It was Sunday afternoon in mid-summer at Greenstreet. The wheat again stood in the shock. The alfalfa waved in scented purple.

Dorian and the old philosopher of Greenstreet sat in the shade of the cottonwood and looked out on the farm scene as they talked.

"I've also been reading 'Natural Law in the Spiritual World'" said   73
Dorian.

"Good," replied Uncle Zed. "I was going to lend you my copy, so we could talk about it intelligently. What message have you found in it for you?"

"Message?"

"Yes; every book should have a message and should deliver it to the reader. Drummond's book thundered a message to me, but it came too late. I am old, and past the time when I could heed any such call. If I were young, if I—if I were like you, Dorian, you who have life before you, what might not I do, with the help of the Lord!"

"What, Uncle Zed?"

"Drummond was a clergyman and a professor of natural history and science. As such, he was a student of the laws of God as revealed both through the written word of inspiration and in nature about him. In his book he aims to prove that the spiritual world is controlled by the same laws which operate in the natural wold; and as you perhaps discovered in your reading, he comes very nearly proving his claim. He presents some wonderfully interesting analogies. Of course, much of his theology is of the perverted sectarian kind, and therein lies the weakness of his argument. If he had had the clear truth of the restored gospel, how much brighter would his facts have been illumed, how much stronger would have been his deductions.   74
Why, even I with my limited scientific knowledge can set him right in many places. So I say, if I were but a young man like you, do you know what I'd do?"

"What?" again questioned Dorian.

"I would devote all my mind, might and strength to the learning of truth, of scientific truth. I would cover every branch of science possible in the limits of one life, especially the natural sciences. Then with my knowledge of the gospel and the lamp of inspiration which the priesthood entitles me to, I could harmonize the great body of truth coming from any and every source. Dorian, what a life work that would be!"

The old man looked smilingly at his companion with a strange, knowing intimation. He spoke of himself, but he meant that Dorian should take the suggestion. Dorian could pick up his beautiful dream and make it come true. Dorian, with life and strength, and a desire for study and truth could accomplish this very desirable end. The old man placed his hand lovingly on the young man's shoulder, as he continued:

"You are the man to do this, Dorian—you, not I."

"I—Uncle Zed, do you believe that?"

"I do. Listen, my boy. I see you looking over the harvested field. It is a fine work you are doing; thousands can plant and harvest year after year; but few there are who can and will devote their lives to the planting of faith and the nourishing and the establishing of faith in the hearts of men; and that's what we need now to properly answer the Lord's cry that when He cometh shall He find faith on the earth?.... Let the call come to you—but there, in the Lord's own good time. Come into the house. I have a new book to show you, also I have a very delicious cherry pie."

They went into the house together, where they inspected both book and pie. Dorian weakly objected to the generous portion which was cut for him, but Uncle Zed explained that the process of division not only increased the number of pieces of pie, but also added to its tastiness. Dorian led his companion to talk about himself.

"Yes," he said in reply to a question, "I was born in England and brought up in the Wesleyan Methodist church. I was a great reader ever since I can remember. I read not only history and some fiction, but even the dry-as-dust sermons were interesting to me. But I never seemed satisfied. The more I read, the deeper grew the mysteries of life. Nowhere did I find a clear, comprehendible statement of what I, an entity with countless other entities, was doing here. Where had I come from, where was I going? I visited the churches within my reach. I heard the preachers and read the philosophers to obtain, if possible, a clue to the mystery of life. I studied, and prayed, and went about seeking, but never finding."

"But you did find the truth at last?"   76

"Yes; thank the Lord. I found the opening in the darkness, and it came through the simple, humble, and not very learned elders of the Church of Jesus Christ of Latter-day Saints."

"What is the principle trouble with all this learning of the world that it does not lead to the truth?"

"The world's ignorance of God. Eternal life consists in knowing the only true God, and the world does not know Him; therefore, all their systems of religion are founded on a false basis. That is the reason there is so much uncertainty and floundering when philosophers and religionists try to make a known truth agree with their conceptions of God."

"Explain that a little more to me, Uncle Zed."

"Some claim that Nature is God, others that God only manifests Himself through nature. I read this latter idea many places. For instance, Pope says:

"'All are but parts of one stupendous whole Whose body nature is, and God the soul.'

"Also Tennyson:

'The sun, the moon, the stars, the seas, the hills and plains Are not these, O soul, the vision of Him who reigns? Speak to Him there, for He hears, and spirit with spirit can meet, Closer is He than breathing, and nearer than hands and feet.'

"This, no doubt, is beautiful poetry, but it tells only a part of the   77
truth. God, by His Spirit is, and can be all the poet here describes. 'Whither shall I go from thy spirit? or whither shall I flee from thy presence?' exclaims the Psalmist. 'In him we live and move and have our being' declares Paul; but these statements alone are not enough for our proper understanding of the subject. We try to see God

behind the veil of nature, in sun and wind and flower and fruit; but there is something lacking. Try now to formulate some distinct idea of what this universal and almighty force back of nature is. We are told that this force is God, whom we must love and worship and serve. We want the feeling of nearness to satisfy the craving for love and protection, but our intellect and our reason must also be some-what satisfied. We must have some object on which to rest—we cannot always be floating about unsuspended in time and space.

"Then there is some further confusion: Christian philosophers have tried to personify this 'soul of the universe,' for God, they say, thinks and feels and knows. They try to get a personality without form or bounds or dimentions, but it all ends in vagueness and confusion. As for me, and I think I am not so different from other men,—for me to be able to think of God, I must have some image of Him. I cannot think of love or good, or power or glory in the abstract. These must be expressed to me by symbols at least as eminating from, or inherent in, or exercised by some person. Love cannot exist alone: there must be one who loves and one who is being loved. God is love. That means to me that a person, a beautiful, glorified, allwise, benevolent being exercises that divine principle which is shed forth on you and me.

"Now, if the world would only leave all this metaphysical meandering and come back to the simple truth, what a clearing of mists there would be! All their philosophies would have a solid basis if they would only accept the truth revealed anew to us through the Prophet Joseph Smith that God is one of a race, the foremost and first, if you wish it, but still one of a race of beings who inhabit the universe; that we humans are His children, begotten of Him in the pre-mortal world in His image; that we are on the upward path through eternity, following Him who has gone before and has marked out the way; that if we follow, we shall eventually arrive at the point where He now is. Ignorance of these things is what I understand to be ignorance of God."

"In England I lost my wife and two children. The gospel came to me shortly after, I am sure, to comfort me in the depths of my despair. Not one church on earth that I knew of, Catholic or Protestant, would hold out any hope of my ever being reunited with wife and children as such. There is no family life in heaven, they teach. At that time I went about listening to the preachers, and I delved into books. 79 I made extensive copyings in my note books. I have them yet, and some day when you are interested I will show them to you."

"I am interested now," said Dorian.

"But I'm not going to talk to you longer on this theme, even though it is Sunday and time for sermonizing. I'm going to meeting, where you also ought to go. You are not attending as regularly as you should."

"No, but I've been very busy."

"No excuse that. There is danger in remaining away too long from the established sources of spiritual inspiration and uplift, especially when one is reading Ingersol and Tom Paine. I have no fault to find with your ambition to get ahead in the world, but with it 'remember thy creator in the days of thy youth.' Are you neglecting your mother?"

"No; I think not, Uncle Zed; but what do you mean about mother?"

"You are all she has. Are you making her days happy by your personal care and presence. Are you giving of yourself to her?"

"Well, perhaps I am not so considerate as I might be; I am away quite a lot; thank you for calling my attention to it."

"Are you neglecting anybody else?"

"Not that I know."

"Good. Now I must clear away my table and get ready for meet- 80 ing. You'll go with me."

"I can't. I haven't my Sunday clothes."

"The Lord will not look at your clothes."

"No; but a lot of people will."

"We go to meeting to worship the Lord, not to be looked at by others. Go home and put on your Sunday best; there is time." The old man was busy between table and cupboard as he talked. "Have you seen Carlia lately?"

"No," replied Dorian.

"The last time she was here I thought she was a little peaked in the face, for you know she has such a rosy, roly-poly one."

"Is that so? She comes to see you, then?"

"Yes; oftener than you do."

"I never meet her here."

"No; she manages that, I surmise."

"What do you mean?"

"I tell you Carlia is a lovely girl," continued Uncle Zed, ignoring his direct question. "Have you ever eaten butter she has churned?"

"Not that I know."

"She used to bring me a nice pat when my cow was dry; and bread of her own baking too, about as good as I myself make." He chuckled as he wiped the last dish and placed it neatly in the rack.

Dorian arose to go. "Remember what I have told you this evening" said Uncle Zed. The old man from behind his window watched his young friend walk leisurely along the road until he reached the cross-lots path which led to the Duke home. Here he saw him pause, go on again, pause once more, then jump lightly over the fence and strike out across the field. Uncle Zed then went on finishing his preparations for meeting.

As Dorian walked across the field, he did think of what Uncle Zed had said to him. Dorian had built his castles, had dreamed his dreams; but never before had the ideas presented to him by Uncle Zed that afternoon ever entered in them. The good old man had seemed so eager to pass on to the young man an unfulfilled work, yes, a high, noble work. Dorian caught a glimpse of the greatness of it and the glory of it that afternoon, and his soul was thrilled. Was he equal to such a task? ... He had wanted to become a successful farmer, then his vision had gone on to the teaching profession; but beyond that he had not ventured. He was already well on the way to make a success of his farms. He liked the work. He could with pleasure be a farmer all his life. But should a man's business be all of life? Dorian realized, not of course in its fuller meaning, that the accumulating of worldly riches was only a means to the accomplishing of other and greater ends of life; and here was before him something worthy of any man's best endeavors. Here was a life's work which at its close would mean something to him and to the world. With these thoughts in his mind he stepped up to the rear of the Duke place where he saw someone in the corral with the cows, busy with her milking.

82

8.

"HELLO, CARLIA", greeted Dorian as he stopped at the yard and stood leaning against the fence.

Carlia was just finishing milking a cow. As she straightened, with a three-legged stool in one hand and a foaming milk pail in the other, she looked toward Dorian. "O, is that you? You scared me."

"Why?"

"A stranger coming so suddenly."

The young man laughed. "Nearly through?" he asked.

"Just one more—Brindle, the kickey one."

"Aren't you afraid of her?"

Carlia laughed scornfully. The girl had beautiful white teeth. Her red cheeks were redder than ever. Her dark hair coiled closely about her shapely head. And she had grown tall, too, the young man noticed, though she was still plump and round-limbed.

"My buckets are full, and I'll have to take them to the house before I can finish," she said. "You stay here until I come back—if you want to."

"I don't want to—here, let me carry them." He took the pails from her hand, and they went to the house together.

The milk was carried into the kitchen where Mrs. Duke was busy with pots and pans. Mr. Duke was before the mirror, giving the finishing touches to his hair. He was dressed for meeting. As he heard rather than saw his daughter enter, he asked:

"Carlia, have you swilled the pigs?"

"Not yet," she replied.

"Well, don't forget—and say, you'd better give a little new milk to the calf. It's not getting along as well as it should—and, if you have time before meetin', throw a little hay to the horses."

"All right, father, I'll see to all of it. As I'm not going to meeting, I'll have plenty of time."

"Not goin'?" He turned, hair brush in hand, and saw Dorian. "Hello, Dorian," he greeted, "you're quite a stranger. You'll come along to meetin' with Carlia, I suppose. We will be late if we don't hurry."

"Father, I told you I'm not going. I—" she hesitated as if not quite certain of her words— "I had to chase all over the hills for the cows, and I'm not through milking yet. Then there are the pigs and the calves and the horses to feed. But I'll not keep Dorian. You had better go with father" —this to the young man who still stood by the kitchen door.

"Leave the rest of the chores until after meetin'," suggested the father, somewhat reluctantly, to be sure, but in concession to Dorian's presence.

"I can't go to meeting either," said Dorian. "I'm not dressed for it, so I'll keep Carlia company, if you or she have no objections."

"Well, I've no objections, but I don't like you to miss your meetin's."

"We'll be good," laughed Dorian.

"But—"

"Come, father," the mother prompted, "you know I can't walk fast in this hot weather."

Carlia got another pail, and she and Dorian went back to the corral.

"Let me milk," offered Dorian.

"No; you're strange, and she'd kick you over the fence."

"O, I guess not," he remarked; but he let the girl finish her milking. He again carried the milk back; he also took the "slop" to the pigs and threw the hay to the horses, while the girl gave the new milk to the butting calf; then back to the house where they strained the milk. Then the young man was sent into the front room while the girl changed from work to Sunday attire.

The front room was very hot and uncomfortable. The young man looked about on the familiar scene. There were the same straight-backed chairs, the same homemade carpet, more faded and threadbare than ever, the same ugly enlarged photographs within their massive frames which the enterprising agent had sold to Mrs. Duke. There was the same lack of books or music or anything pretty or refined; and as Dorian stood and looked about, there came to him more forcibly than ever the barrenness of the room and of the house in general. True, his own home was very humble, and yet there was an air of comfort and refinement about it. The Duke home had always impressed him as being cold and cheerless and ugly. There were no protecting porches, no lawn, no flowers, and the barn yard had crept close up to the house. It was a place to work. The eating and the sleeping were provided, so that work could be done, farm and kitchen work with their dirt and litter. The father and the mother and the daughter were slaves to work. Only in work did the parents companion with the daughter. The visitors to the house were mostly those who came to talk about cattle and crops and irrigation.

As a child, Carlia was naturally cheerful and loving; but her sordid environment seemed to be crushing her. At times she struggled to get out from under; but there seemed no way, so she gradually gave in to the inevitable. She became resentful and sarcastic. Her black eyes frequently flashed in scorn and anger. As she grew in physical strength and beauty, these unfortunate traits of character became more pronounced. The budding womanhood which should have been carefully nurtured by the right kind of home and neighborhood was often left to develop in wild and undirected ways. Dorian Trent as he stood in that front room awaiting her had only a dim conception of all this.

Carlia came in while he was yet standing. She had on a white dress and had placed a red rose in her hair.

"O, say, Carlia!" exclaimed Dorian at sight of her.

"What's the matter?" she asked.

"Here you go dolling up, and look at me."

"You're all right. Open the door, it's terribly stuffy in here."

Dorian opened the tightly stuck door. Then he turned and stood looking at the girl before him. It seemed to him that he had never seen her so grown-up and so beautiful.

"Say, Carlia, when did you grow up?" he asked.

"While you have been away growing up too."

"It's the long dress, isn't it?"

"And milking cows and feeding pigs and pitching hay." She gave a toss to her head and held out her roughened red hands as proof of her assertion. He stepped closer to her as if to examine them more carefully, but she swiftly hid them behind her back. The rose, loosened from the tossing head, fell to the floor, and Dorian picked it up. He sniffed at it then handed it to her.

"Where did you get it?" he asked.

She reddened. "None of your—Say, sit down, can't you."

Dorian seated himself on the sofa and invited her to sit by him, but she took a chair by the table.

"You're not very neighborly," he said.

"As neighborly as you are," she retorted.

"What's the matter with you, Carlia?"

"Nothing the matter with me. I'm the same; only I must have grown up, as you say."

A sound as of someone driving up the road came to them through the open door. Carlia nervously arose and listened. She appeared to be frightened, as she looked out to the road without wanting to be seen. A light wagon rattled by, and the girl, somewhat relieved, went back to her chair.

"Isn't it warm in here?" she asked.

"It's warm everywhere."

"I can't stay here. Let's go out—for a walk."

"All right—come on."

They closed the door, and went out at the rear. He led the way around to the front, but Carlia objected.

"Let's go down by the field," she said. "The road is dusty."

The day was closing with a clear sky. A Sunday calm rested over meadow and field, as the two strolled down by the ripening wheat. The girl seemed uneasy until the house was well out of sight. Then she seated herself on a grassy bank by the willows. 89

"I'm tired," she said with a sigh of relief.

Dorian looked at her with curious eyes. Carlia, grown up, was more of a puzzle than ever.

"You are working too hard," he ventured.

"Hard work won't kill anybody—but it's the other things."

"What other things?"

"The grind, the eternal grind—the dreary sameness of every day."

"You did not finish the high school. Why did you quit?"

"I had to, to save mother. Mother was not only doing her usual house work, but nearly all the outside choring besides. Father was away most of the time on his dry farm too, and he's blind to the work at home. He seems to think that the only real work is the plowing and the watering and the harvesting, and he would have let mother go on killing herself. Gee, these men!" The girl viciously dug the heel of her shoe into the sod.

"I'm sorry you had to quit school, Carlia."

"Sorry? I wanted to keep on more than I ever wanted anything in my life; but—"

"But I admire you for coming to the rescue of your mother. That was fine of you."

"I'm glad I can do some fine thing."

Dorian had been standing. He now seated himself on the bank 90 beside her. The world about them was very still as they sat for a few moments without speaking.

"Listen," said he, "I believe Uncle Zed is preaching. The meeting house windows are wide open, for a wonder."

"He can preach," she remarked.

"He told me you visit him frequently."

"I do. He's the grandest man, and I like to talk to him."

"So do I. I had quite a visit with him this afternoon. I rather fooled him, I guess."

"How?"

"He told me to go home and change my clothes, and then go to meeting; but I came here instead."

"Why did you do that?"

"To see you, of course."

"Pooh, as if I was anything to look at."

"Well, you are, Carlia," and his eyes rested steadily on her to prove his contention. "Why didn't you want to go to meeting this evening?"

"You heard me tell father."

"That wasn't the whole truth. I was not the reason because you had decided not to go before I came."

"Well—how do you know that? but, anyway, it's none of your business, where I go, is it?" She made an effort to stare him out of countenance, but it ended in lowered head and eyes.

91   "Carlia! No, of course, it isn't. Excuse me for asking."

There was another period of silence wherein Dorian again wondered at the girl's strange behavior. Was he annoying her? Perhaps she did not care to have him paying his crude attentions to her; and yet—

"Tell me about your dry farm," she said.

"I've already plowed eighty acres," he informed her. "The land is rich, and I expect to raise a big crop next year. I've quite a cosy house, up there, not far from the creek. The summer evenings are lovely and cool. I can't get mother to stay over night. I wish you would come and go with her, and stay a few days."

"How could I stay away from home that long? The heavens would fall."

"Well, that might help some. But, honestly, Carlia, you ought to get away from this grind a little. It's telling on you. Don't you ever get into the city?"

"Sometimes Saturday afternoons to deliver butter and eggs."

"Well, some Saturday we'll go to see that moving picture show that's recently started in town. They say it's wonderful. I've never been. We'll go together. What do you say?"

"I would like to."

"Let's move on. Meeting is out, and the folks are coming home."

They walked slowly back to the house. Mr. and Mrs. Duke soon arrived and told of the splendid meeting they had had. 92

"Uncle Zed spoke," said Mr. Duke, "and he did well, as usual. He's a regular Orson Pratt."

"The people do not know it," added Dorian; "perhaps their children or their children's children will."

"Well, what have you two been doing?" enquired the father of Carlia.

"We've just been taking a walk," answered Dorian. "Will it be alright if Carlia and I go to the new moving picture theatre in town some Saturday?"

Neither parent made any objection. They were, in fact, glad to have this neighbor boy show some interest in their daughter.

"Your mother was at meeting," said Mrs. Duke; "and she was asking about you."

"Yes; I've neglected her all afternoon; so I must be off. Good night folks."

Carlia went with him to the gate, slipping her arm into his and snuggling closely as if to get the protection of good comradship. The movement was not lost on Dorian, but he lingered only for a moment.

"Goodnight, Carlia; remember, some Saturday."

"I'll not forget. Goodnight" she looked furtively up and down the road, then sped back into the house.

Dorian walked on in the darkening evening. A block or so down the road he came on to an automobile. No one in Greenstreet owned one of these machines as yet, and there were but few in the city. As Dorian approached, he saw a young man working with the machinery under the lifted hood.

"Hello," greeted Dorian. "what's the trouble?"

"Damned if I know. Been stalled here for an hour." The speaker straightened from his work. His hands were grimy, and the sweat was running down his red and angry face. He held tightly the stump of a cigarette between his lips.

"I'm sorry I can't help you," said Dorian, "but I don't know the first thing about an automobile."

"Well, I thought I knew a lot, but this gets me." He swore again, as if to impress Dorian with the true condition of his feelings. Then he went at the machinery again with pliers and wrenches, after which he vigorously turned the crank. The engine started with a wheeze and then a roar. The driver leaped into the car and brought the racing engine to a smoother running. "The cursed thing" he remarked, "why couldn't it have done that an hour ago. O, say, excuse me, have you just been at the house up the road?"

"The Duke house? yes."

"Is the old man—is Mr. Duke at home?"

"Yes; he's at home."

"Thank you." The car moved slowly up the road until it reached the Duke gate where it stopped; but only for a moment, for it turned and sped with increasing hurry along the road leading to the city.

Dorian stood and watched it until its red light disappeared. He wondered why the stranger wanted to know why Mr. Duke was at home, then on learning that he was, why he turned about as if he had no business with him.

Later, Dorian learned the reason.

9.

DORIAN WAS TWENTY-ONE years old, and his mother had planned a little party in honor of the event. The invited guests were Uncle Zed, Bishop Johnson and wife, the teacher of the district school, and Carlia Duke. These arrived during the dusk of the evening, all but Carlia. They lingered on the cool lawn under the colored glow of the Chinese lanterns.

Mrs. Trent realized that it would be useless to make the party a surprise, for she had to have Dorian's help in hanging out the lanterns, and he would necessarily see the unusual activity in front room and kitchen. Moreover, Dorian, unlike Uncle Zed, had not lost track of his birthdays, and especially this one which would make him a full-fledged citizen of these United States.

The little party chatted on general topics for some time until Mrs. Trent, in big white apron, announced that supper was ready, and would they all come right in. Mrs. Trent always served her refreshments at the regular supper time and not near midnight, for she claimed that people of regular habits, which her guests were, are much better off by not having those habits broken into.

"Are we all here?" she asked, scanning them as they passed in. "All but Carlia," she announced. "Where's Carlia?"

No one knew. Someone proffered the explanation that she was usually late as she had so many chores to do, at which the Bishop's wife shook her head knowingly, but said nothing.

"Well, she'll be along presently," said Mrs. Trent. "Sit down all of you. Bishop, will you ask the blessing?"

The hostess, waitress, and cook all combined in the capable person of Mrs. Trent, sat at the table with her party. Everything which was to be served was on the table in plain sight, so that all could nicely guage their eating to various dishes. When all were well served and the eating was well under way, Mrs. Trent said:

"Brothers and sisters, this is Dorian's birthday party. He has been a mighty good boy, and so—"

"Mother," interrupted the young man.

"Now, you never mind—you be still. Dorian is a good boy, and I want all of you to know it."

"We all do, Sister Trent," said the Bishop; "and it is a good thing to sometimes tell a person of his worthiness to his face."

"But if we say more, he'll be uncomfortable," remarked the mother, "so we had better change the subject. The crops are growing, the weather is fine, and the neighbors are all right. That disposes of the chief topics of conversation, and will give Uncle Zed a chance. He always has something worth listening to, if not up his sleeve, then in his white old head. But do not hurry, Uncle Zed; get through with your supper."

The old man was a light eater, so he finished before the others. He looked smilingly about him, noting that those present were eager to listen. He took from his pocket a number of slips of paper and placed them on the table beside his plate. Then he began to talk, the others leisurely finishing their dessert.

"The other evening," he said, "Dorian and I had a conversation which interested us very much, and I think it would interest all of us here. I was telling him my experience in my search for God and the plan of salvation, and I promised him I would read to him some of the things I found. Here is a definition of God which did not help me very much." He picked up one of the slips of paper and read:

"'God is the integrated harmony of all potentialities of good in every actual and possible rational agent.' What do you think of that?"

The listeners knitted their brows, but no one spoke. Uncle Zed continued: "Well, here is a little more. Perhaps this will clear it up: 'The greatest of selves, the ultimate Self of the universe, is God ... My God is my deeper self and yours too. He is the self of the universe, and knows all about it ... By Deity we mean the all-controling consciousness of the universe, as well as the unfathomable, all unknowable, and unknowable abyss of being beyond'." 98

Uncle Zed carefully folded his papers and placed them back in his pocket. He looked about him, but his friends appeared as if they had had a volley of Greek fired at them. "Well" he said, "why don't some of you say something?"

"Please pass the pickles," responded Mrs. Trent.

When the merriment had ceased, uncle Zed continued: "There is some truth in these definitions. God is all that which they try to express, and vastly more. The trouble is these men talk about the attributes of God, and confound these with the being and personality of the Great Parent. I may describe the scent of the rose, but that does not define the rose itself. I cannot separate the rose from its color or form or odor, any more than I can divorce music from the instrument. These vague and incomplete definitions have had much to do with the unbelief in the world. Tom Paine wrote a book which he called the 'Age of Reason' on the premise that reason does away with God. Isn't that it, Dorian?"

"All agnostic writers seem to think that there is no reason in religion, and at times they come pretty near proving it too," replied Dorian.

"That is because they base their arguments on the religions of the world; but the restored gospel of Jesus Christ rests largely on reason. Why, I can prove, contrary to the generally accepted opinion, by reason alone that there must be a God." 99

"We shall be glad to hear it," said the school teacher. The eating was about over, and so they all sat and listened attentively.

"We do not need to quote a word of scripture," continued Uncle Zed. "All we need to know is a little of the world about us, a little of the race and its history, and a little of the other worlds out in space, all of which is open to anybody who will seek it. The rest is simply a little connected thought. Reason tells me that there can be no limits to time or space or intelligence. Time always has been, there can be no end to space, and intelligence cannot create itself. Now, with limitless time and space and intelligence to work with, what have we? The human mind, being limited, cannot grasp the limitless; therefore, we must make arbitrary points of beginning and ending. Now, let us project our thought as far back into duration as we can—count the periods by any thinkable measurements, years, centuries, ages, aeons, anything you please that will help. Have we arrived at a point when there is no world, no life, no intelligence? Certainly not. Somewhere in space, all that we see here and now will be seen to exist. Go back from this point to a previous period, and then count back as far as you wish; there is yet time and space and intelligence.

"There is an eternal law of progress which holds good always and everywhere. It has been operating all through the ages of the past. Now, let us take one of these Intelligences away back in the far distance past and place him in the path of progress so that the eternal law of growth and advancement will operate on him. I care not whether you apply the result to Intelligences as individuals or as the race. Given time enough, this endless and eternal advancement must result in a state of perfection that those who attain to it may with truth and propriety be called Gods. Therefore, there must be a God, yes, many Gods living and reigning throughout the limitless regions of glorified space.

"Here is corroborative evidence: I read in the Doctrine and Covenants, Section 88: 'All kingdoms have a law given; and there are many kingdoms; for there is no space in the which there is no kingdom; and there is no kingdom in which there is no space, either a greater or a lesser kingdom. And unto every kingdom is given a law;

and unto every law there are certain bounds also and conditions.'

"There is a hymn in our hymn book in which W.W. Phelps expresses this idea beautifully. Let me read it:

'If you could hie to Kolob,
    In the twinkling of an eye,
And then continue onward,
    With that same speed to fly.

'Do you think that you could ever,
    Through all eternity,
Find out the generation
    Where Gods began to be?

'Or see the grand beginning
    Where space did not extend?
Or view the last creation,
    Where Gods and matter end?

'Methinks the Spirit whispers:
    No man has found "pure space,"
Nor seen the outside curtains,
    Where nothing has a place.

'The works of God continue,
    And worlds and lives abound;
Improvement and progression
    Have one eternal round.

'There is no end to matter,
    There is no end to space,
There is no end to spirit,
    There is no end to race.

'There is no end to virtue,
     There is no end to might,
There is no end to wisdom,
     There is no end to light.

'There is no end to union,
     There is no end to youth,
There is no end to priesthood,
     There is no end to truth.

102   'There is no end to glory,
     There is no end to love,
There is no end to being,
     Grim death reigns not above.'

"The Latter-day Saints have been adversely criticized for holding out such astounding hopes for the future of the human race; but let us reason a little more, beginning nearer home. What has the race accomplished, even within the short span of our own recollection? Man is fast conquering the forces of nature about him, and making these forces to serve him. Now, we must remember that duration extends ahead of us in the same limitless way in which it reaches back. Give, then, the race today all the time necessary, what cannot it accomplish? Apply it again either to an individual or to the race, in time, some would attain to what we conceive of as perfection, and the term by which such beings are known to us is God. I can see no other logical conclusion."

The chairs were now pushed back, and Mrs. Trent threw a cloth over the table just as it stood, explaining that she would not take the time from her company to devote to the dishes. She invited them into Dorian's little room, much to that young man's uneasiness.

His mother had tidied the room, so it was presentable. His picture, "Sunset in Marshland" had been lowered a little on the wall,

and directly over it hung a photograph of Mildred Brown. To Dorian's questioning look, Mrs. Trent explained, that Mrs. Brown had   103
sent it just the other day. Dorian looked closely at the beautiful picture, and a strange feeling came over him. Had Mildred gone on in
this eternal course of progress of which Uncle Zed had been speaking? Was she still away ahead of him? Would he ever reach her?

On his study table were a number of books, birthday presents.
One was from Uncle Zed's precious store, and one— What? He
picked it up— "David Copperfield." He opened the beautiful volume and read on the fly leaf: "From Carlia, to make up a little for
your loss." He remembered now that Carlia, some time before, had
asked him what books were in the package which had gone down the
canal at the time when he had pulled her out of the water. Carlia had
not forgotten; and she was not here; the supper was over, and it was
getting late. Why had she not come?

The party broke up early, as it was a busy season with them all.
Dorian walked home with Uncle Zed, then he had a mind to run
over to Carlia's. He could not forget about her absence nor about the
present she had sent. He had never read the story, and he would like
to read it to Carlia. She had very little time, he realized, which was all
the more reason for his making time to read it to her.

As every country boy will, at every opportunity, so Dorian cut
crosslots to his objective. He now leaped the fence, and struck off   104
through the meadow up into the corn field. Mr. Duke had a big, fine
field that season, the growing corn already reaching to his shoulder.
The night was dark, save for the twinkling stars in the clear sky; it
was still, save for the soft rustling of the corn in the breeze.

Dorian caught sight of a light as of a lantern up by the ditch from
which the water for irrigating was turned into the rows of corn and
potatoes. He stopped and listened. A tool grated in the gravelly soil.
Mr. Duke was no doubt using his night turn at the water on his corn
instead of turning it on the hay-land as was the custom. He would
inquire of him about Carlia.

As he approached the light, the scraping ceased, and he saw a dark figure dart into the shelter of the tall corn. When he reached the lantern, he found a hoe lying in the furrow where the water should have been running. No man irrigates with a hoe; that's a woman's tool. Ah, the secret was out! Carlia was 'tending' the water. That's why she was not at the party.

He stood looking down into the shadows of the corn rows, but for the moment he could see or hear nothing. He had frightened her, and yet Carlia was not usually afraid. He began to whistle softly and to walk down into the corn. Then he called, not loudly, "Carlia".

105   There was no response. He quickened his steps. The figure ran to another shelter. He could see her now, and he called again, louder than before. She stopped, and then darted through the corn into the more open potatoe patch. Dorian followed.

"Hello, Carlia," he said, "what are you doing?"

The girl stood before him, bareheaded, with rough dress and heavy boots. She was panting as if with fright. When she caught a full sight of Dorian she gave a little cry, and when he came within reach, she grasped him by the arm.

"Oh, is it you, Dorian?"

"Sure. Who else did you think it was? Why, you're all of a tremble. What are you afraid of?"

"I—I thought it was—was someone else. Oh, Dorian, I'm so glad it is you!"

She stood close to him as if wishing to claim his protection. He instinctively placed his arm about her shoulders. "Why, you silly girl, the dark won't hurt you."

"I'm not afraid of the dark. I'm afraid of—Oh, Dorian, don't let him hurt me!" There was a sob in her voice.

"What are you talking about? I believe you're not well. Are your feet wet? Have you a fever?" He put his hand on her forehead, brushing back the dark, towsled hair. He took her plump, work-roughened hand in his bigger and equally rough one. "And this is why you were not to my party," he said.

"Yes; I hated to miss it, but father's rheumatism was so bad that he could not come out. So it was up to me. We haven't any too much water this summer. I'd better turn the water down another row; it's flooding the corn." 106

They went to the lantern on the ditch bank. Dorian picked up the hoe and made the proper adjustment of the water flow. "How long will it take for the water to reach the bottom of the row?" he asked.

"About fifteen minutes."

"And how many rows remain?"

Carlia counted. "Twelve," she said.

"All right. This is a small stream and will only allow for three rows at a time. Three into twelve is four, and four times fifteen is sixty. It is now half past ten. We'll get through by twelve o'clock easy."

"You'd better go home. I'm all right now. I'm not afraid."

"I said we will get home. Sit down here on the bank. Are you cold?" He took off his coat and placed it about her shoulders. She made no objections, though in truth she was not cold.

"Tell me about the party," she said.

He told her who were there, and how they had missed her.

"And did Uncle Zed preach?"

"Preach? O, yes, he talked mighty fine. I wish I could tell you what he said."

"What was it about?"

"About God," he answered reverently.

"Try to tell me, Dorian. I need to know. I'm such a dunce." 107

Dorian repeated in his way Uncle Zed's argument, and he succeeded fairly well in his presentation of the subject. The still night under the shining stars added an impressive setting to the telling, and the girl close by his side drank in hungrily every word. When the water reached the end of the rows, it was turned into others, until all were irrigated. When that was accomplished, Dorian's watch showed half past eleven. He picked up the lantern and the hoe, and they walked back to the house.

"The party was quite complete, after all," he said at the door. "I've enjoyed this little after-affair as much as I did the party."

"I'm glad," she whispered.

"And it was wonderfully good of you to give me that present."

"I'm glad," she repeated.

"Do you know what I was thinking about when I opened the book and saw it was from you?"

"No; what?"

"Why, I thought, we'll read this book together, you and I."

"Wouldn't that be fine!"

"We can't do that now, of course; but after a while when we get more time. I'll not read it until then … Well, you're tired. Go to bed. Good night, Carlia."

108

"Goodnight, Dorian, and thank you for helping me."

They stood close together, she on the step above him. The lamp, placed on the kitchen table for her use, threw its light against the glass door which formed a background for the girl's roughened hair, soiled and sweat-stained face, and red, smiling lips.

"Goodnight," he said again; and then he leaned forward and kissed her.

10.

THAT GOODNIGHT'S KISS should have brought Dorian back to Carlia sooner than it did; but it was nearly a month before he saw her again. The fact that it was the busiest time of the year was surely no adequate excuse for this neglect. Harvest was on again, and the dry-farm called for much of his attention. Dorian prospered, and he had no time to devote to the girls, so he thought, and so he said, when occasion demanded expression.

One evening while driving through the city and seeing the lights of the moving picture theatre, he was reminded of his promise to Carlia. His conscience pricked him just a little, so the very next evening he drove up to Farmer Duke's. Seeing no one choring about, he went into the house and inquired after Carlia. Mrs. Duke told him that Carlia had gone to the city that afternoon. She was expected back any minute, but one could never tell, lately, when she would get home. Since this Mr. Lamont had taken her to the city a number of times, she had been late in getting home.

"Mr. Lamont?" he inquired.

"Yes; haven't you met him? Don't you know him?"

"No; who is he?"

"Dorian, I don't know. Father seems to think he's all right, but I don't like him. Oh, Dorian, why don't you come around oftener?"

Mrs. Duke sank into a chair and wiped away the tears from her eyes with the corner of her apron. Dorian experienced a strange sinking of the heart. Again he asked who this Mr. Lamont was.

"He's a salesman of some kind, so he says. He drives about in one of those automobiles. Surely, you have seen him—a fine-looking fellow with nice manners and all that, but—"

"And does Carlia go out with him?"

"He has taken her out riding a number of times. He meets her in the city sometimes. I don't know what to make of it, Dorian. I'm afraid."

Dorian seemed unable to say anything which would calm the mother's fears. That Carlia should be keeping company with someone other than himself, had never occurred to him. And yet, why not? she was ald enough to accept attention from young men. He had certainly neglected her, as the mother had implied. The girl had such few opportunities for going out, why should she not accept such as came to her. But this stranger, this outsider! Dorian soon took his departure.

He went home, unhitched, and put up his horse; but instead of going into the house, he walked down to the post office. He found nothing in his box. He felt better in the open, so he continued to walk. He had told his mother he was going to the city, so he might as well walk that way. Soon the lights gleamed through the coming darkness. He went on with his confused thoughts, on into the city and to the moving picture show. He bought a ticket and an attendant led him stumbling in the dark room to a seat.

It was the first time he had been there. He and Carlia were going together. It was quite wonderful to the young man to see the actors moving about lifelike on the white screen. The story contained a number of love-making scenes, which, had they been enacted in real life, in public as this was, they would certainly have been stopped by the police. Then there was a comic picture wherein a young fellow was playing pranks on an old man. The presentation could hardly be said to teach respect for old age, but the audience laughed uproariously at it.

111

When the picture closed and the lights went on, Dorian turned about to leave, and there stood Carlia. A young man was assisting her into her light wraps. She saw him, so there was no escape, and they spoke to each other. Carlia introduced her escort, Mr. Lamont.

"Glad to know you," said Mr. Lamont, in a hearty way. "I've known of you through Miss Duke. Going home now?"

"Yes," said Dorian.

"Drive?"

"No; I'm walking."

"Then you'll ride with us. Plenty of room. Glad to have you."

"Thank you, I—"

"Yes, come," urged Carlia.

Dorian hesitated. He tried to carry an independent manner, but Mr. Lamont linked his arm sociably with Dorian's as he said:

"Of course you'll ride home with us; but first we'll have a little ice cream."

"No thanks," Dorian managed to say. What more did this fellow want of him?

However, as Dorian could give no good reason why he should not ride home with them, he found no way of refusing to accompany them to a nearby ice-cream parlor. Mr. Lamont gave the order, and was very attentive to Carlia and Dorian. It was he who kept the flow of conversation going. The other two, plainly, were not adept at this.

"What did you think of the show, Mr. Trent?"

"The moving pictures are wonderful, but I did not like the story very much."

"It was rotten," exclaimed the other in seeming disgust. I did not know what was on, or I should not have gone. Last week they had a fine picture, a regular classic. Did you see it?

"No; in fact, this is my first visit."

"Oh, indeed. This is Miss Duke's second visit only."

Under the bright lights Carlia showed rouge on her cheeks, something Dorian had never seen on her before. Her lips seemed redder

112

113

than ever, and he eyes shone with a bright luster. Mr. Lamont led them to his automobile, and then Dorian remembered the night when this same young man with the same automobile had stopped near Carlia's home. Carlia seated herself with the driver, while Dorian took the back seat. They were soon speeding along the road which led to Greenstreet. The cool night air fanned Dorian's hot face. Conversation ceased. Even Carlia and the driver were silent. The moon peeped over the eastern hills. The country-side was silent. Dorian thought of the strange events of the evening. This Mr. Lamont had not only captured Carlia but Dorian also. "If I were out with a girl," reasoned Dorian, "I certainly wouldn't want a third person along if I could help it." Why should this man be so eager to have his company? Dorian did not understand, not then.

In a short time they drove up to Carlia's gate, and she and Dorian alighted. The driver did not get out. The machine purred as if impatient to be off again and the lamps threw their streams of light along the road.

114 "Well, I shall have to be getting back," said Mr. Lamont. "Goodnight, Miss Duke. Thanks for your company. Goodnight, Mr. Trent; sure glad to have met you."

The machine glided into the well-worn road and was off. The two stood looking at it for a moment. Then Carlia moved toward the house.

"Come in" she said.

He mechanically followed. He might as well act the fool to the end of the chapter, he thought. It was eleven by the parlor clock, but the mother seemed greatly relieved when she saw Dorian with her daughter. Carlia threw off her wraps. She appeared ill at ease. Her gaiety was forced. She seemed to be acting a part, but she was doing it poorly. Dorian was not only ill at ease himself, but he was bewildered. He seated himself on the sofa. Carlia took a chair on the other side of the room and gazed out of the window into the night.

"Carlia, why did you—why do you," he stammered.

"Why shouldn't I?" she replied, somewhat defiantly as if she understood his unfinished question.

"You know you should not. It's wrong. Who is he anyway?"

"He at least thinks of me and wants to show me a good time, and that's more than anybody else does."

"Carlia!"

"Well, that's the truth." She arose, walked to the table in the middle of the room and stood challengingly before him. "Who are you to find fault? What have you done to—"

"I'll admit I've done very little; but you, yourself."

"Never mind me. What do you care for me? What does anybody care?"

"Your mother, at least."

"Yes, mother; poor, dear mother … Oh, my God, I can't stand it, I can't stand it!" With a sob she broke and sank down by the table, hiding her face in her arms. Dorian arose to go to her. The door opened, and the mother appeared.

"What is it, Carlia," she asked in alarm.

The girl raised her head, swiftly dashed the tears from her eyes, then with a sad effort to smile, said:

"Nothing, mother, nothing at all. I'm going to bed. Where's father?"

"He was called out to Uncle Zed's who is sick. Dorian's mother is there with him too, I understand."

"Then I'd better go for her," said the young man. "I'll say goodnight. Poor Uncle Zed; he hasn't been well lately. Goodnight Sister Duke, goodnight Carlia."

Carlia stood in the doorway leading to the stairs. "Goodnight, Dorian," she said. "Forgive me for being so rude."

He stepped toward her, but she motioned him back, and than ran up the carpetless stairs to her room. Dorian went out in the night. With a heavy heart he hurried down the road in the direction of Uncle Zed's home.

11.

UNCLE ZED'S ILLNESS did not prove fatal, though it was
serious enough. In a few days he was up and about again, slowly,
quietly providing for his simple needs. However, it was plainly evident that he had nearly come to the end of his earthly pilgrimage.

After the most pressing fall work had been disposed of, Dorian
spent as much of his spare time as possible with the old man, who
seemed to like the company of the younger man better than anyone
else in the village; and Dorian, for his part, took delight in visiting with
him, in helping him with the heaviest of his not heavy chores. Especially, was it pleasant during the lengthening evening with a small fire
and the lamp newly trimmed. Uncle Zed reclined in his easy chair,
while Dorian sat by the table with books and papers. Their conversa-
tions ranged from flower gardens to dry-farms, and from agnosticism
to the highest degrees of the celestial glory. And how they both reveled
in books and their contents on the occasions when they were alone
and unhampered by the unsympathetic minds of others.

"As you see, Dorian," said Uncle Zed on one such Sunday evening, "my collection of books is not large, but they are such that I can
read and read again."

"Where is your 'Drummond's Natural Law'?" asked Dorian.

Uncle Zed looked about. "I was reading it this morning. There it
is on the window." Dorian fetched him the volume.

"When I read Drummond's work," continued the old man, "I feel keener than ever my lack of scientific knowledge. I have always had a desire to delve into nature's laws through the doors of botany, zoology, mineralogy, chemistry, and all the other sciences. I have obtained a smattering only through my reading. I realize that the great ocean of truth is yet before me who am now an old man and can never hope in this life to explore much further."

"But how is it, Uncle Zed," enquired Dorian, "that so many scientists have such little faith?"

"'The letter killeth, but the Spirit giveth life,' The Spirit has taught us Dorian, that this world is God's world, and that the laws which govern here and now are the same eternal laws which have always been in operation; that we have come to this world of element to get in touch with earthly forms of matter, and become acquainted with the laws which govern them. Drummond has attempted to prove that the laws which prevail in the temporal world about us also hold good in the spiritual world, and he has made out a very good case, I think; but neither Drummond nor anybody else not endowed by the gift of the Holy Ghost, can reach the simple ultimate truth. That's why I have been looking for some young man in the Church who could and would make it his life's mission and work to learn the truths of science and harmonize them where necessary with the revealed truth—in fact, to complete what Henry Drummond has so well begun." The old man paused, then looking steadily at Dorian, said: "That's what I expect you to do."

"I? Oh, do you think I could?"

"Yes; it would not be easy, but with your aptness and your trend of mind, and your ability to study long and hard, you could, with the assistance of the Spirit of God, accomplish wonders by the time you are as old as I."

The young man mildly protested, although the vision of what might be thrilled his being.

"Don't forget what I am telling you, Dorian. Think and pray and dream about it for a time, and the Lord will open the way. Now then, we are to discuss some of Drummond's problems, were we not?"

"Yes; I shall be glad to. Are you comfortable? Shall I move your pillow?"

"I'm resting very easily, thank you. Just hand me the book. 120 Drummond's chapter on Biogenesis interests me very much. I cannot talk very scientifically, Dorian, on these things, but I hope to talk intelligently and from the large viewpoint of the gospel. Here is a paragraph from my book which I have marked and called 'The Wall Between.' I'm sure you will remember it. Let us read it again:

"'Let us first place,' he read from the book, 'vividly in our imagination the picture of the two great Kingdoms of Nature, the inorganic and the organic, as these now stand in the light of the Law of Biogenesis. What essentially is involved in saying that there is no Spontaneous Generation of Life? It is meant that the passage from the mineral world is hermetically sealed on the mineral side. This inorganic world is staked off from the living world by barriers which have never yet been crossed from within. No change of substance, no modification of environment, no chemistry, no electricity, nor any form of energy, nor any evolution can endow any single atom of the mineral world with the attribute of life. Only by bending down into this dead world of some living form can these dead atoms be gifted with the properties of vitality, without this preliminary contact with life they remain fixed in the inorganic sphere forever. It is a very mysterious Law which guards in this way the portals of the living world. And if there is one thing in Nature more worth pondering for its strangeness it is the spectacle of this vast helpless world of the dead 121 cut off from the living by the law of Biogenesis and denied forever the possibility of resurrection within itself. So very strange a thing, indeed, is this broad line in Nature, that Science has long sought to obliterate it. Biogenesis stands in the way of some forms of Evolution with such stern persistency that the assaults upon this law for number and thoroughness have been unparalleled. But, as we have seen, it has stood the test. Nature, to the modern eye, stands broken in two. The physical laws may explain the inorganic world; the biological laws may account for inorganic. But of the point where they meet, of that living borderland between the dead and the living, Science is silent. It is as if God had placed everything in earth and in heaven in the hands of Nature, but reserved a point at the genesis of Life for His direct appearing.'

"Drummond goes on to prove by analogy that the same law which makes such a separation between the higher and the lower in the natural world holds good in the spiritual realm, and he quotes such passages as this to substantiate his argument: 'Except a man is born again, he cannot enter the kingdom of God'. Man must be born from above. 'The passage from the natural world to the spiritual world is hermetically sealed on the natural side.' that is, man cannot by any means make his own unaided way from the lower world to the higher. 'No mental energy, no evolution, no moral effort, no evolution of character, no progress of civilization' can alone lift life from the lower to the higher. Further, the lower can know very little about the higher, for 'the natural man receiveth not the things of the Spirit of God; for they are foolishness to him; neither can he know them, because they are spiritually discerned'. All of which means, I take it, that the higher must reach down to the lower and lift it up. Advancement in any line of progress is made possible by some directing power either seen or unseen. A man cannot simply grow better and better until in his own right he enters the kingdom of God'."

"But, Uncle Zed, are we not taught that we must work out our own salvation?" asked Dorian. "That is also scriptural."

"Yes; but wait; I shall come to that later. Let us go on with our reasoning and see how this law which Drummond points out—how it fits into the larger scheme of things as revealed to us Latter-day Saints. You remember some time ago in our talk on the law of eternal progress we established the truth that there always have been intelligences evolving from lower to higher life, which in the eternity of the past would inevitably lead to the perfection of Gods. This is plainly taught in Joseph Smith's statement that God was once a man like us, perhaps on an earth like this, working out His glorious destiny. He, then, has gone on before into higher worlds, gaining wisdom, power, and glory. 123 Now, there is another law of the universe that no advancing man can live to himself alone. No man can grow by taking selfish thought to the process. He grows by the exercise of his faculties and powers for the benefit of others. Dorian, hand me the 'Pearl of Great price'."

Dorian found the book and handed it to the old man, who, finding the passage he wanted, continued: "Listen to this remarkable statement by the Lord: 'For behold, this is my work and my glory—to bring to pass the immortality and eternal life of man.' Just think what that means."

"What does it mean?"

"It means, my boy, that the way of progress is the way of unselfish labor. 'This is my work,' says the Lord, to labor for those who are yet on the lower rungs of the ladder, to institute laws whereby those below may climb up higher; (note I used the word climb, not float); to use His greater experience, knowledge, and power for others; to pass down to those in lower or primary stages that which they cannot get by self-effort alone. Let me say this in all reverence, they who attain to All Things do not greedily and selfishly cling to it, but pass it on to others. 'As one lamp lights another nor grows less, So kindliness enkindleth kindliness.' Yes; through great stress and sacrifice, they may do this, as witnessed in what our Father has done by endowing His Beloved Son with eternal life, and then giving Him to us. That Son was the 'Prince of Life.' He was the Resurrection and the Life.' He brought Life from 124 the higher kingdom to a lower, its natural course through the ages. That is the only way through which it can come. And herein, to my humble way of thinking is the great error into which the modern evolutionist has fallen. He reasons that higher forms evolve from the initial and unaided movements of the lower. That is as impossible as that a man can lift himself to the skies by his boot-straps."

Dorian smiled at the illustration.

"Now, my boy, I want to make an application of these divine truths to us here and now. I'm not going to live here much longer."

"Uncle Zed!"

"Now, wait; it's a good thing that you nor anybody else can prevent me from passing on. I've wanted to live long enough to get rid of the fear of death. I have reached that point now, and so I am ready at any time, thank the Lord."

Uncle Zed was beautiful to look upon in the clear whiteness of his person and the peaceful condition of his spirit. The young listener was deeply impressed by what he was hearing. (He never forgot that particular Sunday afternoon).

"You asked me about working out our own salvation," continued Uncle Zed. "Let me answer you on that. There are three principles in the law of progress, all of them important: First, there must be an exercise of the will by the candidate for progression. He must be willing to advance and have a desire to act for himself. That is the principle of free agency. Second, he must be willing to receive help from a higher source; that is, he must place himself in a condition to receive life and light from the source of life and light. Third, he must be unselfish, willing, eager to share all good with others. The lack of any of these will prove a serious hindrance. We see this everywhere in the world.

"Coming back now to the application I mentioned. If it is God's work and glory to labor for those below Him, why should not we, His sons and daughters, follow His example as far as possible in our sphere of action? If we are ever to become like Him we must follow in His steps and do the things which He has done. Our work, also must be to help along the road to salvation those who are lower down, those who are more ignorant and are weaker than we."

"Which, Uncle Zed, you have been doing all your life."

"Just trying a little, just a little."

"And this will be as it already has been, your glory. I see that plainly."

"Why shouldn't it be everybody's work and glory! What a beautiful world this would be if this were the case!"

"Yes, truly."

"And see, Dorian, how this principle ties together the race from the beginning to the end, comparatively speaking. Yes, in this way will men and families and races and worlds be linked together in chains of love, which cannot be broken, worlds without end." 126

The old man's voice became sweet and low. Then there was silence for a few minutes. The clock struck ten.

"I must be going," said Dorian. "I am keeping you out of bed."

"You'll come again?"

"Oh, yes."

"Come soon, my boy. I have so much to tell you. I can talk so freely to you, something I cannot do to all who come here, bless their hearts. But you, my boy—"

He reached out his hand, and Dorian took it lovingly. There were tears in the old man's eyes.

"I'll not forget you," said Dorian, "I'll come soon and often."

"Then, good night."

"Good night," the other replied from the door as he stepped out into the night. The cool breeze swept over meadow and field. The world was open and big, and the young man's heart expanded to it. What a comfort to feel that the Power which rules the world and all the affairs of men is unfailing in its operations! What a joy to realize that he had a loving Father to whom he could go for aid! And then 127 also, what a tremendous responsibility was on him because of the knowledge he already had and because of his God-given agency to act for himself. Surely, he would need light from on High to help him to choose the right!

Surely, he would.

12.

AT THE COMING of winter, Uncle Zed was bedfast. He was failing rapidly. Neighbors helped him. Dorian remained with him as much as he could. The bond which had existed between these two grew stronger as the time of separation became nearer. The dying man was clear-minded, and he suffered very little pain. He seemed completely happy if he could have Dorian sitting by him and they could talk together. And these were wonderful days to the young man, days never to be forgotten.

Outside, the air was cold with gusts of wind and lowering clouds. Inside, the room was cosy and warm. A few of the old man's hardiest flowers were still in pots on the table where the failing eyes could see them. That evening Mrs. Trent had tidied up the room and had left Dorian to spend the night with the sick man. The tea-kettle hummed softly on the stove. The shaded lamp was turned down low.

"Dorian."

"Yes, Uncle Zed."

"Turn up the lamp a little. It's too dark in here."

"Doesn't the light hurt your eyes!"

"No; besides I want you to get me some papers out of that drawer in my desk."

Dorian fetched a large bundle of clippings and papers and asked if they were what he wanted.

"Not all of them just now; but take from the pile the few on top. I want you to read them to me. They are a few selections which I have culled and which have a bearing on the things we have lately been talking about."

The first note which Dorian read was as follows. "'The keys of the holy priesthood unlock the door of knowledge to let you look into the palace of truth'."

"That's by Brigham Young. You did not know that he was a poet as well as a prophet," commented the old man. "The next one is from him also."

"'There never was a time when there were not Gods and worlds, and when men were not passing through the same ordeals that we are now passing through. That course has been from all eternity and it is and will be to all eternity'."

"Now you know, Dorian, where I get my inspiration from. Read the next, also from President Young."

"'The idea that the religion of Christ is one thing, and science is another, is a mistaken idea, for there is no true science without religion. The fountain of knowledge dwells with God, and He dispenses it to His children as He pleases, and as they are prepared to receive it; consequently, it swallows up and circumscribes all'."

"Take these, Dorian; have them with you as inspirational mottoes for your life's work. Go on, there are a few more."

Dorian read again: "'The region of true religion and the region of a completer science are one.' —Oliver Lodge."

"You see one of the foremost scientists of the day agrees with Brigham Young," said Uncle Zed. "I think the next one corroborates some of our doctrine also."

Dorian read: "'We do not indeed remember our past, we are not aware of our future, but in common with everything else we must have had a past and must be going to have a future.' —Oliver Lodge."

Again he read: "'We must dare to extend the thought of growth and progress and development even up to the height of all that we can realize of the Supreme Being—In some part of the universe perhaps already the ideal conception has been attained; and the region of such attainment—the full blaze of self-conscious Deity—is too bright for mortal eyes, is utterly beyond our highest thoughts.' —Oliver Lodge."

Uncle Zed held out his hand and smiled. "There," he said in a whisper, "is a hesitating suggestion of the truth which we boldly pro-claim." 131

"Now you are tired, Uncle Zed," said Dorian. "I had best not read more."

"Just one—the next one."

Dorian complied:

"'There are more lives yet, there are more worlds waiting,
    For the way climbs up to the eldest sun,
Where the white ones go to their mystic mating,
    And the holy will is done.
I'll find you there where our love life heightens –
    Where the door of the wonder again unbars,
Where the old love lures and the old fire whitens,
    In the stars behind the stars'."

Uncle Zed lay peacefully on his pillow, a wistful look on his face. The room became still again, and the clock ticked away the time. Dorian folded up the papers which he had been told to keep and put them in his pocket. The rest of the package he returned to the draw-er. He lowered the lamp again. Then he sat down and watched. It seemed it would not be long for the end.

"Dorian."

"Yes, Uncle Zed, can I do anything for you?"

"No" —barely above a whisper— "nothing else matters—you're a good boy—God bless you."

The dying man lay very still. As Dorian looked at the face of his friend it seemed that the mortal flesh had become waxen white so that the immortal spirit shone unhindered through it. The young man's heart was deeply sorrowful, but it was a sanctified sorrow. Twice before had death come near to him. He had hardly realized that of his father's and he was not present when Mildred had passed away; but here he was again with death, and alone. It seemed strange that he was not terrified, but he was not—everything seemed so calm, peaceful, and even beautiful in its serene solemnity.

Dorian arose, went softly to the window and looked out. The wind had quieted, and the snow was falling slowly, steadily in big white flakes, When Dorian again went back to the bedside and looked on the stilled face of his friend, he gave a little start. He looked again closely, listening, and feeling of the cold hands. Uncle Zed was dead.

The Greenstreet meeting house was filled to overflowing at the funeral. Uncle Zed had gone about all his days in the village doing good. All could tell of some kind deed he had done, with the admonition that it should not be talked about. He always seemed humiliated when anyone spoke of these things in his hearing; but now, surely, there could be no objection to letting his good deeds shine before men.

Uncle Zed had left with the Bishop a written statement, not in the form of a will, wherein he told what disposition was to be made of his simple belongings. The house, with its few well tilled acres, was to go to the ward for the use of any worthy poor whom the Bishop might designate. Everything in the house should be at the disposal of Dorian Trent. The books, especially, should belong to him "to have and to hold and to study." Such books which Dorian did not wish to keep were to be given to the ward Mutual Improvement Library. This information the Bishop publicly imparted on the day of the funeral.

"These are the times," said the Bishop, "when the truth comes forcibly to us all that nothing in this world matters much or counts for much in the end but good deeds, kind words, and unselfish service to others. All else is now dross … The mantle of Brother Zed seems to have fallen on Dorian Trent. May he wear it faithfully and well."

A few days after the funeral Dorian and his mother went to Uncle Zed's vacant home. Mrs. Trent examined the furnishings, while Dorian looked over the books.

"Is there anything here you want, mother? he asked.

"No; I think not; better leave everything, which isn't much, for those who are to live here. What about the books?'

"I'm going to take most of them home, for I am sure Uncle Zed would not want them to fall into unappreciating hands; but there's no hurry about that. We'll just leave everything as it is for a few days."

The next evening Dorian returned to look over again his newly-acquired treasures. The ground was covered with snow and the night was cold. He thought he might as well spend the evening, and be comfortable, so he made a fire in the stove.

On the small home-made desk which stood in the best-lighted corner, near to the student's hand were his well-worn Bible, his Book of Mormon, and Doctrine and Covenants. He opened the drawers and found them filled with papers and clippings, covering, as Dorian learned, a long period of search and collecting. He opened again the package which he had out the evening of Uncle Zed's death, and looked over some of the papers. These, evidently, had been selected for Dorian's special benefit, and so he settled himself comfortably to read them. The very first paper was in the old man's own hand, and was a dissertation on "Faith." and read thus: "Some people say that they can believe only what they can perceive with the senses. Let us see: The sun rises, we say. Does it? The earth is still. Is it? We hear music, we see beauty. Does the ear hear or the eye see? We burn our fingers. Is the pain in our fingers? I cut the nerves leading from the brain to these various organs, and then I neither hear nor see nor feel."

"How can God keep in touch with us?" was answered thus: "A ray of light coming through space from a star millions of miles away will act on a photographic plate, will eat into its sensitive surface and

134

135   imprint the image of the star. This we know, and yet we doubt if God can keep in touch with us and answer our prayers."

Many people wondered why a man like Uncle Zed was content to live in the country. The answer seemed to be found in a number of slips:

"How peaceful comes the Sabbath, doubly blessed, In giving hope to faith, to labor rest. Most peaceful here: —no city's noise obtains, And God seems reverenced more where silence reigns."

Once Dorian had been called a "Clod hopper." As he read the following, he wondered whether or not Uncle Zed had not also been so designated, and had written this in reply:

"Mother Earth, why should not I love you? Why should not I get close to you? Why should I plan to live always in the clouds above you, gazing at other far-distant worlds, and neglecting you? Why did I, with others, shout with joy when I learned that I was coming here from the world of spirits? I answer, because I knew that 'spirit and element inseparately connected receiveth a fullness of joy.' I was then to get in touch with 'element' as I had been with 'spirit.' This world which I see with my natural eyes is the 'natural' part of Mother Eearth, even as the flesh and bones and blood of my body is the element of myself, to be inseparately connected with my spirit and to the end that I might receive a fullness of joy. The earth and all things on it known by the

136   term nature is what I came here to know. Nature, wild or tamed, is my schoolroom—the earth with its hills and valleys and plains, with its clouds and rain, with its rivers and lakes and oceans, with its trees and fruits and flowers, its life—about all these I must learn what I can at first hand. Especially, should I learn of the growing things which clothe the earth with beauty and furnish sustenance to life. Some day I hope the Lord will give me a small part of this earth, when it is glorified. Ah, then, what a garden shall I have!"

No one in Greenstreet had ever known Uncle Zed as a married man. His wife had died long ago, and he seldom spoke of her. Dorian had wondered whether he had ever been a young man, with a young man's thoughts and feelings; but here was evidence which dispelled any doubt. On a slip of paper, somewhat yellow with age, were the following lines, written in Uncle Zed's best hand:

"In the enchanted air of spring,
I hear all Nature's voices sing,
     'I love you'.

By bursting buds, by sprouting grass,
I hear the bees hum as I pass,
     'I love you'.

The waking earth, the sunny sky
Are whispering the same as I,
     'I love you'.

The song of birds in sweetest notes   137
Comes from their bursting hearts and throats,'
     'I love you'."

"Oh, Uncle Zed!" said Dorian, half aloud, "who would have thought it!"

Near the top of the pile of manuscript Dorian found an envelope with "To Dorian Trent," written on it. He opened it with keen interest and found that it was a somewhat newly written paper and dealt with a subject they had discussed in connection with the chapter on Death in Drummond's book. Uncle Zed had begun his epistle by addressing it, "Dear Dorian" and then continued as follows:

"You remember that some time ago we talked on the subject of sin and death. Since then I have had some further thought on the subject which I will here jot down for you. You asked me, you remember, what sin is, and I tried to explain. Here is another definition: Man belongs to an order of beings whose goal is perfection. The way to that perfection is long and hard, narrow and straight. Any deviation from that path is sin. God, our Father, has reached the goal. He has told us how we may follow Him. He has pointed out the way by teaching us the law of progress which led Him to His exalted state. Sin lies in not heeding that law, but in following laws of our own making. The Lord says this in the Doctrine and Covenants, Section 88:

138   'That which breaketh a law, and abideth not by law, but seeketh to become a law unto itself, and willeth to abide in sin, and altogether abideth in sin, cannot be sanctified by law, neither by mercy, justice, nor judgement. Therefore, they must remain filthy still.'

"Now, keeping in mind that sin is the straying from the one straight, progressive path, let us consider this expression: 'The wages of sin is death'. This leads us to the question: what is death? Do you remember what Drummond says? He first explains in a most interesting way what life is, using the scientist's phrasing. A human being, for instance, is in direct contact with all about him—earth, air, sun, other human beings, etc. In biological language he is said to be 'in correspondence with his environment,' and by virtue of this correspondence is said to be alive. To live, a human being must continue to adjust himself to his environment. When he fails to do this, he dies. Thus we have also a definition of death. 'Dying is that breakdown in an organization which throws it out of correspondence with some necessary part of the environment.'

"Of course, these reasonings and deductions pertain to what we term he physical death; but Drummond claims that the same law holds good in the spiritual world. Modern revelation seems to agree with him. We have an enlightening definition of death in the following quotation from the Doctrine and Covenants, Section 29: 'Where-

139   fore I the Lord God caused that he (Adam) should be cast out from the Garden of Eden, from my presence, because of his transgression, wherein he became spiritually dead, which is the first death, even that same death, which is the last death, which is spiritual, which shall be pronounced upon the wicked when I shall say Depart ye cursed'.

"It seems to me that there is a most interesting agreement here. Banishment from the place where God lives is death. By the operations of a natural law, a person who fails to correspond with a celestial environment dies to that environment and must go or be placed in some other, where he can function with that which is about him. God's presence is exalted, holy, glorified. He who is not pure, holy, glorified cannot possibly live there, is dead to that higher world. A soul who cannot function in the celestial glory, may do so in the terrestrial glory; one who cannot function in the terrestrial, may in the telestial; and one who cannot 'abide the law' or function in the telestial must find a place of no glory. This is inevitable—it cannot be otherwise. Immutable law decrees it, and not simply the ruling of an allwise power. The soul who fails to attain to the celestial glory, fails to walk in the straight and narrow path which leads to it. Such a person wanders in the by-paths called sin, and no power in the universe can arbitrarily put him in an environment with which he cannot function. 'To be carnally minded is death', said Paul. 'The wages of sin is death', or in other words, he who persistently avoids the Celestial Highway will never arrive at the Celestial Gate. He who works evilly will obtain evil wages. Anyway, what would it profit a man with dim eyesight to be surrounded with ineffable glory? What would be the music of the spheres to one bereft of hearing? What gain would come to a man with a heart of stone to be in an environment of perfect and eternal love!"

Dorian finished the reading and laid the paper on the desk. For some time he sat very still, thinking of these beautiful words from his dear friend to him. Surely, Uncle Zed was very much alive in any environment which his beautiful life had placed him. Would that he, Dorian, could live so that he might always be alive to the good and be dead to sin.

The stillness of the night was about him. The lamplight grew dim, showing the oil to be gone, so he blew out the smoking wick. He opened the stove door, and by the light of the dying fire he gathered up some books to take home. He heard a noise as if someone were outside. He listened. The steps were muffled in the snow. They seemed to approach the house and then stop. There was silence for a few minutes, then plainly he heard sobbing close to the door.

141

What could it mean? who could it be? Doubtless, some poor soul to whom Uncle Zed had been a ministering angel, had been drawn to the vacant house, and could not now control her sorrow. Then the sobbing ceased, and Dorian realized he had best find out who was there and give what help he could. He opened the door, and a frightened scream rang out from the surprised Carlia Duke who stood in the faint light from the open doorway. She stood for a second, then as if terror stricken, she fled.

"Carlia," shouted Dorian. "Carlia!"

But the girl neither stopped nor looked back. Across the pathless, snow-covered fields she sped, and soon became only a dark-moving object on the white surface. When she had entirely disappeared, Dorian went back, gathered up his bundles, locked the door, and went wonderingly and meditatingly home.

13.

IT IS NO DOUBT a wise provision of nature that the cold of winter closes the activity in field and garden, thus allowing time for study by the home fire. Dorian Trent's library, having been greatly enlarged, now became to him a source of much pleasure and profit. Books which he never dreamed of possessing were now on his shelves. In some people's opinion, he was too well satisfied to remain in his cosy room and bury himself in his books; but his mother found no fault. She was always welcome to come and go; and in fact, much of the time he sat with her by the kitchen fire, reading aloud and discussing with her the contents of his book.

Dorian found, as Uncle Zed had, wonderful arguments for the truth of the gospel in Orson and Parley P. Pratt's works. In looking through the "Journal of Discourses," he found markings by many of the sermons, especially by those of Brigham Young. Dorian always read the passages thus indicated, for he liked to realize that he was following the former owner of the book even in his thinking. The early volumes of the "Millennial Star" contained some interesting reading. Very likely, the doctrinal articles of these first elders were no better than those of more recent writers, but their plain bluntness and their very age seemed to give them charm.

By his reading that winter Dorian obtained an enlarged view of his religion. It gave him vision to see and to comprehend better the whole and thus to more fully understand the details. Besides, he was laying a broad and firm foundation for his faith in God and the restored gospel of Jesus Christ, a faith which would stand him well in need when he came to delve into a faithless and a Godless science.

Not that Dorian became a hermit. He took an active part in the Greenstreet ward organizations. He was secretary of the Mutual, always attended Sunday School, and usually went to the ward dances. As he became older he overcame some of his shyness with girls; and as prosperity came to him, he could dress better and have his mass of rusty-red hair more frequently trimmed by the city barber. More than one of the discerning Greenstreet girls laid their caps for the big, handsome young fellow.

And Dorian's thoughts, we must know, were not all the time occupied with the philosophy of Orson Pratt. He was a very natural young man, and there were some very charming girls in Greenstreet. When, arrayed in their Sunday best, they sat in the ward choir, he, not being a member of the choir, could look at them to his heart's content, first at one and then at another along the double row. Carlia Duke usually sat on the front row where he could see her clearly and compare her with the others—and she did not suffer by the comparison.

Dorian now begin to realize that it was selfish, if not foolish, to think always of the dead Mildred to the exclusion of the very much alive Carlia. Mildred was safe in the world of spirits, where he would some day meet her again; but until that time, he had this life to live and those about him to think of. Carlia was a dear girl, beautiful, too, now in her maturing womanhood. None of the other girls touched his heart as Carlia. He had taken a number of them to dances, but he had always come back, in his thought, at least, to Carlia. But her actions lately had been much of a puzzle. Sometimes she seemed to welcome him eagerly when he called, at other times she tried to evade him. No doubt this Mr. Jack Lamont was the disturbing element. That winter he could be seen coming quite openly to the Duke home, and when the weather would permit, Carlia would be riding with him in his automobile. The neighbors talked, but the father could only shake his head and explain that Carlia was a willful girl.

Now when it seemed that Carlia was to be won by this very gallant stranger, Dorian began to realize what a loss she would be to 145 him. He was sure he loved the girl, but what did that avail if she did not love him in return. He held to the opinion that such attractions should be mutual. He could see no sense in the old-time custom of the knight winning his lady love by force of arms or by the fleetness of horse's legs.

However, Dorian was not easy in his mind, and it came to the point when he suffered severe heartaches when he knew of Carlia's being with the stranger. The Christmas holidays that season were nearly spoiled for him. He had asked Carlia a number of times to go to the parties with him, but she had offered some excuse each time.

"Let her alone," someone had told him.

"No; do not let her alone," his mother had counseled; and he took his mother's advice.

Carlia had been absent from the Sunday meetings for a number of weeks, so when she appeared in her place in the choir on a Sunday late in January, Dorian noticed the unusual pallor of her face. He wondered if she had been ill. He resolved to make another effort, for in fact, his heart went out to her. At the close of the meeting he found his way to her side as she was walking home with her father and mother. Dorian never went through the formality of asking Carlia if he might accompany her home. He had always taken it for granted that he was welcome; and, at any rate, a man could always tell by the girl's actions whether or not he was wanted.

"I haven't seen you for a long time," began Dorian by way of 146 greeting.

The girl did not reply.

"Been sick?" he asked.

"Yes—no, I'm all right."

The parents walked on ahead, leaving the two young people to follow. Evidently, Carlia was very much out of sorts, but the young man tried again.

"What's the matter, Carlia?"

"Nothing."

"Well, I hope I'm not annoying you by my company."

No answer. They walked on in silence, Carlia looking straight ahead, not so much at her parents, as at the distant snow-clad mountains. Dorian felt like turning about and going home, but he could not do that very well, so he went on to the gate, where he would have said goodnight had not Mrs. Duke urged him to come in. The father and mother went to bed early, leaving the two young people by the dining-room fire.

They managed to talk for some time on "wind and weather". Despite the paleness of cheek, Carlia was looking her best. Dorian was jealous.

"Carlia," he said, "why do you keep company with this Mr. Lamont?"

She was standing near the book-shelf with its meagre collection. She turned abruptly at his question.

"Why shouldn't I go with him?" she asked.

147   "You know why you shouldn't."

"I don't. Oh, I know the reasons usually given, but—what am I to do. He's so nice, and a perfect gentleman. What harm is there?"

"Why do you say that to me, Carlia?"

"Why not to you?" She came and sat opposite him by the table. He was silent, and she repeated her question, slowly, carefully, and with emphasis. "Why not to you? Why should you care?"

"But I do care."

"I don't believe it. You have never shown that you do."

"I am showing it now."

"Tomorrow you will forget it—forget me for a month."

"Carlia!"

"You've done it before—many times—you'll do it again."

The girl's eyes flashed. She seemed keyed up to carry through something she had planned to do, something hard. She arose and stood by the table, facing him.

"I sometimes have thought that you cared for me—but I'm through with that now. Nobody really cares for me. I'm only a rough farm hand. I know how to milk and scrub and churn and clean the stable—an' that's what I do day in and day out. There's no change, no rest for me, save when he takes me away from it for a little while. He understands, he's the only one who does."

"But, Carlia!"

"You," she continued in the same hard voice, "you're altogether too good and too wise for such as I. You're so high up that I can't touch you. You live in the clouds, I among the clods. What have we two in common?"

"Much, Carlia—I—"

He arose and came to her, but she evaded him.

"Keep away, Dorian; don't touch me. You had better go home now."

"You're not yourself, Carlia. What is the matter? You have never acted like this before."

"It's not because I haven't felt like it, but it's because I haven't had the courage; but now it's come out, and I can't stop it. It's been pent up in me like a flood—now it's out. I hate this old farm—I hate everything and everybody—I—hate you!"

Dorian arose quickly as if he had been lifted to his feet. What was she saying? She was wild, crazy wild.

"What have I done that you should hate me?" he asked as quietly as his trembling voice would allow.

"Done? nothing. It's what you haven't done. What have you done to repay—my—Oh, God, I can't stand it—I can't stand it!"

She walked to the wall and turned her face to it. She did not cry. The room was silently tense for a few moments.

"I guess I'd better go," said Dorian.

She did not reply. He picked up his hat, lingered, then went to the door. She hated him. Then let him get out from her presence. She hated him. He had not thought that possible. Well, he would go. He would never annoy any girl who hated him, not if he knew it. How his heart ached, how his very soul seemed crushed! yet he could not appeal to her. She stood with her face to the wall, still as a statue, and as cold.

"Good night," he said at the door.

She said nothing, nor moved. He could see her body quiver, but he could not see her face. He perceived nothing clearly. The familiar room, poorly furnished, seemed strange to him. The big, ugly enlarged photographs on the wall blurred to his vision. Carlia, with head bowed now, appeared to stand in the midst of utter confusion. Dorian groped his way to the door, and stepped out into the wintry night. When he had reached the gate, Carlia rushed to the door.

"Dorian!" she cried in a heart-breaking voice, "O, Dorian, come back—come back!"

But Dorian opened the gate, closed it, then walked on down the road into the darkness, nor did he once look back.

14.

CARLIA'S RINGING CRY persisted with Dorian all the way home, but he hardened his heart and went steadily on. His mother had gone to bed, and he sat for a time by the dying fire, thinking of what he had just passed through.

After that, Dorian kept away from Carlia. Although the longing to see her surged strongly through his heart from time to time, and he could not get away from the thought that she was in some trouble, yet his pride forbade him to intrude. He busied himself with chores and his books, and he did not relax in his ward duties. Once in a while he saw Carlia at the meeting house, but she absented herself more and more from public gatherings, giving as an excuse to all who inquired, that her work bound her more closely than ever at home.

Dorian and his mother frequently talked about Uncle Zed and the hopes the departed one had of the young man. "Do you really think, mother, that he meant I should devote my life to the harmo- nizing of science and religion?" he asked.

"I think Uncle Zed was in earnest. He had great faith in you."

"But what do you think of it, mother?"

After a moment's thought, the mother replied.

"What do you think of it?"

"Well, it would be a task, though a wonderfully great one."

"The aim is high, the kind I would expect of you. Do you know, Dorian, your father had some such ambition. That's one of the reasons we came to the country in hopes that some day he would have more time for studying."

"I never knew that, mother."

"And now, what if your father and Uncle Zed are talking about the matter up there in the spirit world."

Dorian thought of that for a few moments. Then: "I'll have to go to the University for four years, but that's only a beginning. Ill have to go East to Yale or Harvard and get all they have. Then will come a lot of individual research, and—Oh, mother, I don't know."

"And all the time you'll have to keep near to God and never lose your faith in the gospel, for what doth it profit if you gain the whole world of knowledge and lose your own soul." The mother came to him and ran her fingers lovingly through his hair. "But you're equal to it, my son; I believe you can do it."

152   This was a sample of many such discussions, and the conclusion was reached that Dorian should work harder than ever, if that were possible, for two or perhaps three years, by which time the farms could be rented and the income derived from them be enough to provide for the mother's simple needs and the son's expenses while at school.

Spring came early that year, and Dorian was glad of it, for he was eager to be out in the growing world and turn that growth to productiveness. When the warm weather came for good, books were laid aside, though not forgotten. From daylight until dark, he was busy. The home farm was well planted, the dry-farm wheat was growing beautifully. Between the two, prospects were bright for the furthering of their plans.

"Mother, when and where in this great plan of ours, am I to get married?"

Dorian and his mother were enjoying the dusk and the cool of the evening within odorous reach of Mrs. Trent's flowers, many of which had come from Uncle Zed's garden. They had been talking over some details of their "plan." Mrs. Trent laughed at the abruptness of the question.

"Oh, do you want to get married?" she asked, wondering what there might be to this query.

"Well—sometimes, of course, I'll have to have a wife, won't I?"

"Certainly, in good time; but you're in no hurry, are you?"

"Oh, no; I'm just talking on general principles. There's no one   153
who would have me now."

The mother did not dispute this. She knew somewhat of his feelings toward Carlia. These lovers' misunderstandings were not serious, she thought to herself. All would end properly and well, in good time.

But Carlia was in Dorian's thought very often, much to his bewilderment of heart and mind. He often debated with himself if he should not definitely give her up, cease thinking about her as being anything to him either now or hereafter; but it seemed impossible to do that. Carlia's image persisted even as Mildred's did. Mildred, away from the entanglements of the world, was safe to him; but Carlia had her life to live and the trials and difficulties of mortality to encounter and to overcome; and that would not be easy, with her beauty and her impulsive nature. She needed a man's clear head and steady hand to help her, and who was more fitting to do that than he himself, Dorian thought without conscious egotism.

If it were possible, Dorian always spent Sunday at home. If he was on his dry farm in the hills, he drove down on Saturday evenings. One Saturday in midsummer, he arrived home late and tired. He put up his team, came in, washed, and was ready for the good supper which his mother always had for him. The mother busied herself about the kitchen and the table.

"Come and sit down, mother," urged Dorian. "What's the fuss-   154
ing about! Everything I need is here on the table. You're tired, I see. Come, sit down with me and tell me all the news."

"The news? what news!"

"Why, everything that's happened in Greenstreet for the past week. I haven't had a visitor up on the farm for ten days."

"Everything is growing splendidly down here. The water in the canal is holding out fine and Brother Larsen is fast learning to be a farmer."

"Good," said Dorian. "Our dry wheat is in most places two feet high, and it will go from forty to fifty bushels, with good luck. If now, the price of wheat doesn't sag too much."

Dorian finished his supper, and was about to go to bed, being in need of a good rest. His mother told him not to get up in the morning until she called him.

"All right, mother," he laughed as he kissed her good night, "but don't let me be late to Sunday School, as I have a topic to treat in the Theological class. By heck, they really think I'm Uncle Zed's successor, by the subjects they give me."

He was about to go to his room when his mother called him by name.

"Yes, mother, what is it?"

"You'll know tomorrow, so I might as well tell you now."

"Tell me what?"

"Some bad news."

155   "Bad news! What is it?"

The mother seemed lothe to go on. She hesitated.

"Well, mother?"

"Carlia is gone."

"Gone? Gone where?"

"Nobody knows. She's been missing for a week. She left home last Saturday to spend a few days with a friend in the city, so she said. Yesterday her father called at the place to bring her home and learned that she had never been there."

"My gracious, mother!"

"Yes; it's terrible. Her father has inquired for her and looked for her everywhere he could think of, but not a trace of her can he find. She's gone."

Mother and son sat in silence for some time. He continued to ask questions, but she know no more than the simple facts which she had told. He could do nothing to help, at least, not then, so he reluctantly went to bed. He did not sleep until past midnight.

15.

DORIAN WAS NOT tardy to Sunday School, and, considering his mental condition, he gave a good account of himself in the
class. He heard whispered comment on Carlia's disappearance.

After Sunday school Dorian went directly to Carlia's home. He
found the mother tear-stained and haggard with care. The tears
flowed again freely at the sight of Dorian, and she clung to him as if
she had no other means of comfort.

"Do you know where Carlia is?" she wailed.

"No, Sister Duke, I haven't the last idea. I haven't seen her for
some time."

"But what shall we do, Dorian, what shall we do! She may be
dead, lying dead somewhere!"

"I hardly think that," he tried to comfort her. "She'll turn up
again. Carlia's well able to take care of herself."

The father came in. He told what had been done to try to find
the missing girl. Not a word had they heard, not a clue or a trace had
been discovered. The father tried hard to control his emotions as he
talked, but he could not keep the tears from slowly creeping down
his face.

"And I suppose I'm greatly to blame" he said. "I have been told as
much by some, who I suppose, are wiser than I am. The poor girl has
been confined too much to the work here."

"Work doesn't hurt anybody," commented Dorian.

"No; but all work and no play, I was plainly reminded just the other day, doesn't always make Jack a dull boy: sometimes, it makes dissatisfaction and rebellion—and it seems it has done that here. Carlia, I'll admit had very little company, saw very little of society. I realize that now when it may be too late."

"Oh, I hope not," said Dorian.

"Carlia, naturally, was full of life. She wanted to go and see and learn. All these desires in her were suppressed so long that this is the way it has broken loose. Yes, I suppose that's true."

Dorian let the father give vent to his feelings in his talk. He could reply very little, for truth to say, he realized that the father was stating Carlia's case quite accurately. He recalled the girl when he and she had walked back and forth to and from the high school how she had rapidly developed her sunny nature in the warm, somewhat care-free environment of the school life, and how lately with the continual drudgery of her work, she had changed to a pessimism unnatural to one of her years. Yes, one continual round of work at the farm house is apt either to crush to dullness or to arouse to rebellion. Carlia was of the kind not easily crushed ... But what could they now do? What could he do? For, it came to him with great force that he himself was not altogether free from blame in this matter. He could have done more, vastly more for Carlia Duke.

"Well, Brother Duke," said Dorian. "Is there anything that I can do?"

"I don't think of anything," said he.

"Not now," added the mother in a tone which indicated that she did not wish the implied occasion to be too severe.

The father followed Dorian out in the yard. There Dorian asked:

"Brother Duke, has this Mr. Lamont been about lately?"

"He was here yesterday. He came, he said, as soon as he heard of Carlia's disappearance. He seemed very much concerned about it."

"And he knew nothing about it until yesterday?"

"He said not—do you suspect—he—might—?"

"I'm not accusing anybody, but I never was favorably impressed with the man."

"He seemed so truly sorry, that I never thought he might have had something to do with it."

"Well, I'm not so sure; but I'll go and see him myself. I suppose I can find him in his office in the city?"

"I think so—Well, do what you can for us, my boy; and Dorian, don't take to heart too much what her mother implied just now."   159

"Not any more than I ought," replied Dorian. "If there is any blame to be placed on me—and I think there is—I want to bear it, and do what I can to correct my mistakes. I think a lot of Carlia, I like her more than any other girl I know, and I should have shown that to her both by word and deed more than I have done. I'm going to help you find her, and when I find her I'll not let her go so easily."

"Thank you. I'm glad to hear you say that."

Monday morning Dorian went to the city and readily found the man whom he was seeking. He was in his office.

"Good morning. Glad to see you," greeted Mr. Lamont, as he swung around on his chair. "Take a seat. What can I do for you?"

As the question was asked abruptly, the answer came in like manner.

"I want to know what you know about Carlia Duke."

Mr. Lamont reddened, but he soon regained his self-possession.

"What do you mean!" he asked.

"You have heard of her disappearance?"

"Yes; I was very sorry to hear of it."

"It seems her father has exhausted every known means of finding her, and I thought you might, at least, give him a clew."

"I should be most happy to do so, if I could; but I assure you I   160
haven't the least idea where she has gone. I am indeed sorry, as I expressed to her father the other day."

"You were with her a good deal."

"Well, not a good deal, Mr. Trent—just a little," he smilingly corrected. "I will admit I'd liked to have seen more of her, but I soon learned that I had not the ghost of a chance with you in the field."

"You are making fun, Mr. Lamont."

"Not at all, my good fellow. You are the lucky dog when it comes to Miss Duke. A fine girl she is, a mighty fine girl—a diamond, just a little in the rough. As I'm apparently out of the race, go to it, Mr. Trent and win her. Good luck to you. I don't think you'll have much trouble."

Dorian was somewhat nonplused by this fulsome outburst. He could not for a moment find anything to say. The two men looked at each other for a moment as if each were measuring the other. Then Mr. Lamont said:

"If at any time I can help you, let me know—call on me. Now you'll have to excuse me as I have some business matters to attend to."

Dorian was dismissed.

The disappearance of Carlia Duke continued to be a profound mystery. The weeks went by, and then the months. The gossips found other and newer themes. Those directly affected began to think that all hopes of finding her were gone.

161 Dorian, however, did not give up. In the strenuous labors of closing summer and fall he had difficulty in keeping his mind on his work. His imagination ranged far and wide, and when it went into the evil places of the world, he suffered so that he had to throw off the suggestion by force. He talked freely with his mother and with Carlia's parents on all possible phases of the matter, until, seemingly, there was nothing more to be said. To others, he said nothing.

Ever since Dorian had been taught to lisp his simple prayers at his mother's knee, he had found strength and comfort in going to the Lord. With the growth of his knowledge of the gospel and his enlarged vision of God's providences, his prayers became a source of power. Uncle Zed had taught him that this trustful reliance on a higher power was essential to his progress. The higher must come to the help of the lower, but the lower must seek for that help and sincerely accept it when offered. As a child, his prayers had been very largely a set form, but as he had come in contact with life and its experiences, he had learned to suit his prayers to his needs. Just now, Carlia and her welfare was the burden of his petitions.

The University course must wait another year, so Dorian and his mother decided. They could plainly see that one more year would be needed, besides Dorian was not in a condition to concentrate his mind on study. So, when the long evenings came on again, he found solace in his books, and read again many of dear Uncle Zed's writings which had been addressed so purposely to him.

One evening in early December Dorian and his mother were cosily "at home" to any good visitors either of persons or ideas. Dorian was looking over some of his papers.

"Mother, listen to this," he said. "Here is a gem from Uncle Zed which I have not seen before." He read:

"'The acquisition of wealth brings with it the obligation of helping the poor; the acquisition of knowledge brings with it the obligation of teaching others; the acquisition of strength and power brings with it the obligation of helping the weak. This is what God does when He says that His work and His glory is to bring to pass the immortality and eternal life of man'."

"How true that is," said the mother.

"Yes," added Dorian after a thoughtful pause, "I am just wondering how and to what extent I am fulfilling any obligation which is resting on me by reason of blessings I am enjoying. Let's see—we are not rich, but we meet every call made on us by way of tithing and donations; we are not very wise, but we impart of what we have by service; we are not very strong—I fear, mother, that's where I lack. Am I giving of my strength as fully as I can to help the weak. I don't know—I don't know."

"You mean Carlia?"

"Yes; what am I doing besides thinking and praying for her?"

"What more can we do?"

"Well, I can try doing something more."

"What, for instance!"

"Trying to find her."

"But her father has done that."

"Yes; but he has given up too soon. I should continue the search. I've been thinking about that lately. I can't stay cosily and safely at home any longer, mother, when Carlia may be in want of protection."

"And what would you be liable to find if you found her?"

That question was not new to his own mind, although his mother had not asked it before. Perhaps, in this case, ignorance was more bliss than knowledge. Whatever had happened to her, would it not be best to have the pure image of her abide with him? But he know when he thought of it further that such a conclusion was not worthy of a strong man. He should not be afraid even of suffering if it came in the performance of duty.

That very night Dorian had a strange dream, one unusual to him because he remembered it so distinctly the day after. He dreamed that he saw Mildred in what might well be called the heavenly land. She seemed busy in sketching a beautiful landscape and as he approached her, she looked up to him and smiled. Then, as she still gazed at him, her countenance changed and with concern in her voice, she asked, "Where's Carlia?"

164   The scene vanished, and that was all of the dream. In the dim consciousness of waking he seemed to hear Carlia's voice calling to him as it did that winter night when he had left her, not heeding. The call thrilled his very heart again:

"Dorian, Dorian, come back—come back!"

16.

THE SECOND WEEK in December Dorian went into action in search of Carlia Duke. He acknowledged to himself that it was like searching for the proverbial needle in the haystack, but inaction was no longer possible.

Carlia very likely had no large amount of money with her, so she would have to seek employment. She could have hidden herself in the city, but Dorian reasoned that she would be fearful of being found, so would have gone to some nearby town; but which one, he had no way of knowing. He visited a number of adjacent towns and made diligent enquiries at hotels, stores, and some private houses. Nothing came of this first week's search.

A number of mining towns could easily be reached by train from the city. In these towns many people came and went without notice or comment. Dorian spent nearly a week in one of them, but he found no clue. He went to another. The girl would necessarily have to go to a hotel at first, so the searcher examined a number of hotel registers. She had been gone now about six months, so the search had to be in some books long since discarded, much to the annoyance of the clerks.

Dorian left the second town for the third which was situated well up in the mountains. The weather was cold, and the snow lay two feet deep over the hills and valleys. He became disheartened at times, but always he reasoned that he must try a little longer; and then one day in a hotel register dated nearly five monhs back, he found this entry:

"Carlia Davis."

Dorian's heart gave a bound when he saw the name. Carlia was not a common name, and the handwriting was familiar. But why Davis? He examined the signature closely. The girl, unexperienced in the art of subterfuge, had started to write her name, and had gotten to the D in Duke, when the thought of disguise had come to her. Yes; there was an unusual break between that first letter and the rest of the name. Carlia had been here. He was on the right track, thank the Lord!

Dorian enquired of the hotel clerk if he remembered the lady. Did he know anything about her? No; that was so long ago. His people came and went. That was all. But Carlia had been here. That much was certain. Here was at least a fixed point in the sea of nothingness from which he could work. His wearied and confused mind could at least come back to that name in the hotel register.

167

He began a systematic search of the town. First he visited the small business section, but without results. Then he took up the residential district, systematically, so that he would not miss any. One afternoon he knocked on the door of what appeared to be one of the best residences. After a short wait, the door was opened by a girl, highly painted but lightly clad, who smiled at the handsome young fellow and bade him come in. He stepped into the hall and was shown into what seemed to be a parlor, though the parlors he had known had not smelled so of stale tobacco smoke. He made his usual inquiry. No; no such girl was here, she was sorry, but—the words which came from the carmine lips of the girl so startled Dorian that he stood, hat in hand, staring at her, and shocked beyond expression. He know, of course, that evil houses existed especially in mining towns, inhabited by corrupt women, but this was the first time he had ever been in such a place. When he realized where he was, a real terror seized him, and with unceremonious haste he got out and away, the girl's laughter of derision ringing in his ears.

Dorian was unnerved. He went back to his room, his thoughts in a

whirl, his apprehensions sinking to gloomy depths. What if Carlia   168
should be in such a place? A cold sweat of suffering broke over him
before he could drive away the thought. But at last he did get rid of it.
His mind cleared again, and he set out determined to continued the
search. However, he went no more into the houses by the invitation of
inmates of doubtful character, but made his inquiries at the open door.

Then it occurred to Dorian that Carlia, being a country bred girl
and accustomed to work about farm houses, might apply to some of
the adjacent farms down in the valley below the town for work. The
whole country lay under deep snow, but the roads were well broken.
Dorian walked out to a number of the farms and made enquiries. At
the third house he was met by a pleasant faced, elderly woman who
listened attentively to what he said, and then invited him in. When
they were both seated, she asked him his name. Dorian told her.

"And why are you interested in this girl?" she continued.

"Has she been here?" he asked eagerly.

"Never mind. You answer my question."

Dorian explained as much as he thought proper, but the woman
still appeared suspicious.

"Are you her brother?"

"No."

"Her young man?"

"Not exactly; only a dear friend."

"Well, you look all right, but looks are deceivin'." The woman tried
to be very severe with him, but somehow she did not succeed very well.
She looked quite motherly as she sat with her folded hands in her ample   169
lap and a shrewd look in her face. Dorian gained courage to say:

"I believe you know something about the girl I am seeking. Tell me."

"You haven't told me the name of the girl you are looking for."

"Her name is Carlia Duke."

"That isn't what she called herself."

"Oh, then you do know."

"This girl was Carlia Davis."

"Yes—is she here!"

"No."

"Do you know where she is?"

"No, I don't."

Dorian's hopes fell. "But tell me what you know about her—you know something."

"It was the latter part of August when she came to us. She had walked from town, an' she said she was wanting a place to work. As she was used to farm life, she preferred to work at a country home, she said."

"Was she a dark-haired, rosy-cheeked girl?"

"Her hair was dark, but there was no roses in her cheeks. There might have been once. I was glad to say yes to her for I needed help bad. Of course, it was strange, this girl comin' from the city a' wanting to work in the country. It's usually the other way."

"Yes; I suppose so."

"So I was a little suspicious."

"Of what?"

170

"That she hadn't come to work at all; though I'll say that she did her best. I tried to prevent her, but she worked right up to he last."

"To the last? I don't understand?"

"Don't you know that she was to be sick? That she came here to be sick?"

"To be sick?" Dorian was genuinely at loss to understand.

"At first I called her a cheat, and threatened to send her away; but the poor child pleaded so to stay that I hadn't the heart to turn her out. She had no where to go, she was a long way from home, an' so I let her stay, an' we did the best for her."

Dorian, in the simplicity of his mind, did not yet realize what the woman was talking about. He let her continue.

"We had one of the best doctors in the city 'tend her, an' I did the nursing myself which I consider was as good as any of the new-fangled trained nurses can do; but the poor girl had been under a strain so long that the baby died soon after it was born."

"The baby?" gasped Dorian.

"Yes," went on the woman, all unconsciously that the listener had not fully understood. "Yes, it didn't live long, which, I suppose, in such cases, is a blessing."

Dorian stared at the woman, then in a dazed way, he looked about the plain farm-house furnishings, some details of which strangely impressed him. The woman went on talking, which seemed 171 easy for her, now she had fairly started; but Dorian did not hear all she said. One big fact was forcing itself into his brain, to the exclusion of all minor realities.

"She left a month ago," Dorian heard the woman say when again he was in a condition to listen. "We did our best to get her to stay, for we had become fond of her. Somehow, she got the notion that the scoundrel who had betrayed her had found her hiding place, an' she was afraid. So she left."

"Where did she go? Did she tell you?"

"No; she wouldn't say. The fact is, she didn't know herself. I'm sure of that. She just seemed anxious to hide herself again. Poor girl." The woman wiped a tear away with the corner of her apron.

Dorian arose, thanked her, and went out. He looked about the snow-covered earth and the clouds which threatened storm. He walked on up to the road back to the town. He was benumbed, but not with cold. He went into his room, and, although it was mid-afternoon, he did not go out any more that day. He sat supinely on his bed. He paced the floor. He looked without seeing out of the window at the passing crowds. He could not think at all clearly. His whole being was in an uproar of confusion. The hours passed. Night came on with its blaze of lights in the streets. What could he do now? What should he do now? "Oh, God, help me," he prayed, "help me 172 to order my thoughts, tell me what to do."

If ever in his life Dorian had need of help from higher power, it was now.

17.

DORIAN HAD NOT found Carlia Duke; instead, he had found something which appeared to him to be the end of all things. Had he found her dead, in her virginal purity, he could have placed her, with Mildred, safely away in his heart and his hopes; but this! … What more could he now do? That he did not take the first train home was because he was benumbed into inactivity.

The young man had never before experienced such suffering of spirit. The leaden weight on his heart seemed to be crushing, not only his physical being, but his spirit also into the depths of despair. As far back in his boyhood as he could remember, he had been taught the enormity of sexual sin, until it had become second nature for him to think of it as something very improbable, if not impossible, as pertaining to himself. And yet, here it was, right at the very door of his heart, casting its evil shadow into the most sacred precincts of his being. He had never imagined it coming to any of his near and dear ones, especially not to Carlia—Carlia, his neighbor, his chummy companion in fields and highways, his schoolmate. He pictured her in many of her wild adventures as a child, and in her softer moods as a grown-up girl. He saw again her dark eyes flash with anger, and then her pearly teeth gleam in laughter at him. He remembered how she used to run from him, and then at other times how she would cling to him as if she pleaded for a protection which he had not given. The weak had reached out to the strong, and the stronger one had failed. If 'remorse of conscience' is hell, Dorian tasted of its bitter depths, for it came to him now that perhaps because of his neglect, Carlia had been led to her fall.

But what could he now do? Find her. And then, what? Marry her? He refused to consider that for a moment. He drove the thought fiercely away. That would be impossible now. The horror of what had been would always stand as a repellent specter between them … Yes,, he had loved her—he knew that now more assuredly than ever; and he tried to place that love away from him by a play upon words in the past tense; but deep down in his heart he knew that he was merely trying to deceive himself. He loved her still; and the fact that he loved her but could not marry her added fuel to the flames of his torment.

That long night was mostly a hideous nightmare and even after he awoke from a fitful sleep next morning, he was in a stupor. After a while, he went out into the wintry air. It was Sunday, and the town was comparatively quiet. He found something to eat at a lunch counter, then he walked about briskly to try to get his blood into active circulation. Again he went to his room.

Presently, he heard the ringing of church bells. The folks would be going to Sunday school in Greenstreet. He saw in the vision of his mind Uncle Zed sitting with the boys about him in his class. He saw the teacher's lifted hand emphasize the warning against sin, and then he seemed to hear a voice read:

"For the Son of man is come to save that which is lost.

"How think ye if a man have an hundred sheep, and one of them be gone astray, doth he not leave the ninety and nine, and goeth into the mountains, and seeketh that which is gone astray?

"And if so be that he find it, verily, I say unto you, he rejoiceth more of that sheep than of the ninety and nine which went not astray."

Dorian seemed to awaken with a start. Donning coat and hat, he went out again, his steps being led down the country road toward the farmhouse. He wanted to visit again the house where Carlia had been. Her presence there and her suffering had hallowed it.

"Oh, how do you do?" greeted the woman, when she saw Dorian at the door. "Come in."

Dorian entered, this time into the parlor which was warm, and where a man sat comfortably with his Sunday paper.

"Father," said the woman, "this is the young man who was here 176 yesterday."

The man shook hands with Dorian and bade him draw up his chair to the stove.

"I hope you'll excuse me for coming again," said Dorian; "but the fact of the matter is I seemed unable to keep away. I left yesterday without properly thanking you for what you did for my friend, Miss Carlia. I also want to pay you a little for the expense you were put to. I haven't much money with me, but I will send it to you after I get home, if you will give me your name and address."

The farmer and his wife exchanged glances.

"Why, as to that," replied the man, "nothing is owing us. We liked the girl. We think she was a good girl and had been sinned against."

"I'm sure you are right," said Dorian. "As I said, I went away rather abruptly yesterday. I was so completely unprepared for that which I learned about her. But I'm going to find her if I can, and take her home to her parents."

"Where do you live?" asked the man.

Dorian told him.

"Are you a 'Mormon'?"

"Yes, sir."

"And not ashamed of it?"

"No; proud of it—grateful, rather."

"Well, young man, you look like a clean, honest chap. Tell me why you are proud to be a 'Mormon'."

Dorian did his best. He had had very little experience in presenting 177 the principles of the gospel to an unbeliever, but Uncle Zed's teachings, together with his own studies, now stood him well in hand.

"Well," commented the farmer, "that's fine. You can't be a very bad man if you believe in and practice all what you have been telling us."

"I hope I am not a bad man. I have some light on the truth, and woe is me if I sin against that light."

The farmer turned to his wife. "Mother," he said," I think you may safely tell him."

Dorian looked enquiringly at the woman.

"It's this," she said. "My husband brought home a postcard from the office last evening after you had left—a card from Miss Davis, asking us to send her an article of dress which she had forgotten. Here is the card. The address may help you to find her. I am sure you mean no harm to the girl."

Dorian made note of the address, as also that of the farmer's with whom he was visiting. Then he arose to go.

"Now, don't be in such a hurry," admonished the man. "We'll have dinner presently."

Dorian was glad to remain, as he felt quite at home with these people, Mr. and Mrs. Whitman. They had been good to Carlia. Perhaps he could learn a little more about her. The dinner was enjoyed very much. Afterward, Mrs. Whitman, encouraged by Dorian's attentiveness, poured into his willing ear all she had learned of the girl he was seeking; and before the woman ceased her freely-flowing talk, a most important item had been added to his knowledge of the case. Carlia, it seems, had gone literally helpless to her downfall. "Drugged" was the word Mrs. Whitman used. The villainy of the foul deed moved the young man's spirit to a fierce anger against the wretch who had planned it, and the same time his pity increased for the unfortunate victim. As Dorian sat there and listened to the story which the woman had with difficulty obtained from the girl, he again suffered the remorse of conscience which comes from a realization of neglected duty and disregarded opportunity. It was late in the afternoon before he got back to the town.

The next day Dorian made inquiries as to how he could reach the place indicated by the address, and he learned that it was a ranch house well up in the mountains. There was a daily mail in that direction, except when the roads and the weather hindered; and it seemed that these would now be hinderances. The threatened storm came, and with it high wind which piled the snow into deep, hard drifts, making the mountain road nearly impassable. Dorian found the mail-carrier who told him that it would be impossible to make a start until the storm had ceased. All day the snow fell, and all day Dorian fretted impatiently, and was tempted to once more go out to Mr. and Mrs. Whitman; but he did not. Christmas was only three days off. He could reach home and spend the day with his mother, but there would be considerable expense, and he felt as if he must be on the ground so that at the soonest possible moment he could continue on the trail which he had found. The pleasure of the home Christmas must this time be sacrificed, for was not he in very deed going into the mountains to seek that which was lost.

179

The storm ceased toward evening, but the postman would not make a start until next morning. Dorian joined him then, and mounted beside him. The sky was not clear, the clouds only breaking and drifting about as if in doubt whether to go or to stay. The road was heavy, and it was all the two horses could do to draw the light wagon with its small load. Dorian wondered how Carlia had ever come that way. Of course, it had been before the heavy snow, when traveling was not so bad.

"Who lives at this place?" asked Dorian of the driver, giving the box number Carlia had sent.

"That? Oh, that's John Hickson's place."

"A rancher?"

"No; not exactly. He's out here mostly for his health."

"Does he live here in the mountains the year around?"

"Usually he moves into town for the winter. Last year the winter was so mild that he decided to try to stick one through; but surely, he's got a dose this time. Pretty bad for a sick man, I reckon."

180

"Anybody with him?"

"Wife and three children—three of the cutest kiddies you ever saw. Oh, he's comfortable enough, for he's got a fine house. You know, it's great out here among the pine hills in the summer; but just now, excuse me."

"Is it far?"

"No." The driver looked with concern at the storm which was coming again down the mountain like a great white wave. "I think perhaps we'll have to stop at the Hickson's tonight," he said.

The travelers were soon enwrapped in a swirling mantle of snow. Slowly and carefully the dug-ways had to be traversed. The sky was dense and black. The storm became a blizzard, and the cold became intense. The men wrapped themselves in additional blankets. The horses went patiently on, the driver peering anxiously ahead; but it must have been well after noon before the outlines of a large building near at hand bulked out of the leaden sky.

"I'm glad we're here," exclaimed the driver.

"Where?" asked Dorian.

"At Hickson's."

They drove into the yard and under a shed where the horses were unhitched and taken into a stable. A light as if from a wood fire in a grate danced upon the white curtain of the unshaded windows. With his mail-bag, the driver shuffled his way through the snow to the kitchen door and knocked. The door opened immediately and Mrs. Hickson, recognizing the mail-driver, bade him come in. Two children peered curiously from the doorway of another room. Dorian a little nervously awaited the possibility of Carlia's appearing.

It was pleasant to get shelter and a warm welcome in such weather. After the travelers had warmed themselves by the kitchen stove, they were invited into another room to meet Mr. Hickson, who was reclining in a big arm chair before the grate. He welcomed them without rising, but pointed them to chairs by the fire. They talked of the weather, of course. Mr. Hickson reasoned that it was foolish to complain about something which they could not possible control.

Dorian was introduced as a traveler, no explanation being asked or given as to his business. He was welcome. In fact, it was a pleasure, said the host, to have company even for an evening, as very few people ever stopped over night, especially in the winter. Dorian soon discovered that this man was not a rough mountaineer, but a man of culture, trying to prolong his earth-life by the aid of mountain air, laden with the aroma of the pines. The wife went freely in and out of the room, the children also; but somewhat to Dorian's surprise, no Carlia appeared. If she were there in the house, she surely would be helping with the meal which seemed to be in the way of preparation.

The storm continued all afternoon. There could be no thought of moving on that day. And indeed, it was pleasant sitting thus by the blazing log in the fireplace and listening, for the most part, to the intelligent talk of the host. The evening meal was served early, and the two guests ate with the family in the dining room . Still no Carlia. 182

When the driver went out to feed his horses and to smoke his pipe, and Mr. Hickson had retired, the children, having overcome some of their timidity, turned their attention to Dorian. The girl, the oldest, with dark hair and rosy cheeks, reminded him of another girl just then in his thoughts. The two small boys were chubby and light haired, after the mother. When Dorian managed to get the children close to him, they reminded him that Christmas was only one day distant. Did he live near by? Was he going home for Christmas? What was Santa Claus going to bring him?

Dorian warmed to their sociability and their clatter. He learned from them that their Christmas this year would likely be somewhat of a failure. Daddy was sick. There was no Christmas tree, and they doubted Santa Claus' ability to find his way up in the mountains in the storm. This was the first winter they had been here. Always they had been in town during the holidays, where it was easy for Santa to reach them; but now—the little girl plainly choked back the tears of disappointment.

"Why, if it's a Christmas tree you want," said Dorian, "that ought to be easy. There are plenty up on the nearby hills."

183

"Yes; but neither papa nor mama nor we can get them."

"But I can."

"Oh, will you? Tomorrow?"

"Yes; tomorrow is Christmas Eve. We'll have to have it then."

The children were dancing with glee as the mother came in and learned what had been going on. "You mustn't bother the gentleman," she admonished, but Dorian pleaded for the pleasure of doing something for them. The mother explained that because of unforeseen difficulties the children were doomed to disappointment this holiday season, and they would have to be satisfied with what scanty preparation could be made.

"I think I can help," suggested the young man, patting the littlest confiding fellow on the head. "We cannot go on until tomorrow, I understand, and I should very much like to be useful."

The big pleading eyes of the children won the day. They moved into the kitchen. All the corners were ransacked for colored paper and cloth, and with scissors and flour paste, many fantastic decorations were made to hang on the tree. Corn was popped and strung into long white chains. But what was to be done for candles? Could Dorian make candles? He could do most everything, couldn't he? He would try. Had they some parafine, used to seal preserve jars. Oh, yes, large pieces were found. And this with some string was soon made into some very possible candles. The children were intensely interested, and

184

even the mail-driver wondered at the young man's cleverness. They had never seen anything like this before. The tree and its trimmings had always been bought ready for their use. Now they learned, which their parents should have known long ago, that there is greater joy in the making of a plaything than in the possession of it.

The question of candy seemed to bother them all. Their last hopes went when there was not a box of candy in the postman's bag. What should they do for candy and nuts and oranges and—

"Can you make candy?" asked the girl of Dorian as if she was aware she was asking the miraculous.

"Now children," warned the happy mother. "You have your hands full" she said to Dorian. "There's no limit to their demands."

Dorian assured her that the greater pleasure was his.

"Tomorrow," he told the clammering children, "we'll see what we can do about the candy."

"Chocolates?" asked one.

"Caramels," chose another.

"Fudge," suggested the third.

"All these?" laughed Dorian. "Well, we'll see—tomorrow," and with that the children went to bed tremulously happy.

The next morning the sun arose on a most beautiful scene. The snow lay deep on mountain and in valley. It ridged the fences and trees. Paths and roads were obliterated.

The children were awake early. As Dorian dressed, he heard them scampering down the stairs. Evidently, they were ready for him. He looked out of the window. He would have to make good about that tree.

As yet, Dorian had found no traces of the object of his search. He had not asked direct questions about her, but he would have to before he left. There seemed some mystery always just before him. The mail-driver would not be ready to go before noon, so Dorian would have time to get the tree and help the children decorate it. Then he would have to find out all there was to know about Carlia. Surely, she was somewhere in the locality.

After breakfast, Dorian found the axe in the wood-shed, and began to make his way through the deep snow up the hill toward a small grove of pine. Behind the shoulder of a hill, he discovered another house, not so large as Mr. Hickson's, but neat and comfortably looking. The blue smoke of a wood fire was rising from the chimney. A girl was vigorously shoveling a path from the house to the wood-pile. She was dressed in big boots, a sweater, and a red hood. She did not see Dorian until he came near the small clearing by the house. Straightening from her work, she stood for a moment looking intently at him. Then with a low, yet startled cry, she let the shovel fall, and sped swiftly back along the newly-made path and into the house.

It was Carlia.

18.

DORIAN STOOD KNEE-DEEP in the snow and watched the girl run back into the house. In his surprise, he forgot his immediate errand. He had found Carlia, found her well and strong; but why had she run from him with a cry of alarm? She surely had recognized him; she would not have acted thus toward a stranger. Apparently, she was not glad to see him. He stood looking at the closed door, and a feeling of resentment came to him. Here he had been searching for her all this time, only to be treated as if he were an unwelcome intruder. Well, he would not force himself on her. If she did not want to see him, why annoy her? He could go back, tell her father where she was, and let him come for her. He stood, hesitating.

The door opened again and a woman looked out inquiringly at the young man standing in the snow with an axe on his shoulder. Dorian would have to offer a word of explanation to the woman, at least, so he stepped into the path toward the house.

"Good morning," he said, lifting his hat. "I'm out to get a Christ- mas tree for the children over there, and it seems I have startled the young lady who just ran in."

"Yes," said the woman.

"I'm sorry to have frightened her, but I'm glad to have found her. You see, I've been searching for her."

The woman stood in the doorway, saying nothing, but looking with some suspicion at the young man.

"I should like to see her again," continued Dorian. "Tell her it's Dorian Trent."

"I'll tell her," said the woman as she withdrew and closed the door.

The wait seemed long, but it was only a few minutes when the door opened and Dorian was invited to come in. They passed through the kitchen into the living room where a fire was burning in a grate. Dorian was given a chair. He could not fail to see that he was closely observed. The woman went into another room, but soon returned.

"She'll be in shortly," she announced.

"Thank you."

The woman retired to the kitchen, and presently Carlia came in. She had taken off her wraps and now appeared in a neat house dress. As she stood hesitatingly by the door. Dorian came with outstretched hands to greet her; but she was not eager to meet him, so he went back to his chair. Both were silent. He saw it was the same Carlia, with something added, something which must have taken much experience if not much time to bring to her. The old-time roses, somewhat modified, were in her cheeks, the old-time red tinted the full lips; but she was more mature, less of a girl and more of a woman; and to Dorian she was more beautiful than ever.

188

"Carlia," he again ventured, "I'm glad to see you; but you don't seem very pleased with your neighbor. Why did you run from me out there?"

"You startled me."

"Yes; I suppose I did. It was rather strange, this coming so suddenly on to you. I've been looking for you quite a while."

"I don't understand why you have been looking for me."

"You know why, Carlia."

"I don't."

"You're just talking to be talking—but here, this sounds like quarreling, and we don't want to do that so soon, do we?"

"No, I guess not."

"Won't you sit down."

The girl reached for a chair, then seated herself.

"The folks are anxious about you. When can you go home?"

"I'm not going home."

"Not going home? Why not? Who are these people, and what are you doing here?"

"These are good people, and they treat me fine. I'm going to stay—here."

"But I don't see why. Of course, it's none of my business; but for the sake of your father and mother, you ought to go home." 189

"How—how are they?"

"They are as well as can be expected. You've never written them, have you, nor ever told where you were. They do not know whether you are dead or alive. That isn't right."

The girl turned her bowed head slightly, but did not speak, so he continued: "The whole town has been terribly aroused about you. You disappeared so suddenly and completely. Your father has done everything he could think of to find you. When he gave up, I took up the task, and here you are in the hills not so far from Greenstreet."

Carlia's eyes swam with tears. The kitchen door opened, and the woman looked at Carlia and then at Dorian.

"Breakfast is ready," she announced. "Come, Miss Davis, and have your friend come too."

Dorian explained that he had already eaten.

"Please excuse me just now," pleaded Carlia, to the woman. "Go eat your breakfast without me. Mrs. Carlston, this is Mr. Trent, a neighbor of ours at my home. I was foolish to be so scared of him. He—he wouldn't hurt anyone." She tried bravely to smile.

Alone again, the two were ill at ease. A flood of memories, a confusion of thoughts and feelings swept over Dorian. The living Carlia in all her attractive beauty was before him, yet back of her stood the grim 190 skeleton. Could he close his eyes to that? Could he let his love for her overcome the repulsion which would arise like a black cloud into his thoughts? Well, time alone would tell. Just now he must be kind to her, he must be strong and wise. Of what use is strength and wisdom if it is unfruitful at such times as these? Dorian arose to his feet and stood in the strength of his young manhood. He seemed to take Carlia with him, for she also stood looking at him with her shining eyes.

"Well, Carlia," he said, "go get your breakfast, and I'll finish my errand. You see, the storm stopped the mail carrier and me and we had to put up at your neighbour's last night. There I found three children greatly disappointed in not having their usual Christmas tree. I promised I would get them one this morning, and that's what I was out for when I saw you. You know, Carlia, it's Christmas Eve this morning, if you'll allow that contradiction."

"Yes, I know."

"I'll come back for you. And mind, you do not try to escape. I'll be watching the house closely. Anyway," he laughed lightly, "the snow's too deep for you to run very far."

"O, Dorian—"

"Yes."

He came toward her, but she with averted face, slipped toward the kitchen door.

191   "I can't go home, I can't go with you—really, I can't," she said. "You go back home and tell the folks I'm all right now, won't you, please."

"We'll talk about that after a while. I must get that tree now, or those kiddies will think I am a rank impostor." Dorian looked at his watch. "Why, it's getting on toward noon. So long, for the present."

Dorian found and cut a fairly good tree. The children were at the window when he appeared, and great was their joy when they saw him carry it to the woodshed and make a stand for it, then bring it in to them. The mail carrier was about ready to continue his journey, and he asked Dorian if he was also ready. But Dorian had no reason for going on further; he had many reasons for desiring to remain.

And here was the Christmas tree, not dressed, nor the candy made. How could he disappoint these children?

"I wonder," he said to the mother, "if it would be asking too much to let me stay here until tomorrow. I'm in no hurry, and I would like to help the children with the tree, as I promised. I've been hindered some this morning, and—"

"Stay," shouted the children who had heard this. "Stay, do stay."

"You are more than welcome," replied Mrs. Hickson; "but I fear that the children are imposing on you."

Dorian assured her that the pleasure was his, and after the mail carrier had departed, he thought it wise to explain further.

"A very strange thing has happened," said Dorian. "As I was going after the tree for the children, I met the young lady who is staying at Mrs. Carlston." 192

"Miss Davis."

"Yes; she's a neighbor of mine. We grew up together as boy and girl. Through some trouble, she left home, and—in fact, I have been searching for her. I am going to try to get her to go home to her parents. She—she could help us with our tree dressing this evening."

"We'd like to have both our neighbors visit with us," said Mrs. Hickson; "but the snow is rather deep for them."

By the middle of the afternoon Dorian cleared a path to the neighboring house, and then went stamping on to the porch. Carlia opened the door and gave him a smiling welcome. She had dressed up a bit, he could see, and he was pleased with the thought that it was for him. Dorian delivered the invitation to the two women. Carlia would go immediately to help, and Mrs. Carlston would come later. Carlia was greeted by the children as a real addition to their company.

"Did you bring an extra of stockings?" asked Mrs. Hickson of her. "An up-to-date Santa Claus is going to visit us tonight, I am sure." She glanced toward Dorian, who was busy with the children and the tree.

That was a Christmas Eve long to be remembered by all those 193 present in that house amid solitude of snow, of mountain, and of pine forests. The tree, under the magic touches of Dorian and Carlia grew to be a thing of beauty, in the eyes of the children. The home-made candles and decorations were pronounced to be as good as the "boughten ones." And the candy—what a miracle worker this sober-laughing, ruddy-haired young fellow was!

Carlia could not resist the spirit of cheer. She smiled with the older people and laughed with the children. How good it was to laugh again, she thought. When the tree was fully ablaze, all, with the exception of Mr. Hickson joined hands and danced around it. Then they had to taste of the various and doubtful makings of candies, and ate a bread-pan of snow-white popcorn sprinkled with melted butter. Then Mr. Hickson told some stories, and his wife in a clear, sweet voice led the children in some Christmas songs. Oh, it was a real Christmas Eve, made doubly joyful by the simple helpfulness and kindness of all who took part.

At the close of the evening, Dorian escorted Mrs. Carlston and Carlia back to their house, and the older woman graciously retired, leaving the parlor and the glowing log to the young people.

They sat in the big armchairs facing the grate.

"We've had a real nice Christmas Eve, after all," said he.

"Yes."

194 "Our Christmas Eves at home are usually quiet. I'm the only kid there, and I don't make much noise. Frequently, just mother and Uncle Zed and I made up the company; and then when we could get Uncle Zed to talking about Jesus, and explain who He was, and tell his story before He came to this earth as the Babe of Bethlehem, there was a real Christmas spirit present. Yes; I believe you were with us on one of these occasions."

"Yes, I was."

Dorian adjusted the log in the grate. "Carlia, when shall we go home?" he asked.

"How can I go home?"

"A very simple matter. We ride on the stage to the railroad, and then—"

"O! I do not mean that. How can I face my folks, and every-body?"

"Of course, people will be inquisitive, and there will be a lot of speculation; but never mind that. Your father and mother will be mighty glad to get you back home, and I am sure your father will see to it that you—that you'll have no more cause to run away from home."

"What—what?"

"Why, he'll see that you do not have so much work-man's work, to do. Yes, regular downright drudgery it was. Why, I hardly blame you for running away, that is, taking a brief vacation." He went on talking, she looking silently into the fire. "But now," he said finally, "you have had a good rest, and you are ready to go home."

She sat rigidly looking at the glow in the grate. He kept on talking 195 cheerfully, optimistically, as if he wished to prevent the gloom of night to overwhelm them. Then, presently, the girl seemed to shake herself free from some benumbing influence, as she turned to him and said:

"Dorian, why, really why have you gone to all this trouble to find me?"

"Why, we all wanted to know what had become of you. Your father is a changed man because of your disappearance, and your mother is nearly broken hearted."

"Yes, I suppose so; but is that all?"

"Isn't that enough?"

"No."

"Well, I—I—"

"Dorian, you're neither dull nor stupid, except in this. Why did not someone else do this hunting for a lost girl? Why should it be you?"

Dorian arose, walked to the window and looked out into the win-try night. He saw the shine of the everlasting stars in the deep blue. He sensed the girl's pleading eyes sinking into his soul as if to search him out. He glimpsed the shadowy specter lurking in her back-ground. And yet, as he fixed his eyes on the heavens, his mind cleared, his purpose strengthened. As he turned, there was a grim smile on his face. He walked back to the fire-place and seated himself on the arm of Carlia's chair.

"Carlia," he said, "I may be stupid—I am stupid—I've always been stupid with you. I know it. I confess it to you. I have not always acted toward you as one who loves you. I don't know why—lay it to my stupidity. But, Carlia, I do love you. I have always loved you. Yes, ever since we were children playing in the fields and by the creek and the ditches. I know now what that feeling was. I loved you then, I love you now."

The girl arose mechanically from her chair, reached out as if for support to the mantle. "Why, Oh, why did you not tell me before— before" —she cried, then swayed as if to a fall. Dorian caught her and placed her back in the seat. He took her cold hands, but in a moment, she pulled them away.

"Dorian, please sit down in this other chair, won't you?"

Dorian did as she wanted him to do, but he turned the chair to face her.

"I want you to believe me, Carlia."

"I am trying to believe you."

"Is it so hard as all that?"

"What I fear is that you are doing all this for me out of the good-ness of your heart. Listen, let me say what I want to say—I believe I can now ... You're the best man I know. I have never met anyone as good as you, no, not even my father—nobody. You're far above me. You always have been willing to sacrifice yourself for others; and now—what I fear is that you are just doing this, saying this, out of the goodness of your heart and not because you really—really love me."

"Carlia, stop—don't."

"I know you, Dorian. I've heard you and Uncle Zed talk, some-times when you thought I was not listening. I know your high ideals of service, how you believe it is necessary for the higher to reach down to help and save the lower. Oh, I know, Dorian; and it is this that I think of. You cannot love poor me for my sake, but you are doing this for fear of not doing your duty. Hush—Listen! Not that I don't honor you for your high ideals—they are noble, and belong to just such as I believe you are. Yes, I have always, even as a child, looked up to you as someone big and strong and good—Yes, I have always worshiped you, loved you! There, you know it, but what's the use!"

Dorian moved his chair close to her, then said:

"You are mistaken, of course, in placing my goodness so high, though I've always tried to do the right by everybody. That I have failed with you is evidence that I am not so perfect as you say. But now, let's forget everything else but the fact that we love each other. Can't we be happy in that?"

The roses faded from Carlia's cheeks ,though coaxed to stay by the firelight.

"My dear," he continued, "we'll go home, and I'll try to make up to you my failings. I think I can do that, Carlia, when you become my wife."

"I can't, Dorian, Oh, I can't be that."

"Why not Carlia?"

198

"I can't marry you. I'm not—No, Dorian."

"In time, Carlia. We will have to wait, of course; but some day" —he took her hands, and she did not seem to have power to resist— "some day" he said fervently, "you are going to be mine for time and for eternity."

They looked into each others faces without fear. Then: "Go now, Dorian" she said. "I can't stand any more tonight. Please go."

"Yes; I'll go. Tomorrow, the stage comes again this way, and we'll go with it. That's settled. Goodnight."

They both arose. He still held her hands.

"Goodnight," he repeated, and kissed her gently on the cheek.

19.

THE SUDDEN RETURN of Carlia Duke to her home creat-
ed as much talk as her disappearance had done. Dorian was besieged
with enquirers whom he smilingly told that he had just come across
her taking a little vacation up in the hills. What, in the hills in the
depths of winter? Why, yes; none but those who have tried it know
the comfort and the real rest one may obtain shut out by the snow
from the world, in the solitude of the hills. He told as little as possible of the details of his search, even to Carlia's parents. Any unpleas-
ant disclosures would have to come from her to them, he reasoned.
Not being able to get Dorian talking about the case, the good people
of Greenstreet soon exhausted their own knowledge of the matter, so
in a short time, the gossip resumed its every-day trend.

Hardly a day passed without Dorian spending some time with
Carlia. She would not go to Sunday School or to Mutual, and it was
some time before he could convince her that it was a matter of wisdom as well as of right that she should attend some of the public
ward meetings. Frequently, he took his book to the Duke home and
read aloud to Carlia. This she enjoyed very much. Sometimes the
book was a first class novel, but oftener it was a scientific text or a
religions treatise. Carlia listened attentively to his discussion of deep
problems, and he was agreeably surprised to learn that she could
readily follow him in the discussion of these themes; so that the long

winter evenings spent with her either at her home or at his own became a source of great inspiration to the young man who had not
lost sight or the mission assigned to him by the beloved Uncle Zed.
Dorian talked freely to Carlia on how he might best fulfill the high
destiny which seemed to lay before him; and Carlia entered enthusiastically into his plans.

"Fine, fine," she would say. "Carry it out. You can do it."

"With your help, Carlia."

"I'll gladly help you all I can; but that is so little; what can I do?"

"Trust me, have faith in me; and when the time comes, marry me."

This was usually the end of the conversation for Carlia; she became silent unless he changed the subject.

Dorian, naturally undemonstrative, was now more careful than
ever in his love making. The intimacy between them never quite returned to the earlier state. Complete forgetfulness of what had been,
was, of course, impossible, either for Carlia or for Dorian; but he
tried manfully not to let the "specter" come too often between him
and the girl he loved. He frequently told her that he loved her, but it
was done by simple word or act. Dorian's greater knowledge gave
him the advantage over her. He was bound by this greater knowledge
to be the stronger, the wiser, the one who could keep all situations
well in hand.

One evening, when Carlia was unusually sweet and tempting, he
asked if he might kiss her goodnight. She set her face as if it were
hard to deny him, but she finally said:

"No; you must not."

"Why not, Carlia?"

"We're not engaged yet."

"Carlia!"

"We are not. I have never promised to marry you, have I?" She
smiled.

"No; I guess not; but that's understood."

"Don't be so sure."

"There are some things definitely fixed without the spoken word."

"Good night, Dorian." She was smiling still.

"Good night, Carlia." Their hands met and clasped, atoning the best they could for the forbidden kiss.

ONE EVENING WHEN the feeling of spring was in the air, Dorian was going to call on Carlia, when he heard the approach of an automobile. As it turned into the bystreet, leading to the Duke home, Dorian saw the driver to be Mr. Jack Lamont. Dorian kept in the road, and set his face hard. As the machine had to stop to prevent running over him, Dorian turned, walked deliberately to the side of the car, and looking steadily into Mr. Lamont's face, said:

"I'm going to Mr. Duke's also. If I find you there, I'll thrash you within an inch of your life. Drive on."

For a moment, the two glared at each other, then the automobile went on—on past the Duke house toward town. When Dorian arrived at his destination, Carlia greeted him with:

"Dorian, what's the matter?"

"Nothing," he laughed.

"You're as pale as a ghost."

"Am I? Well, I haven't seen any ghosts—Say, mother wants you to come to supper. She has something you specially like. Can you?"

"Sure, she can," answered her mother, for she was glad to have Carlia out away from the work which she was determined to stick to closer than ever. Carlia was pleased to go, and kept up a merry chatter until she saw that Dorian was exceptionally sober-minded. She asked him what was the matter with him, but he evaded. His thoughts were on the man whom he had prevented from calling at her home that evening. What was his errand? What was in the scoundrel's mind? Dorian struggled to put away from him the dark thoughts which had arisen because of his recent encounter with Mr. Lamont. All the evening at home and during their walk back he was unusually silent, and Carlia could only look at him with questioning anxiety.

Spring, once started, came on with a rush. The melting snow filled the river with a muddy flood; the grass greened the slopes; the bursting willows perfumed the air; the swamp awakened to the warm touch of the sun. Dorian's busy season also began.

As soon as the roads were passible, Dorian drove up to his dry-farm. On one of these first trips he fell in with a company of his neighboring dry-farmers, and they traveled together. While they were stopping for noon at a small hotel in the canyon, a rain storm came up, which delayed them. They were not impatient, however, as the moisture was welcome; so the farmers rested easily, letting their horses eat a little longer than usual.

The conversation was such which should be expected of Bishop's counselors, president of Elders' quorums, and class leaders in the Mutual, which these men were. On this occasion some of the always-present moral problems were discussed. Dorian was so quiet that eventually some one called on him for an opinion.

"I don't think I can add anything to the discussion," replied Dorian. "Only this, however: One day in Sunday school Uncle Zed painted the terrors of sin to us boys in such colours that I shall never forget it. The result in my case is that I have a dreadful fear of moral wrong doing. I am literally scared, I—"

Dorian turned his eyes to the darkened doorway. Mr. Jack Lamont stood there with a cynical expression on his face. His hat was tilted back on his head, and a half-smoked cigarette sagged from his lips. The genial warmth of the room seemed chilled by the newcomer's presence.

"G'day, gentlemen," said Mr. Lamont. "Mr. Trent, here, is afraid, I understand."

The men arose. Outside the clouds were breaking. Dorian stepped forward, quite close to Jack Lamont.

"Yes, I am afraid," said Dorian, his face white with passion, "but not of what you think, not of what you would be afraid, you dirty, low, scoundrel!"

Lamont raised a riding whip he had in his hand, but the men interfered, and they all moved outside into the yard. Dorian, still tense with anger, permitted himself to be taken to the teams where they began hitching up. Dorian soon had himself under control, yet he was not satisfied with the matter ending thus. Quietly slipping back to where Mr. Lamont stood looking at the men preparing to drive on, he said, "I want a word with you."

The other tried to evade.

"Don't try to get away until I'm through with you. I want to tell you again what a contemptable cur you are. No one but a damned scoundrel would take advantage of a girl as you did, and then leave her to bear her shame alone."

"Do you mean Carlia—"

"Don't utter her name from your foul lips."

"For if you do, I might say, what have I got to do with that? You were her lover, were you not? you were out with her in the fields many times until midnight, you—"

The accusing mouth closed there, closed by the mighty impact of Dorian's fist. The blood spurted from a gashed lip, and Mr. Lamont tried to defend himself. Again Dorian's stinging blow fell upon the other's face. Lamont was lighter than Dorian, but he had some skill as a boxer which he tried to bring into service; but Dorian, mad in his desire to punish, with unskilled strength fought off all attacks. They grappled, struggled, and fell, to arise again and give blow for blow. It was all done so suddenly, and the fighting was so fierce, that Dorian's fellow travelers did not get to the scene before Jack Lamont lay prone on the ground from Dorian's finishing knockout blow.

"Damn him!" said Dorian, as he shook himself back into a somewhat normal condition and spat red on the ground. "He's got just a little of what's been coming to him for a long time. Let him alone. He's not seriously hurt. Let's go."

205

20.

ON A SATURDAY afternoon in early July Dorian and a neighbor were coming home from a week's absence up in the hills. They were on horseback, and therefore they cut across by way of the new road in course of construction between Greenstreet and the city.

The river was high. The new bridge was not yet open for traffic, but horses could safely cross. As the two riders passed to the Greenstreet side, they saw near the bridge down on the rocks by the rushing river, an automobile, overturned and pretty well demolished. Evidently, someone had been trying to reach the bridge, had missed the road, and had gone over the bank, which at this point was quite steep.

The two men stopped, dismounted, and surveyed the wreck. Someone was under the car, dead or alive, they could not tell. Dorian unslung his rope from his saddle, and took off his coat. "I'll go down and see," he said.

"Be careful," admonished the other, "if you slip into the river, you'll be swept away."

Dorian climbed down to where the broken machine lay. Pinned under it with his body half covered by the water was Mr. Jack Lamont. He was talking deliriously, calling in broken sentences for help. Dorian's hesitancy for an instant was only to determine what was the best thing to do.

"Hold on a bit longer, Mr. Lamont," said Dorian; but it was

doubtful whether the injured man understood. He glared at his rescuer with unseeing eyes. Part of the automobile was already being
moved by the force of the stream, and there was danger that the
whole car, together with the injured man, would be swept down the
stream. Dorian, while clinging to the slippery rocks, tried to pull the
man away, but he was so firmly pinned under the wreck that he
could not be moved. Dorian then shouted to his companion on the
bank to bring the rope and come to his assistance; but even while it
was being done, a great rush of water lifted the broken car out into
the stream. Lamont was released, but he was helpless to prevent the
current from sweeping him along.

Dorian reached for the man, but missed him and stepped into a
deep place. He went in to his arms, but he soon scrambled on to a
shallower point where he regained his balance. The unconscious Lamont was beginning to drift into the current and Dorian knew that
if he was to be saved he must be prevented from getting into the
grasp of the mid-stream. Dorian took desperate chances himself, but
his mind was clear and his nerves were steady as he waded out into
the water. His companion shouted a warning to him from the bank,
but he heeded it not. Lamont's body was moving more rapidly, so
Dorian plunged after it, and by so doing got beyond wading depths.
He did not mind that as he was a good swimmer, and apparently,
Mr. Lamont was too far gone to give any dangerous death grip. Dorian got a good hold of the man's long hair and with the free arm he
managed to direct them both to a stiller pool lower down where by
the aid of his companion, he pulled Lamont out of the water and laid
him on the bank. He appeared to be dead, but the two worked over
him for some time. No other help appeared, so once more they tried
all the means at their command to resuscitate the drowned.

"I think he's gone," said Dorian's companion.

"It seems so. He's received some internal injury. He was not
drowned."

"Who is he, I wonder."

"His name is Jack Lamont."

"Do you know him?"

"I know him. Yes; let's carry him up the bank. We'll have to notify somebody."

The man was dead when he was laid on the soft warm grass. Dorian covered the lifeless form with his own coat.

"I'll stay here," suggested Dorian's companion, "while you go and telephone the police station in the city. Then you go right on home and get into some dry clothes."

Dorian did as he was told. After reaching the nearest telephone, and delivering his message, he went on home and explained to his mother what had happened. Then he changed his clothes.

"What a terrible thing!" exclaimed his mother. "And you also might have been drowned."

"Oh, no; I was all right. I knew just what I could do. But the poor fellow. I—I wish I could have saved him. It might have been a double salvation for him."

The mother did not press him for further explanations, for she also had news to tell. As soon as Dorian came from his room in his dry clothes, she asked him if he had seen Brother Duke on the way.

"No, mother; why?"

"Well, he was here not long ago, asking for you. Carlia, it seems, has had a nervous breakdown, and the father thinks you can help."

"I'll go immediately."

"You'll have some supper first. It will take me only a moment to place it on the table."

"No, mother, thank you; after I come back; or perhaps I'll eat over there. Don't wait for me." He was out of the house, and nearly running along the road.

Dorian found Carlia's father and mother under great mental strain. "We're so glad you came," they said; "we're sure you can help her."

"What is the matter?"

"We hardly know. We don't understand. This afternoon—that

Mr. Jack Lamont—you remember him—he used to come here. Well, he hasn't been around for over a year, for which we were very thankful, until this afternoon when he came in his automobile. Carlia was in the garden, and she saw him drive up to the gate. When he alighted and came toward her, she seemed frightened out of her wits, for she ran terror stricken into the house. She went up to her bedroom and would not come down."

"He did not see her, then, to talk to her?"

"No; he waited a few moments only, then drove off again."

"Where is Carlia now?"

"Still up in her room."

"May I go up to her?"

"Yes; but won't you have her come down?"

"No, I'd rather go up there, if you don't mind."

"Not at all. Dorian, you seem the only help we have."

He went through the living room to the stairway. He noticed that the bare boards of the stairs had been covered with a carpet, which made his ascending steps quite noiseless. Everything was still in Carlia's room. The door was slightly ajar, so he softly pushed it open. Carlia was lying on her bed asleep.

211   Dorian tiptoed in and stood looking about. The once bare, ugly room had been transformed into quite a pretty chamber, with carpet and curtains and wall-paper and some pretty furniture. The father had at last done a sensible thing for his daughter.

Carlia slept on peacefully. She had not even washed away the tear-stains from her cheeks, and her nut-brown hair lay in confusion about her head. Poor, dear girl! If there ever was a suffering penitent, here was one.

In a few moments, the girl stirred, then sensing that someone was in the room, she awoke with a start, and sprang to her feet.

"It's only Dorian," said he.

"Oh!" she put her hand to her head, brushing back her hair.

"Dorian, is it you?"

"Sure, in real flesh and blood and rusty-red hair." He tried to force cheerfulness into his words.

"I'm so glad, so glad it's you."

"And I'm glad that you're glad to see me."

"Has he gone? I'm afraid of him."

"Afraid of whom, Carlia?"

"Don't you know? Of course you don't know. I—"

"Sit down here, Carlia." He brought a chair; but she took it nearer the open window, and he pushed up the blind that the cool air might the more freely enter. The sun was nearing the western hills, and the evening sounds from the yard came to them. He drew a chair close to hers, and sat down by her, looking silently into the troubled face.

"I'm a sight," she said, coming back to the common, everyday cares as she tried to get her hair into order.

"No, you're not. Never mind a few stray locks of hair. Never mind that tear-stained face. I have something to tell you."

"Yes?"

"You said you were afraid, afraid of Mr. Jack Lamont."

"Yes," she whispered.

"Well, you never need be afraid of him again."

"I—I don't understand."

"Jack Lamont is dead."

She gave a startled cry.

"Dorian—you—?"

"No; I have not killed him. He was and is in the hands of the Lord." Then he told her what had happened that afternoon.

Carlia listened with staring eyes and bated breath. And Dorian had actually risked his life in an attempt to save Jack Lamont! If Dorian only had known! But he would never know, never now. She had heard of the fight between Dorian and Lamont, as that had been common gossip for a time; but Carlia had no way of connecting that event with herself or her secret, as no one had heard what words passed between them that day, and Dorian had said nothing. And now he had tried to save the life of the man whom he had so thoroughly trounced. "What a puzzle he was! And yet what a kind, open face was his, as he sat there in the reddening evening light telling her in his simple way what he had done. What did he know, anyway? For it would be just like him to do good to those who would harm him; and had she not proved in her own case that he had been more patient and kind to her after her return than before. What did he know?

"Shall I close the window?" he asked. "Is there too much draught?"

"No; I must have air or I shall stifle. Dorian, tell me, what do you know about this Mr. Lamont?"

"Why, not much, Carlia; not much good, at any rate. You know I met him only a few times." He tried to answer her questions and at the same time give her as little information as possible.

"But Dorian, why did you fight with him?"

"He insulted me. I've explained that to you before."

"That's not all the reason. Jack Lamont could not insult you. I mean, you would pay no attention to him if only yourself were involved."

"Now, Carlia, don't you begin to philosophize on my reasons for giving Jack Lamont a licking. He's dead, and let's let him rest in as much peace as the Lord will allow."

"All right."

"Now, my dear, you feel able to go down and have some supper. Your father and mother should be told the news, and perhaps I can do that better than anybody else. I'll go with you, and, if your mother has something good for supper, I'll stay."

But the girl did not respond to his light speech. She sat very still by the window. For a long, long time—ages it seemed to her, she had suffered in silent agony for her sin, feeling as if she were being smothered by her guilty secret. She could not bring herself to tell it even to her mother. How could she tell it to anyone else, certainly not Dorian. And yet, as she sat there with him she felt as if she might confide in him. He would listen without anger or reproach. He would forgive. He—her heart soared, but her brain came back with a jolt to her daily thinking again. No, no, he must not know, he must never know; for if he knew, then all would surely be over between them, and then, she might as well die and be done with it!

"Come, Carlia."

She did not even hear him.

But Dorian must know, he must know the truth before he asked her again to marry him. But if he knew, he would never urge that again. That perhaps would be for the best, anyway. And yet she could not bear the thought of sending him away for good. If he deserted her, who else would she have? No; she must have him near her, at least. Clear thinking was not easy for her just then, but in time she managed to say:

"Dorian, sit down ... Do you remember that evening, not so long ago, when you let me 'browse', as you called it, among Uncle Zed's books and manuscripts?"

"Yes; you have done that a number of times."

"But there is one time which I shall remember. It was the time when I read what Uncle Zed had written about sin and death."

"O, I had not intended you to see that."

"But I did, and I read carefully every word of it. I understood most of it, too. 'The wages of sin is death' —That applies to me. I am a sinner. I shall die. I have already died, according to Uncle Zed."

"No, Carlia, you misapply that. We are all sinners, and we all die in proportion to our sinning. That's true enough; but there is also the blessed privilege of repentance to consider. Let me finish the quotation: 'The wages of sin is death; but the gift of God is eternal life through Jesus Christ our Lord'; also let me add what the Lord said about those who truly repent; 'Though your sins be as scarlet, they shall be white as snow; though they be red like crimson, they shall be as wool'. That is a great comfort to all of us, Carlia."

"Yes; thank you, Dorian ... but—but now I must tell you. The Lord may forgive me, but you cannot."

"Carlia, I have long since forgiven you."

"Oh, of my little foolish ways, of course; but, Dorian, you don't know—"

"But, Carlia, I do know. And I tell you that I have forgiven you."

"The terrible thing about me?"

"The unfortunate thing and the great sorrow which has come to you, and the suffering—yes, Carlia, I know."

"I can't understand your saying that."

"But I understand."

"Who told you?"

"Mrs. Whitman."

"Have you been there?"

"Yes."

"Dorian!" She stared past him through the open window into the western sky. The upper disk of the sun sank slowly behind the purple mountain. The flaming underlining of a cloud reflected on the open water of the marshland and faintly into the room and on to the pale face of the girl. Presently, she arose, swayed and held out her arms as if she was falling. Dorian caught her. Tears, long pent up, save in her own lonely hours, now broke as a torrent from her eyes, and her body shook in sobs. Gone was her reserve now, her holding him away, her power of resistance. She lay supinely in his arms, and he held her close. O, how good it was to cry thus! O, what a haven of rest! Would the tears and sobs never cease? ... The sun was down, the color faded from the sky, a big shadow enveloped the earth.

Then when she became quieter, she freed her arms, reached up and clasped her hands behind his neck, clinging to him as if she never wanted to leave him. Neither could speak. He stroked her hair, kissed her cheeks, her eyes, wiped away her tears, unaware of those which ran unhindered down his own face ...

"Carlia, my darling, Carlia," he breathed.

"Dorian, Oh, Dorian, *how—good—you—are!*"

21.

IT WAS A DAY in June—nearly a year from the time of the
"understanding"—a day made more beautiful because of its being in
the mountains and on a Sunday afternoon. Dorian and Carlia lived
in the midst of its rarity, seated as they were on the grassy hill-side
overlooking the dry-land farms near at hand and the valley below,
through which tumbled the brook. The wild odor of hill plants mingled with the pungent fragrance of choke-cherry blossoms. The air
was as clear as crystal. The mountains stood about them in silent,
solemn watchfulness, strong and sure as the ages. The red glowed in
Carlia's lips again, and the roses in her cheeks. The careworn look
was gone from her face. Peace had come into her heart, peace with
herself, with the man she loved, and with God.

Dorian pointed out to her where the wild strawberries grew down
in the valley, and where the best service berries could be found on the
hills. He told her how the singing creek had, when he was alone in
the hills, echoed all his varied moods.

Then they were silent for a time, letting the contentment of their
love suffice. For now all barriers between these two were down. There
was no thought they could not share, no joy neither trouble they could
not meet together. However, they were very careful of each other; their
present peace and content had not easily been reached. They had come
"up through great tribulation," even thus far in their young lives. The

period of their purification seemed now to be drawing to a close, and they were entering upon a season of rest for the soul.

"Blessed are the pure in heart, for they shall see God." This promise is surely not limited to that hoped-for future time when we shall have laid aside mortality, but the pure in heart see much of God here and now—see Him in the beauty of hill and dale, in cloud and blue sky, in placid pool and running water, in flowers and insect, and in the wonderful workings of the human heart! And so Dorian Trent and Carlia Duke, being of the pure in heart, saw much of God and His glory that afternoon.

Then they talked again of the home folks, of Mildred Brown, and of Uncle Zed; and at length came to their own immediate affairs.

That fall Dorian was to enter the University. The farm at Greenstreet would have to be let to others, but he thought he could manage the dry-farm, as most of the work came in vacation season. Mrs. Trent did not want to leave her home in the country; but she would likely become lonesome living all by herself; so there would always be a room for her with Dorian and Carlia in the little house they would rent near the school. Then, after the University, there would be some Eastern College for a period of years, and after that, other work. The task Dorian had set before him was a big one, but it was a very important one, and no one seemed to be doing it as yet. He might fail in accomplishing what he and Uncle Zed and perhaps the Lord had in mind regarding him, but he would do his very best, anyway.

"You'll not fail," the girl at his side assured him.

"I hope not. But I know some men who have gone in for all the learning they could obtain, and in the process of getting the learning, they have lost their faith. With me, the very object of getting knowledge is to strengthen my faith. What would it profit if one gains the whole world of learning and loses his soul in the process. Knowledge is power, both for good and for ill. I have been thinking lately of the nature of faith, the forerunner of knowledge. I can realize somewhat the meaning of the scripture which says that the worlds were framed and all things in them made by the power of faith. As Uncle Zed used to say—"

"You always put it that way. Don't you know anything of your own?"   221

"No; no one does. There is no such thing as knowledge of one's own making. Knowledge has always existed from the time when there has been a mind to conceive it. The sum of truth is eternal. We can only discover truth, or be told it by someone who has already found it. God has done that. He comprehends all truth, and therefore all power and all glory is found in Him. It is the most natural thing in the world, then, that we should seek the truth from the fountain head or source to us, and that is God."

Although it was after the usual time of the Sunday sermon, Dorian felt free to go on.

"'When the Son of Man cometh, shall He find faith on the earth?' I hope to help a little to make the answer, Yes. I know of nothing which the world needs more than faith. Not many are specializing in that field. Edison is bringing forth some of the wonders of electricity; Burbank is doing marvelous things in the plant world; we have warriors and statesmen and philosophers and philanthropists and great financiers a-plenty; we have scientists too, and some of them are helping. Have you ever heard of Sir Oliver Lodge and Lord Kelvin?"

No; she never had.

"Well" —and Dorian laughed softly to himself at the apparent egotism of the proposition— "I must be greater than either of them.   222 I must know all they know, and more; and that is possible, for I have the 'Key of Knowledge' which even the most learned scholar cannot get without obedience to the laws and ordinances of the gospel."

Carlia silently worshiped.

"Now," he continued in a somewhat lighter vein, "do you realize what you are doing when you say you will be my wife and put up with all the eccentricities of such a man as I am planning to be? Are you willing to be a poor man's wife, for I cannot get money and this knowledge I am after at the same time? Are you willing to go without the latest in dresses and shoes and hats—if necessary?"

"Haven't I heard you say that the larger part of love is in giving and not in getting?" replied she.

"Yes, I believe that's true."

"Well, then, that's my answer. Don't deny me the joy I can get by the little I can give."

The sun was nearing the western mountains, the sharpest peaks were already throwing shadows across the valley.

"Come," said Dorian. "We had better go down. Mother has come out of the cabin, and I think she is looking for us. Supper must be ready."

223   He took Carlia's hand and helped her up. Then they ran like care-free children down the gentler slopes.

"Wait a minute," cried Carlia, "I'm out of breath. I—I want to ask you another question."

"Ask a hundred."

"Well, in the midst of all this studying, kind of in between the great, serious subjects, we'll find time, will we not, to read 'David Copperfield'—together?"

He looked into her laughing eyes, and then kissed her.

"Why, yes, of course," he said.

Then they went on again, hand in hand, down into the valley of sunshine and shadow.

THE END.

CHRISTIAN NEPHI ANDERSON was born in Norway on January 22, 1865. His family emigrated to Utah to join other members of the Church of Jesus Christ of Latter-day Saints in 1871. As an adult, Anderson worked as an educator, author, and genealogist; he served two missions to Europe where he worked in publishing in addition to other missionary tasks. His first wife, Asenath, died in 1904. He married his second, Maud, in 1908. He died on January 6, 1923.

NOTES ON THE TEXT

ERIC W JEPSON

Some notes were written by or with Tyler Gardner or Blair Hodges, and include some additional information, suggestions, direction, and phrasing from Scott Hales, Rachel Gillie, Larry W. Draper, and Kjerste Christensen.

I

DORIAN TRENT

Arguments over whether or not Anderson's upright hero was intended as an antithesis to the decadent protagonist of Oscar Wilde's (1854 – 1900) *The Picture of Dorian Gray* (1891) remain unproven, though they are not unreasonable: it appears true that Wilde was the first to use the word Dorian as a name. Whether Dorian's last name carries significance is equally uncertain, but a potential irony does exist when comparing Dorian's life plans to the Council of Trent, which condemned Protestant heresies while simultaneously being one of Catholicism's great reform councils. At times, in the original manuscript, Anderson wrote Donald rather than Dorian.

Wilde had visited Utah in April 1882 as part of an American tour. Utah audiences were excited by his arrival—the front row of his lecture audience consisted of young men—but his lecture did not go over well. Wilde was similarly disenchanted with Utah and his visit with President John Taylor (1808 – 1887), and said as much in interviews in other cities. In a letter to Mrs. Bernard Beere, written a week later from Kansas City, Wilde wrote more kindly: "I have lectured to the Mormons ... The President, a nice old man, sat with five wives in the stage box. I visited him in the afternoon and saw a charming daughter of his" (this transcription taken from Wilde's letters as collected and edited by Merlin Holland and Rupert Hart-Davis).

OLD NIG
"Old Nig" seems to have been a common name of the era for animals such as mules and dogs. From the 1892 book *Where is my dog?: or, Is man alone immortal?* by Charles Josiah Adams (1850 – 1924) we learn of "a horse, whose color and woolly hair procured for him the name, which fitted him, Nig, which in the lapse of years grew Old Nig." In general, the color and texture of the animal's coat appears to have been an important precedent for the name. The titular character of Anderson's *John St. John* (1917) also has a horse named Nig.

GREENSTREET
Greenstreet is a fictional town, presumably in Utah. Described as a community of several family farms on the outskirts of a larger town, Greenstreet seems to match the description of just about every farming community in early twentieth-century Utah. Although the book refrains from naming geographical features that correlate to a specific place, Anderson spent much of his life in and around Ogden, Utah, 15 miles up the Weber River from which is a town called Mountain Green in Morgan County. Mountain Green may have something to do with Anderson's Greenstreet as it appears to fit the novel's geography (a river runs between Greenstreet and the unnamed larger town). Yet, if we consider the name "Greenstreet," there is also a town in Sanpete County, Utah, called Fountain Green, which—with a total area of 1.4 square miles—is the size of a single street.

DICKENS'S *DAVID COPPERFIELD, TALE OF TWO CITIES, DOMBEY AND SON*
David Copperfield by Charles Dickens (1812 – 1870) was first published in serial form from 1849 – 1850. *Dombey and Son* was first published in serial form from 1846 – 1848 and *Tale of Two Cities* was first published in 1859. As wildly popular as most of Dickens's novels were, many, including Leo Tolstoy

(1828 – 1910), consider *David Copperfield* Dickens's masterpiece—and it is that novel that receives the most attention throughout *Dorian*.

THACKERAY'S *VANITY FAIR*

After Charles Dickens, William Makepeace Thackeray (1811 – 1863) was considered the nineteenth century's most popular English novelist. Unlike Dickens, Thackeray was known for his satire. His most famous work, *Vanity Fair*—a name he retrieved from a chapter title in John Bunyan's *Pilgrim's Promise*—was a satire in which Thackeray took every opportunity to critique Britain's nineteenth-century culture and persona. The story follows two women with opposing temperaments (one culturally acceptable and one unacceptable) as they navigate through Victorian society from school life to adulthood. In contrast to the social-problem novels of Dickens, *Vanity Fair* focuses on the personal shortcomings of his characters and suggests inherent weaknesses in the human condition (Monsarrat, Ann. *An Uneasy Victorian: Thackeray the Man, 1811 – 1863*. New York: Dodd, Mead & Company, 172).

MRS. HUMPHREY WARD

Mrs. Humphrey Ward (1851 – 1920) was the married and professional name of Mary Augusta Ward (née Arnold). She was born in Australia, the niece of Matthew Arnold and a noted anti-suffragette. Her most popular novel was *Robert Elsmere* which Oscar Wilde described as "simply Arnold's *Literature and Dogma* with the literature left out." The novel's eponymous hero is an Anglican clergyman who begins to doubt his faith after encountering the German rationalists, but instead of wallowing in despair, takes on "constructive liberalism" and serves the poor. The novel's enormous success is generally attributed to its concern "with the fairly common Victorian crisis of faith occasioned by the failing belief in the historical veracity of the Bible" and how that lent itself to frequent and vigorous public debate (Freed, Mark M. "The Moral Irrelevance of Dogma: Mary Ward and Critical Theology in England." *Women's Theology in Nineteenth-century Britain: Transfiguring the Faith of Their Fathers*. Ed. Julie Melnyk. New York: Garland, 133 – 146).

MARGARET DELAND

Of the list of authors whose books mesmerize Dorian in the bookstore, Margaret Deland (1857 – 1945) is the only author still alive when *Dorian* was published, although Mrs. Humphrey Ward died only one year before. Anderson's

American, though "non-Mormon" (for lack of a better term), contemporary, Deland also wrote novels, short stories, and poetry. Along with some of the other writers on Dorian's list, Deland's work was known to deal with religious ideas and sentiment. Her first novel, *John Ward, Preacher* (1888), inspired a significant amount of controversy as it centered around the strained relationship of a Calvinist preacher and his Episcopalian wife, exposing the genuine familial conflicts that occur over divergent religious beliefs (Reep, Diana. *Margaret Deland*. Boston: Twayne, 1985).

ROBINSON CRUSOE, A BIG BOOK WITH FINE PICTURES
Written by Daniel Defoe (1660 – 1731), *Robinson Crusoe* was first published in 1719 with both fine pictures and a fine title: *The Life and Strange Surprizing Adventures of Robinson Crusoe, of York, Mariner: Who lived Eight and Twenty Years, all alone in an un-inhabited Island on the Coast of America, near the Mouth of the Great River of Oroonoque; Having been cast on Shore by Shipwreck, wherein all the Men perished but himself. With An Account how he was at last as strangely deliver'd by Pyrates.*

PRESCOTT'S *CONQUEST OF PERU*
William Heckling Prescott (1796 – 1859) was the most prominent American historian of the nineteenth century, and his work *The History of the Conquest of Peru,* published in 1847, was his most famous. The two volumes to which Dorian here refers are the first two volumes of that history. Upon their original publication, the volumes sold for a dollar each.

STOGY
According to the Oxford English Dictionary, before "stogy" referred to a roughly made cigar, it was, as we see here, a common epithet used to describe a heavy and rough pair of boots or shoes.

PIZARRO, THE BAD, BOLD SPANIARD
Francisco Pizarro (d. 1541) was the protagonist of Prescott's *Conquest of Peru.*

BEN HUR
The 1880 novel by Lew Wallace (1827 – 1905) was the bestselling American novel until Margaret Mitchell's *Gone with the Wind* (1936). In an era when many considered novels sinful, *Ben Hur*'s tale of a Jew who becomes Christian was required reading in many American primary schools.

HEADGATE
The gate that controls water flowing into an irrigation ditch. The term dates to at least 1832.

I CAN BACK YOU OUT.
A curious and apparently extremely localized expression. Carlia is indirectly daring the boys; in essence, she is suggesting that she is proposing a task so treacherous that even if they were to accept her dare, they would later back out. This transitive use of *back out* is unusual and, in this particular sense of being connected to a dare, may have only been used in the particular time and place documented in *Dorian*.

CARLIA
As Dorian will note later, the name Carlia is an unusual one. Carlia is a rare feminine for Carl from the German name meaning "free man." It's also, likely irrelevantly, one of the genus names for skinks. Carlia's last name, Duke, is perhaps most striking given its apparent loftiness in comparison to Mildred's last name, Brown. Prepublication, Anderson had written Carlia's last name as Davis.

II

AN ARTIST'S CONCEPTION OF *LORNA DOONE*
Lorna Doone is the eponymous heroine of the novel by R.D. Blackmore (1825 – 1900). Laced with Blackmore's love for and attention to the English woods and countryside, *Lorna Doone: A Romance of Exmoor* revolves around a young woman raised among outlaws who eventually discovers royal origins. First published in 1869, *Lorna Doone* has never been out of print and several of the various editions have included detailed and elaborate illustrations (Madison,

R.D. "Introduction." *Lorna Doone: A Romance of Exmoor*. New York: Penguin Books, 2005). According to one biography on Blackmore, the "Yale College Class of 1906 voted *Lorna Doone* their favourite novel, it having received nine more votes than its closest rival, *Vanity Fair*" (Dunn, W.H. *R.D. Blackmore: The Author of Lorna Doone*. London: Robert Hale, 1956, 142).

LUCERNE
Here, another name for alfalfa.

SALERATUS
Sodium bicarbonate. High alkaline levels can result in a chalky soil that results in fine dust and brackish water, both of which can be irritating and even dangerous.

MILDRED
The name Mildred was popular around the time Mildred Brown would have been born, peaking as the United States's sixth most popular girl name, according to the Social Security Administration, in 1912, 1913, and 1915 to 1920. The popularity of the name at the time and its ubiquity for decades previous makes any particular allusion difficult to determine. The archetypal Mildred remains Saint Mildthryth (694 – 716). As an abbess, Mildthyth was well educated and, although she lived before enforced celibacy for nuns, it seems she never married. The journalist and civil-rights activist Mildred Brown was still a child at the time of *Dorian*'s publication.

BULWARK
A rampart or defensive wall.

MUCH FEAR AND SOME INVISIBLE TREMBLING
A common scriptural combination found throughout the standard works of the Church of Jesus Christ of Latter-day Saints. For an idea of just how common, here are a few examples: "Fear came upon me, and trembling, which made all my bones to shake" (Job 4:14); "And I was with you in weakness, and in fear, and in much trembling" (1 Corinthians 2:3); "And it came to pass that when my father beheld the things which were written upon the ball, he did fear and tremble exceedingly" (1 Nephi 16:27); "Wherefore, fear and tremble, O ye people, for what I the Lord have decreed in them shall be fulfilled" (Doctrine and Covenants 1:7).

III

THE KILLDEER'S SHRILL CRY

A type of plover, a shorebird, with a range all over the Americas, from Canada to Peru. In the September 1895 edition of Smithsonian-affiliated periodical *The Nidologist* is written, "The Killdeer Plover or 'Killdee,' as it is commonly called, that word expressing fairly well the bird's plaintive cry … " The article goes on to express the birder's frustration with the killdeer's ability to hide its nest and eggs—and itself—from the eager seeker. Nidology, being the study of birds' nests and similar forms of study, consisted largely of specimen collection.

I GOT THROUGH SHOCKING THE WHEAT …

Shocking wheat consists of tying the wheat into bundles called shocks for easier removal later for threshing or sale.

SALERATUS SWAMP

This same unusual phrase appears in a January 12, 1851, entry of the *Journal of the Iron County [Utah] Mission* kept by John D. Lee.

SUCH AS MILTON AND SHAKESPEARE

Perhaps a reference to the 1888 talk by Orson F. Whitney (1855 – 1931) entitled "Home Literature" widely credited with galvanizing Mormon literary artists including Anderson. The relevant passage:

> We will yet have Miltons and Shakespeares of our own. God's ammunition is not exhausted. His brightest spirits are held in reserve for the latter times. In God's name and by his help we will build up a literature whose top shall touch heaven, though its foundations may now be low in earth. Let the smile of derision wreathe the face of scorn; let the frown of hatred darken the brow of bigotry. Small things are the seeds of great things, and, like the acorn that brings forth the oak, or the snowflake that forms the avalanche, God's kingdom will grow, and on wings of light and power soar to the summit of its destiny.

IV

THE FINEST GIRL HE HAD EVER SEEN WAS CHUMMING WITH HIM
Here, *chumming* means socializing.

MAKES QUITE A CHUM OF HER
Chum is a more familiar synonym of *friend*, more akin to *pal*.

ZEDEKIAH MANNING
Uncle Zed's most obvious namesake is the king of Judah, most noted in Mormon circles for not only ignoring Jeremiah while ruling at the time of Jerusalem's destruction, but also for allegedly siring a son named Mulek who was to found a people coexistent with the Nephites (see Mosiah 25). Although tempting to extrapolate the connection into a purposeful allusion, Anderson's intent is unclear. Other, even less tempting references could be a high priest of Solomon's Temple, a pair of false prophets, and the thirteenth-century scholar Zedekiah ben Abraham Anaw. The family name Manning is derived from an old Norse word meaning "a valiant man."

AUTUMN TINTED IVY EMBOWERED HIS FRONT DOOR …
The word "embowered," meaning to create a shelter, especially of ornamental plants, was falling out of usage at the time of *Dorian* and would continue to do so until about 2000. Since then it has been experiencing a slight renaissance.

THAT TIME OF YOUTH WHEN THEY ALSO WERE "TRAILING CLOUDS OF GLORY" FROM THEIR HEAVENLY HOME
A reference to William Wordsworth's "Ode. Intimations of Immortality":

> Our birth is but a sleep and a forgetting:
> The Soul that rises with us, our life's Star,
>   Hath had elsewhere its setting,
>   And cometh from afar:
>   Not in entire forgetfulness,
>   And not in utter nakedness,
> But trailing clouds of glory do we come
>   From God, who is our home:
> Heaven lies about us in our infancy!

The poem's suggestion of a premortal existence has long made it popular with Mormon audiences. In fact, since its first quotation in General Conference (Clifford E. Young, 1947), it has only gained in popularity with the majority of Conference references coming in the last few decades, primarily in talks by popular apostles: Ezra Taft Benson, Gordon B. Hinckley, Jeffrey R. Holland, Neal A. Maxwell, Thomas S. Monson, and Dieter F. Uchtdorf.

MILLENNIAL STAR

Beginning in England from 1840, *Millennial Star* (usually and hereinafter referred to as *Millennial Star*) was published until 1970, making it the longest-running publication of The Church of Jesus Christ of Latter-day Saints. During a mission to Great Britain from 1904 – 1906, Anderson served as an assistant editor on the *Millennial Star* to Heber J. Grant (1856 – 1945), then a member of the Quorum of the Twelve Apostles.

JOURNAL OF DISCOURSES

Twenty-six volumes of sermons from early LDS leaders. The most represented speaker is Brigham Young (1801 – 1877) with 390. Highly prized for generations, the *Journal of Discourses* (hereinafter referred to as JD) enjoyed a quasi-scriptural status for many years. How many of the volumes (each composed of one year's collection of the twice-monthly periodical) Uncle Zed owned is unclear. The early volumes were published in large runs, but the final volumes at only a tenth the number. A full description of the publication history can be found in the third volume of Peter Crawley's *A Descriptive Bibliography of the Mormon Church*.

DOCTRINE AND COVENANTS

According to the current LDS edition's introduction, "The Doctrine and Covenants is a collection of divine revelations and inspired declarations given for the establishment and regulation of the kingdom of God on the earth in the last days. Although most of the sections are directed to members of The Church of Jesus Christ of Latter-day Saints, the messages, warnings, and exhortations are for the benefit of all mankind and contain an invitation to all people everywhere to hear the voice of the Lord Jesus Christ, speaking to them for their temporal well-being and their everlasting salvation." Along with the Bible, the Book of Mormon, and the Pearl of Great Price, the Doctrine and Covenants (hereinafter referred to as D&C) is one of the four standard works, or books of canonized scripture recognized by the Church. The 1921 edition of the D&C removed the "Lectures on Faith" as, according to the introduction, they "were never presented to nor accepted by the Church as being otherwise than theological lectures or lessons." The "Lectures"—written by founding Church President Joseph Smith (1805 – 1844) and his then-First Counselor Sidney Rigdon (1793 – 1876)—had been part of the D&C since its first publication in 1835. It is almost certain that any discussion of the scripture in *Dorian* assumes a version including the "Lectures" as *Dorian* was published only about one year after the release of the new edition.

Some parts of the Lectures in Faith were prominently promoted by a small branch of the Church that ended in the excommunication of its leadership just as *Dorian* was coming into print. The apostle visiting this branch during this time and observing their apostasy was James E. Talmage (1862 – 1933), who was simultaneously serving on the committee which made the final recommendation to remove the "Lectures." (See "Sacrificing the Lectures on Faith" by James P. Harris in the August 2013 issue of *Sunstone*.)

THE REVELATION ON THE ETERNITY
OF THE MARRIAGE COVENANT
Likely a reference to D&C 132. Consider verse 15:

> Therefore, if a man marry him a wife in the world, and he marry her not by me nor by my word, and he covenant with her so long as he is in the world and she with him, their covenant and marriage are not of force when they are dead, and when they are out of the world; therefore, they are not bound by any law when they are out of the world.

ORSON PRATT
Orson Pratt (1811 – 1881) was a significant though sometimes controversial philosopher and theologian in the early days of the LDS Church. He was the last surviving member of the original Quorum of the Twelve Apostles.

PARLEY PRATT
Parley P. Pratt (1807 – 1857) was a popular autobiographer, theologian, preacher, and hymnist among early Mormons. The younger brother of Orson Pratt (whom he introduced to the faith), Parley is often credited with writing the first work of Mormon fiction, a closet drama entitled *A Dialogue between Joe Smith and the Devil* (1844).

SPENCER'S LETTERS

Orson Spencer (1802 – 1855) was frequently cited as an example of a well-educated person aligning himself with the Mormon faith. His letters, including one to a former colleague, the Baptist pastor William Crowell, explaining his conversion, were published and often used as a missionary tool. The volume was one of the most ubiquitous among Mormons at the time.

A SECOND EDITION OF THE DOCTRINE AND COVENANTS, PRINTED BY JOHN TAYLOR IN NAUVOO IN 1844

This edition, published the year of Joseph Smith's death, added eight new sections (103, 105, 112, 119, 124, 127, 128, and 135 by the current system). John Taylor (1808 – 1887) was present at Joseph Smith's assassination and would later replace him as the Church's third president.

THE CONTRIBUTOR

Published from 1879 to 1896, this periodical was aimed at the youth of the Church.

ERA

The *Improvement Era* (1897 – 1970) began as a replacement to *The Contributor* but would serve a variety of functions and organizations within the Church over its run.

DRUMMOND'S NATURAL LAW IN THE SPIRITUAL WORLD

Henry Drummond (1851 – 1897) was a Scottish missionary and university lecturer who proposed a "God of the gaps," in which knowledge unexplained by science can be laid with God. Not everyone shared Uncle Zed's favorable opinion of Drummond; biblical scholar William Kelly (1821 – 1906) found Drummond's popular work to have

> ...unworthy and dangerously corrupting peculiarities, which have made it so palatable, at a moment when men crave the exciting food which it supplies, conceiving that they stand well abreast of the science of the age.
> Mr. D. is a Christian. But his enthusiasm evidently goes in the direction of natural science; and so blinding is its influence that he seems completely under the spell of the fashionable evolutionist reveries of the day.

SOME OF THE SIMPLE HEART MELODIES

For examples of what sort of music was intended by this phrase, consider this passage from *History of American Literature* (1919) by Leonidas Warren Payne (1873 – 1945):

> Pennsylvania may also lay claim to Stephen C. Foster (1826 – 1864), since he was born in Pittsburgh, though he lived most of his life in Cincinnati and is frequently thought of as a Middle Westerner. Foster had a fine sense for simple heart melodies, and several of his songs have become fixed in the American popular ear more securely than any other native song except perhaps "Home, Sweet Home." The best known of his songs are "Old Black Joe," "My Old Kentucky Home," and "Old Folks at Home" (138).

V

OF ALL THE MARVELS OF GOD'S WORKMANSHIP ...

As collected in the posthumous 1873 collection *Notes of Thought: Charles Buxton* (1823 – 1871), an English philanthropist and politician. It is number 113 of 684.

LADY OF THE LAKE

Likely she means the 1810 narrative poem by Sir Walter Scott (1771 – 1832), which sets the Arthurian legend in Scotland.

WARD

A term used by Latter-day Saints to describe a congregation, defined by shared geography. At the time of the novel, the number of people attending a ward could vary greatly, as could the number of wards in a community. Greenstreet seems to have had a single ward and the bulk of the community appears to have been Latter-day Saints.

HITCH YOUR WAGON TO A STAR.

From Ralph Waldo Emerson's essay "American Civilization" first published in *The Atlantic* in April 1862, in which he argued largely that civilization depends on morality and for emancipation of the slaves. The paragraph the phrase comes from:

Now that is the wisdom of a man, in every instance of his labor, to hitch his wagon to a star, and see his chore done by the gods themselves. That is the way we are strong, by borrowing the might of the elements. The forces of steam, gravity, galvanism, light, magnets, wind, fire, serve us day by day, and cost us nothing.

VI

SHE WAS THINNER AND PALER THAN EVER ...

Although Mildred's disease is never identified, it bears many of the markers of consumption, tuberculosis—the poet's disease—the traditional killer in Western literature of those too alive to live. As Clark Lawlor observes in his 2007 study *Consumption and Literature: The Making of the Romantic Disease*, even after germ theory overtook medical understanding of medicine, the romantic tradition of consumption affected even scientific explanations of the disease; some even claimed that tuberculosis must in some way lead the brain to a greater capacity for art or love.

VII

THE FIRST SEGO BLOSSOMS

The sego lily (*Calochortus nuttallii*) was selected as the state flower of Utah in 1911 because it is native to the state, produces lovely blossoms, and was an important food source for early settlers.

DRY-FARMING HAD TAKEN THE ATTENTION

Farming without ready water, such as from irrigation.

HOWELL'S [sic] EASY-GOING NOVELS

In addition to writing novels, William Dean Howells (1837 – 1920) was an important editor and critic at *The Atlantic* and *Harper's*. He was a leading proponent of the realist novel over the sentimental novel. In his book *Criticism and*

Fiction (1892), Howells makes an argument striking in its contrast with Mildred's views on art:

> I am in hopes that the communistic era in taste … is approaching, and … will occur within the lives of men now overawed by the foolish old superstition that literature and art are anything but the expression of life … The time is coming, I hope, when each new author, each new artist, will be considered, not in his proportion to any other author or artist, but in his relation to the human nature, known to us all, which it is his privilege, his high duty, to interpret … but hitherto the mass of common men have been afraid to apply their own simplicity, naturalness, and honesty to the appreciation of the beautiful. They have always cast about for the instruction of some one [*sic*] who professed to know better, and who browbeat wholesome common-sense into the self-distrust that ends in sophistication … They have been taught to compare what they see and what they read, not with the things that they have observed and known, but with the things that some other artist or writer has done. Especially if they have themselves the artistic impulse in any direction they are taught to form themselves, not upon life, but upon the masters who became masters only by forming themselves upon life. The seeds of death are planted in them, and they can produce only the still-born, the academic. They are not told to take their work into the public square and see if it seems true to the chance passer, but to test it by the work of the very men who refused and decried any other test of their own work. The young writer who attempts to report the phrase and carriage of everyday life, who tries to tell just how he has heard men talk and seen them look, is made to feel guilty of something low and unworthy by people who would like to have him show how Shakespeare's men talked and looked … he is instructed … to take the life-likeness out of them, and put the book-likeness into them … I hope the time is coming when not only the artist, but the common, average man, who always "has the standard of the arts in his power," will have also the courage to apply it, and will reject the ideal … wherever he finds it, in science, in literature, in art … (8 – 12)

DARWIN
Charles Darwin (1809 – 1882), author of *On the Origin of Species* (1859).

HUXLEY
Thomas Henry Huxley (1825 – 1895), the English biologist known as "Darwin's Bulldog," coined the word agnosticism. Biographies of Huxley and Darwin, both written by Thomas Henry Huxley's son Leonard Huxley (1860 – 1933), had been recently published at the time of *Dorian*'s release. Leonard Huxley's children include evolutionary biologist Julian Huxley (1887 – 1975),

Nobel-prize-winning biophysicist Andrew Huxley (1917 – 2012), and novelist and essayist Aldous Huxley (1894 – 1963).

INGERSOL

A reference to Robert Ingersoll (1833 – 1899) —note the spelling— "The Great Agnostic." His father was John Ingersoll, the Congregationalist minister and abolitionist whose radical views negatively affected Robert's growing-up years. Ingersoll was a friend of Walt Whitman, who considered him to "embod[y] the individuality I preach." In 1890, Canadian preacher A.B. Simpson (1843 – 1919) published a short volume, *Wholly Sanctified*, about becoming such. Of his experience with Ingersoll, he wrote:

> The writer was once tempted to read Robert Ingersol's [*sic*] lectures with a view of answering them, but after reading a single page he felt so deluged with the shower of brimstone that poured from every page upon his whole being that he dared not go farther, and felt that he could only warn his people from any contact with such things, and tell them that "evil communications corrupt good manners," and that God's ground was to abstain from the very appearance of evil and have no fellowship with the unfruitful works of darkness, not even so far as to hear them. He was once called upon by a young convert, a very earnest Christian woman, who had gone one Sabbath night, under strong pressure, to hear this daring blasphemer. Her face was fairly shining with the light of the pit, and she had called to tell her pastor that she was fascinated and knew not what was the matter, but that she had been so captivated by his brilliant blasphemy that she seemed to have lost her power of resisting. Therefore the very first thing in order to the sanctification of the mind is to separate it from all evil by absolutely ignoring evil and refusing any contact with it.

Clearly Dorian, though unconvinced by Ingersoll, takes a more liberal view.

Anderson had written about Ingersoll previously in his article "Wisdom of God—Agency of Man" published in *The Contributor*, August 1890:

> Ingersoll, in a late issue of the Chicago *Herald*, is reported to have made the following utterance: "I believe the only reason or excuse for our existence is that the result shall be happiness. If the result of life is not happiness, then back of life is a fiend and not a being that is God."
>
> Compare that with the following from the Book of Mormon (II. Nephi 2:25): "Men are that they might have joy." Here then we have a doctrine teaching that the real purpose of human life is happiness; a doctrine that unhesitatingly pronounces true that which the unbeliever can alone look

towards in hope, as the only object of his existence.

The skeptic hints that there is a "something" back of this life. It is true. That "something" is a wise Creator, a kind Father who knows what is best for the good of his creations …

By suffering, our natures are perfected. The overcoming of obstacles, the surmounting of trials, adds a new strength to our weakness. Progression is the removing of difficulties in the way of our growth …

To say, then, that God cannot be a being of infinite power and mercy because He allows His children to pass through affliction is to reason as a child, having none of the wisdom of a man.

Even Ingersoll, if he is reported rightly, has admitted the possibility of the above conclusions, as notice in the following, taken from the same article as the preious [sic] quotation:

> "It may be possible that a God of infinite love and compassion will so reward those who suffer through suffering itself—that all that happens will be consistent with wisdom and compassion."

The world is in a conflict of theories. The mightiest among the creeds and beliefs are testing their skill in the arena of discussion. The Latter day [sic] Saint can be an interested spectator. High above the din of battle, he can sit judging the merits of each. With the Spirit of God for his guide, with the Gospel of Christ as his assurance, he can say to each and all … Come, enjoy a "Religion that will satisfy the intellect with its truths; touch the heart with its love; sway the will with its persuasiveness; gratify the taste with its beauties; and fill the imaginations with its sublimities."

The final quotation was likely taken by Anderson from a letter published February 1, 1890, in the *Deseret Weekly*, written by one J.H. Ward of "Europe" in a letter dated January 6, 1890. Ward had in 1884 published a combative volume entitled *Absurdities of Infidelity, and the Harmony of the Gospel, with Science and History*, which contains the same sentence.

The lead story in the issue of *the Improvement Era* in which appeared Anderson's 1898 essay "A Plea for Fiction" (included in this volume) was a paragraph-by-paragraph rebuttal of Ingersoll's "Best Argument Ever Advanced Against Christianity" by assistant Church historian (and later apostle) Charles W. Penrose (1832 – 1925).

TOM PAYNE

Presumably Thomas Paine (1737 – 1809), the American revolutionary best remembered today for his influential 1776 pamphlets *Common Sense* and *The*

American Crisis, together generally considered to have essentially affected the American mindset for independence. Likely what Dorian is including in his list is *The Age of Reason; Being an Investigation of True and Fabulous Theology* (published in three parts: 1794, 1795, 1807). From the introductory chapter:

> Soon after I had published the pamphlet COMMON SENSE, in America, I saw the exceeding probability that a revolution in the system of government would be followed by a revolution in the system of religion. The adulterous connection of church and state, wherever it had taken place, whether Jewish, Christian, or Turkish, had so effectually prohibited, by pains and penalties, every discussion upon established creeds, and upon first principles of religion, that until the system of government should be changed, those subjects could not be brought fairly and openly before the world; but that whenever this should be done, a revolution in the system of religion would follow. Human inventions and priest-craft would be detected; and man would return to the pure, unmixed, and unadulterated belief of one God, and no more.

He then goes on to criticize the Bible using only its own words, thus revealing "the three frauds, *mystery*, *miracle*, and *prophecy*."

IN HIS BOOK HE AIMS TO PROVE THAT THE SPIRITUAL WORLD ...
From Drummond:

> ... we do not demand of Nature directly to prove Religion. That was never its function. Its function is to interpret ... The position we have been led to take up is not that the Spiritual Laws are analogous to the Natural Laws, but that *they are the same Laws*. It is not a question of analogy but of *Identity*. The Natural Laws are not the shadows or images of the Spiritual in the same sense as autumn is emblematical of Decay, or the falling leaf of Death. The Natural Laws, as the Law of Continuity might well warn us, do not stop with the visible and then give place to a new set of Laws bearing a strong similitude to them. The Laws of the invisible are the same Laws, projections of the natural not supernatural. Analogous Phenomena are not the fruit of parallel Laws, but of the same Laws—Laws which at one end, as it were, may be dealing with Matter, at the other end with Spirit ...
>
> Let us now look for a moment at the present state of the question. Can it be said that the Laws of the Spiritual World are in any sense considered even to have analogies with the Natural World? Here and there certainly one finds an attempt, and a successful attempt, to exhibit on a rational basis one or two of the great Moral Principles of the Spiritual World. But the Physical World has not been appealed to. Its magnificent system of Laws remains outside, and its contribution meanwhile is either silently

ignored or purposely set aside. The Physical, it is said, is too remote from the Spiritual. The Moral World may afford a basis for religious truth, but even this is often the baldest concession; while the appeal to the Physical universe is everywhere dismissed as, on the face of it, irrelevant and unfruitful. From the scientific side, again, nothing has been done to court a closer fellowship. Science has taken theology at its own estimate. It is a thing apart. The Spiritual World is not only a different world, but a different kind of world, a world arranged on a totally different principle, under a different governmental scheme.

The Reign of Law has gradually crept into every department of Nature, transforming knowledge everywhere into Science. The process goes on, and Nature slowly appears to us as one great unity, until the borders of the Spiritual World are reached. There the Law of Continuity ceases, and the harmony breaks down. And men who have learned their elementary lessons truly from the alphabet of the lower Laws, going on to seek a higher knowledge, are suddenly confronted with the Great Exception ...

In the recent literature of this whole region there nowhere seems any advance upon the position of "Nature and the Supernatural." All are agreed in speaking of Nature *and* the Supernatural. Nature *in* the Supernatural, so far as Laws are concerned, is still an unknown truth.

THE WESLEYAN METHODIST CHURCH

Likely Uncle Zed was affiliated with the Wesleyan Methodist Connection, which split from the Methodist Episcopal Church in 1842 at a conference in Utica, New York. The faith was one of several to come out of the holiness movement, placing a large emphasis on the claim of John Wesley (1703 – 1791) that it is possible for Christians, through grace, to live without sin.

FOR INSTANCE, POPE SAYS:

This couplet is from *An Essay on Man* (1734) by Alexander Pope (1688 – 1744), who did not admit his authorship until the following year. The selection may seem an odd choice for Uncle Zed, as Pope was complaining about overreliance on reason while Uncle Zed says intellect and reason must also be satisfied. It is from the ninth section of the second chapter of the first epistle, which chapter is introduced thus:

Of Man in the abstract. I. That we can judge only with regard to our own system, being ignorant of the relations of systems and things. II. That Man is not to be deemed imperfect, but a being suited to his place and rank in the creation, agreeable to the general order of things, and conformable to ends and relations to him unknown. III. That it is partly upon his ignorance of future events, and partly upon the hope of a future state, that all his happiness in the present depends. IV. The pride of aiming at more knowledge, and pretending to more perfection, the cause of Man's error and misery. The impiety of putting himself in the place of God, and judging of the fitness or unfitness, perfection or imperfection, justice or injustice, of his dispensations. V. The absurdity of conceiting himself the final cause of creation, or expecting that perfection in the moral world which is not in the natural. VI. The unreasonableness of his complaints against Providence, while, on the one hand, he demands the perfections of the angels, and, on the other, the bodily qualifications of the brutes; though to possess any of the sensitive faculties in a higher degree would render him miserable. VII. That throughout the whole visible world a universal order and gradation in the sensual and mental faculties is observed, which causes a subordination of creature to creature, and of all creatures to man. The gradations of Sense, Instinct, Thought, Reflection, Reason: that Reason alone countervails all the other faculties. VIII. How much further this order and subordination of living creatures may extend above and below us; were any part of which broken, not that part only, but the whole connected creation must be destroyed. IX. The extravagance, madness, and pride of such a desire. X. The consequence of all, the absolute submission due to Providence, both as to our present and future state.

ALSO TENNYSON

Alfred, Lord Tennyson (1809 – 1892) included "The Higher Pantheism" in *The Holy Grail and Other Poems* (London: Strahan, 1870). The full poem:

The sun, the moon, the stars, the seas, the hills and the plains,
Are not these, O Soul, the Vision of Him who reigns?

Is not the Vision He, tho' He be not that which He seems?
Dreams are true while they last, and do we not live in dreams?

Earth, these solid stars, this weight of body and limb,
Are they not sign and symbol of thy division from Him?

Dark is the world to thee; thyself art the reason why,
For is He not all but thou, that hast power to feel "I am I"?

Glory about thee, without thee; and thou fulfillest thy doom,
Making Him broken gleams and a stifled splendour and gloom.

Speak to Him, thou, for He hears, and Spirit with Spirit can meet—
Closer is He than breathing, and nearer than hands and feet.

God is law, say the wise; O soul, and let us rejoice,
For if He thunder by law the thunder is yet His voice.

Law is God, say some; no God at all, says the fool,
For all we have power to see is a straight staff bent in a pool;

And the ear of man cannot hear, and the eye of man cannot see;
But if we could see and hear, this Vision—were it not He?

WHITHER SHALL I GO FROM THY SPIRIT?
Psalm 139:7

IN HIM WE LIVE AND MOVE AND HAVE OUR BEING
Acts 17:28

THEY TRY TO GET A PERSONALITY WITHOUT
FORM OR BOUNDS OR DIMENSIONS ...
As an example of what Uncle Zed is speaking, consider this excerpt from the
Westminster Confession of Faith (1646):

> There is but one only living and true God, who is infinite in being and per-
> fection, a most pure spirit, invisible, without body, parts, or passions, immu-
> table, immense, eternal, incomprehensible, almighty, most wise, most holy,
> most free, most absolute, working all things according to the counsel of His
> own immutable and most righteous will, for His own glory; most loving,
> gracious, merciful, long-suffering, abundant in goodness and truth, forgiv-
> ing iniquity, transgression, and sin; the rewarder of them that diligently seek
> Him; and withal most just and terrible in His judgments, hating all sin, and
> who will by no means clear the guilty.

GOD IS LOVE.
1 John 4 is the source of this phrase, but Uncle Zed's surrounding philosophy is
distinctly Mormon.

REMEMBER THY CREATOR IN THE DAYS OF THY YOUTH
Ecclesiastes 12:1

I'M GOING TO MEETING ...
At this time, "going to meeting" among Mormons referred specifically to attending sacrament meeting ("sacrament" referring specifically to the ordi-
nance in which members partake of bread and water in remembrance of Jesus
Christ's sacrifice, although the meeting also consists of hymns, sermons, etc).

From Anderson's novella *Almina*, serialized in *The Contributor* from November 1891 to May 1892:

> She had not even been to Sunday school or meeting since her marriage. What a time it seemed! Mr. Garnett and his mother had both told her that they did not attend "church," as they called it, when she had proposed going to meeting.

DORIAN HAD BUILT HIS CASTLES ...

May be a reference to Henry David Thoreau (1817 – 1862), who wrote in *Walden* (1854), "If you have built castles in the air, your work need not be lost; that is where they should be. Now put the foundations under them."

Anderson used the castle motif heavily in his 1902 novel *The Castle Builder*; the reference emphasizes Dorian's role as the final in a long line of Andersonian protagonists who dream big and, through Mormonism, build strong foundations for their dreams.

A NICE PAT

These days, a pat of butter is about one and a half teaspoons. At the time of *Dorian* however, it was somewhat larger and did not necessarily refer to a specific quantity. This is described well in the 1808 *British Farmer's Cyclopaedia*:

> ... a pound-lump of butter is placed in the bowl, and with a stroke of the hand, proportioned to the stiffness of the butter, is beaten with the cloth. As the pat of the butter becomes flat and thin, it is rolled up with the cloth (by a kind of dexterity which can only be acquired by practice) and again beaten flat; the dairy-woman every three or four strokes, rolling up either one side or the other of the pat, and moving it about in the bowl to prevent its sticking ... Each pound of butter requires in cool weather four or five minutes to be beaten thoroughly, but two minutes are at any time of essential service.
>
> In warm weather it is well to beat it two or three times over, as the coolness of the cloth assists in giving firmness to the butter.
>
> A pound of butter will lose about half an ounce in beating.

VIII

CARLIA, HAVE YOU SWILLED THE PIGS?

Swill is a mixture of solid and liquid food, usually kitchen waste and usually intended for pigs. As a verb, in this case, it means to give the swill to the swine.

COMING SO SUDDENLY

This phrasing brings scriptural weight, both positive and negative. Consider:

> Therefore shall his calamity come suddenly; suddenly shall he be broken without remedy. (Proverbs 6:15)

> For when they shall say, Peace and safety; then sudden destruction cometh upon them … (1 Thessalonians 5:3)

> And, behold, I come quickly; and my reward is with me, to give every man according as his work shall be. (Revelation 22:12)

BRINDLE

Like Dorian's horse, Carlia's cow has a name that describes its color. Brindle suggests a coat with darker and lighter streaks, sometimes described as tiger-like, though less pronouncedly striped.

IX

A FULL-FLEDGED CITIZEN OF THESE UNITED STATES

Until 1971, the federal voting age in the United States was 21.

GOD IS THE INTEGRATED HARMONY …

This line is from *Some Outlines of the Religion of Experience* (1916) by Horace James Bridges (1880 – 1955).

I MAY DESCRIBE THE SCENT OF THE ROSE …

A not uncommon position. Two similar passages, both from fictionalized reportings of conversation:

> Oh, confound definitions! They are humbugs. Leave that sort of thing to Blackstone and the scientific gentlemen. Can you define the scent of a rose, the light in woman's eye, or the music in her voice? (from *Scott's Monthly Magazine*, 1867)
>
> I see no reason why a sermon paint is essential, nor why virtuosity in excelsis, we esteem only at its lawful value in music, should be more highly valued in painting. You cannot explain the scent of a rose in words, you even describe it so that one who had never even smelt a rose would identify it by its odour. If a common experience in scent, in sound, or in taste cannot be expressed in words, how much more is it unlikely that 'Art' can be explained so that those use who feel it not can recognise it thereby? (from *The Studio: An Illustrated Magazine of Fine and Applied Art*, 1898)

THE DOCTRINE AND COVENANTS, SECTION 88

Verses 36 – 38

W.W. PHELPS

Phelps (1792 – 1872) was an early Mormon leader, printer, editor, hymnist, and a scribe to Joseph Smith. Fifteen of his hymns are in the current LDS hymnal.

IF YOU COULD HIE TO KOLOB …

Still a Latter-day Saint favorite, in part because of its distinctly Mormon viewpoint. As Hodges footnotes in his essay elsewhere in this volume:

> Interestingly, [Latter-day Saint theologian B.H.] Roberts quotes a section of W.W. Phelps's hymn, "If You Could Hie to Kolob," just like Uncle Zed does for Dorian (100 – 102).

More on Roberts below.

THE GREATEST OF SELVES, THE ULTIMATE SELF …

This line is from *The New Theology* by Reginald John Campbell (1867 – 1956), a book Campbell later had recalled. The quotations come (and Uncle Zed has apparently not jotted them down with absolute fidelity) from the following passages:

The Self is God. — A third inference, already hinted at and presumed in all that has gone before, is that the highest of all selves, the ultimate Self of the universe, is God. The New Testament speaks of man as body, soul, and spirit. The body is the thought-form through which the individuality finds expression on our present limited plane; the soul is a man's consciousness of himself as apart from all the rest of existence and even from God—it is the bay seeing itself as the bay and not as the ocean; the spirit is the true being thus limited and expressed—it is the deathless divine within us. The soul therefore is what we make it; the spirit we can neither make nor mar, for it is at once our being and God's. What we are here to do is to grow the soul, that is to manifest the true nature of the spirit, to build up that self-realisation which is God's objective with the universe as a whole and with every self-conscious unit in particular.

Where, then, someone will say, is the dividing line between our being and God's? There is no dividing line except from our side. The ocean of consciousness knows that the bay has never been separate from itself, although the bay is only conscious of the ocean on the outer side of its own being. But, the reader may protest, This is Pantheism. No, it is not. Pantheism is a technical term in philosophic parlance and means something quite different from this. It stands for a Fate-God, a God imprisoned in His universe, a God who cannot help Himself and does not even know what He is about, a blind force which here breaks out into a rock and there into Ruskin and is equally indifferent to either. But that is not my God. My God is my deeper Self and yours too; He is the Self of the universe and knows all about it. He is never baffled and cannot be baffled; the whole cosmic process is one long incarnation and uprising of the being of God from itself to itself. With Tennyson you can call this doctrine the Higher Pantheism if you like, but it is the very antithesis of the Pantheism which has played such a part in the history of thought (34 – 35).

Godhead and manhood. — The first in order of thought is that of the Godhead of Jesus. As regards this tenet I think it should be easily possible to show that the most convinced adherent of the traditional theology does not believe and never has believed what he professes to hold. The terms with which we have to deal are Deity, divinity, and humanity. A good deal of confusion exists concerning the interrelation of these three. It is supposed that humanity and divinity are mutually exclusive, and that divinity and Deity must necessarily mean exactly the same thing. But this is not so. It follows from the first principle of the New Theology that all the three are fundamentally and essentially one, but in scope and extent they are different. By the Deity we mean—and I suppose everyone means—the all-controlling consciousness of the universe as well as the infinite, unfathomable, and unknowable abyss of being beyond. By divinity we mean the essence of the nature of the immanent God, the innermost and all-determining quality of that nature; we have already seen that according to the Christian religion the innermost quality of the divine nature is perfect love. Show us perfect love and you have shown us the divinest thing the universe can produce, whether it knows itself to be immediately directed and controlled by the infinite consciousness of Deity or whether it does not. It is clear, then, that although Deity and divinity are essentially one, the latter is the lesser term and is dependent for its validity upon the former. Humanity is a lesser term still. It stands for that expression of the divine nature which we associate with our limited human consciousness. Strictly speaking, the human and divine are two categories which shade into and imply each other; humanity is divinity viewed from below, divinity is humanity viewed from above. If any human being could succeed in living a life of perfect love, that is a life whose energies were directed toward impersonal ends, and which was lived in such a way as to be and do the utmost for the whole, he would show himself divine, for he would have revealed the innermost of God. (73 – 75)

X

MR. LAMONT

Jack Lamont's surname is generally Scottish though a French name with the same spelling also exists. The name Jack was gaining popularity in the United States in the decades prior to *Dorian*'s publication, peaking at fourteenth in the decade following its publication, according to the Social Security Administration. The name simultaneously was used in the variety of generic uses it has long held. The term Jack Mormon, which had begun as a label for Mormon sympathizers would, by the 1940s, transition to its modern meaning of a Mormon friendly with the Church if no longer living by its precepts. Just where in this transition of meaning the term was in 1921 is uncertain.

XI

THE GREAT OCEAN OF TRUTH

Widely attributed to Isaac Newton (1642 – 1727):

> I don't know what I may seem to the world, but as to myself, I seem to have been only like a boy playing on the sea-shore and diverting myself in now and then finding a smoother pebble or a prettier shell than ordinary, whilst the great ocean of truth lay all undiscovered before me.

THE LETTER KILLETH …
2 Corinthians 3:6

BIOGENESIS
Coined by Henry Charlton Bastian (1837 – 1915) to mean what Thomas Henry Huxley would later rename abiogenesis: the idea that living things can come from unliving material. Bastian believed he had observed the spontaneous generation of microorganisms from nonliving material. Louis Pasteur (1822 – 1895) demonstrated that bacteria come from other bacteria rather than inorganic matter, leading to the current usage of the term. While Pasteur had proven the primacy of biogenesis over spontaneous generation, the question of the beginning of life remained for science to solve. In 1871, Darwin wrote, "It is often said that all the conditions for the first production of a living organism are now present, which could ever have been present. But if (and oh! what a big if!) we could conceive in some warm little pond, with all sorts of ammonia and phosphoric salts, light, heat, electricity, &c., present, that a proteine compound was chemically formed ready to undergo still more complex changes, at the present day such matter would be instantly devoured or absorbed, which would not have been the case before living creatures were formed."

JOSEPH SMITH'S STATEMENT THAT
GOD WAS ONCE A MAN LIKE US

> These are incomprehensible ideas to some, but they are simple. It is the first principle of the Gospel to know for a certainty the Character of God, and to know that we may converse with him as one man converses with another, and that he was once a man like us; yea, that God himself, the Father of us all, dwelt on an earth, the same as Jesus Christ himself did; and I will show it from the Bible (*Teachings of the Prophet Joseph Smith* [first published 1938]. Ed. Joseph Fielding Smith).

The expression comes from transcriptions of the speech Smith gave shortly after the funeral of King Follett (1788 – 1844). The speech was heard by twenty thousand or more Latter-day Saints and has become a classic sermon. The King

Follett Discourse, as it is commonly called, was dramatized by Anderson in his novel *John St. John* and the doctrine explicated in this excerpt is thematically important to that work.

PEARL OF GREAT PRICE
The fourth standard work of The Church of Jesus Christ of Latter-day Saints. Originally compiled in 1851 by apostle Franklin D. Richards (1821 – 1899) in Liverpool, England. Before *Dorian* was published, it had reached its current form.

FOR BEHOLD, THIS IS MY WORK ...
Moses 1:39

AS ONE LAMP LIGHTS ...
From the poem "Yussouf" by James Russell Lowell (1819 – 1891).

PRINCE OF LIFE
> But ye denied the Holy One and the Just, and desired a murderer to be granted unto you;
> And killed the Prince of life, whom God hath raised from the dead; whereof we are witnesses. (Acts 3:14 – 15)

THE RESURRECTION AND THE LIFE
> Jesus said unto her, I am the resurrection, and the life: he that believeth in me, though he were dead, yet shall he live:
> And whosoever liveth and believeth in me shall never die. (John 11:25 – 26)

XII

DAYS NEVER TO BE FORGOTTEN
Phraseology echoes an 1834 letter from Oliver Cowdery (1806 – 1850) to W.W. Phelps:

> These were days never to be forgotten; to sit under the sound of a voice dictated by the inspiration of heaven, awakened the utmost gratitude of this bosom!

Day after day I continued, uninterrupted, to write from his mouth, as he translated with the *Urim* and *Thummim*, or, as the Nephites would have said, "interpreters," the history or record called "The Book of Mormon."

THE KEYS OF THE HOLY PRIESTHOOD UNLOCK THE DOOR ...

Brigham Young, "Discourse delivered by President B. Young in the Tabernacle, G.S.L. City, August 15th, 1852," *Millennial Star* 25, supplement (1853): 58 – 59. This extended quotation taken from *The Contributor* (January 1890):

There are your father and your mother—your ancestors for many genera-tions back—the people that have lived upon the earth since the Priesthood was taken away, thousands and millions of them, who have lived according to the best light and knowledge in their possession. They will expound the Scriptures to you, and open your minds, and teach you of the resurrection of the just and the unjust, of the doctrine of salvation: they will use the keys of the holy Priesthood and unlock the door of knowledge, to let you look into the palace of truth. You will exclaim, That is all plain; why did I not understand it before? and you will begin to feel your hearts burn within you as they walk and talk with you.

THERE NEVER WAS A TIME WHEN THERE WERE NOT GODS ...

JD 7:333, "Progress in Knowledge, &c."

THE IDEA THAT THE RELIGION OF CHRIST IS ONE THING ...

JD 17:53, untitled sermon delivered May 3, 1874.

THE REGION OF TRUE RELIGION ...

From *Science and Immortality* page 47 (1908) by Oliver Lodge (1851 – 1940), a physicist, inventor, and convert to Spiritualism. Dorian will refer to Lodge again in the final chapter of the novel.

WE DO NOT INDEED REMEMBER OUR PAST ...

Page 73

WE MUST DARE TO EXTEND ...

Page 289

THERE ARE MORE LIVES YET ...
From "The Crowning Hour" by Edwin Markham (1852 – 1940), collected in *The Shoes of Happiness and Other Poems* (1915). Markham was a popular Western poet based in Oregon.

THE WARD MUTUAL IMPROVEMENT LIBRARY
The Young Men's Mutual Improvement Society was founded in 1875 by Brigham Young as a counterpart to the Young Ladies' Cooperative Retrenchment Association (1869, renamed in 1877 to the Young Ladies' National Mutual Improvement Association). Anderson himself was called to the MIA's General Board in 1910 where he served until his death.

THE MANTLE OF BROTHER ZED ...
A reference to 2 Kings 2:11 – 14, and a motif that carries throughout the novel:

> And it came to pass, as they still went on, and talked, that, behold, there appeared a chariot of fire, and horses of fire, and parted them both asunder; and Elijah went up by a whirlwind into heaven.
> And Elisha saw it, and he cried, My father, my father, the chariot of Israel, and the horsemen thereof. And he saw him no more: and he took hold of his own clothes, and rent them in two pieces.
> He took up also the mantle of Elijah that fell from him, and went back, and stood by the bank of Jordan;
> And he took the mantle of Elijah that fell from him, and smote the waters, and said, Where is the Lord God of Elijah? and when he also had smitten the waters, they parted hither and thither: and Elisha went over.

CLOD HOPPER
A large and heavy boot or, as here, a rustic who is clumsy or uncouth.

MOTHER EARTH
A common phrase in the *Journal of Discourses*, usually in the sense of the dead returning to their Mother Earth. Even those moments not explicitly about the bodies of the dead returning to molder frequently echo Uncle Zed's suggestion that spirit and element are one. A few examples:

> Why will the Latter-day Saints wander off after the things of this world? But are they not good? We cannot do very well without them, for we are of the world, we are in the world, we partake of the elements of which it is

composed; it is our mother earth, we are composed of the same native material. It is all good, the air, the water, the gold and silver; the wheat, the fine flour, and the cattle upon a thousand hills are all good; but, why do men set their hearts upon them in their present organized state? (1.272; Brigham Young: August 14, 1853)

But are the inhabitants of the earth the only portion of nature that is not uniform? No ... look at mother earth, at the ocean, at the rocks, at the planets that bespangle the blue vault of heaven; in short, at nature in all her works, which you will find stamped with the insignia of continual change. (1.346; Jedediah M. Grant: August 7, 1853)

There was a man here a few days ago, who has been in the Church nearly as long as I have, who told me we should have to leave the valleys and flee into the mountains—into the secret chambers, and close our doors around us. I told him the mountains were nothing more than sloping masses of Mother Earth—that we were now in the chambers, and should not yet go on to the roof. You need not trouble yourselves upon that matter. (7.347; Heber C. Kimball: January 1, 1860)

The devil has had great power and dominion over the generations of the earth; and the earth itself has groaned under the load of sin and corruption which has been upon its face. Enoch when enveloped in the vision of the Almighty, beheld and heard the earth groan under this load of wickedness. ... He was informed that there was a day of rest coming for old mother earth,—for he was grieved in his heart for the earth itself, as well as the inhabitants thereof; for he saw how the earth was afflicted, until she groaned to be relieved. But the time will come, when it will be sanctified ... It is for this purpose you have come to these mountains. (21.205; Orson Pratt: November 12, 1879)

THE D&C, SECTION 88
Verse 35

THE D&C, SECTION 29
Verse 41

BANISHMENT FROM THE PLACE WHERE GOD LIVES IS DEATH.
Given later events, echoes of *Romeo and Juliet* may be intentional. Both eponymous characters speak on the topic. This is Romeo:

Ha, banishment! be merciful, say 'death;'
For exile hath more terror in his look,
Much more than death: do not say 'banishment.' (III:iii, 12 – 14)

A SOUL WHO CANNOT FUNCTION IN THE CELESTIAL GLORY ...
Cf. D&C 88:22 – 24

> For he who is not able to abide the law of a celestial kingdom cannot abide a celestial glory.
> And he who cannot abide the law of a terrestrial kingdom cannot abide a terrestrial glory.
> And he who cannot abide the law of a telestial kingdom cannot abide a telestial glory; therefore he is not meet for a kingdom of glory. Therefore he must abide a kingdom which is not a kingdom of glory.

As regards the above comments on Mother Earth, note verses 25 and 26 as well:

> And again, verily I say unto you, the earth abideth the law of a celestial kingdom, for it filleth the measure of its creation, and transgresseth not the law—
> Wherefore, it shall be sanctified; yea, notwithstanding it shall die, it shall be quickened again, and shall abide the power by which it is quickened, and the righteous shall inherit it.

TO BE CARNALLY MINDED IS DEATH
Romans 8:6

THE WAGES OF SIN IS DEATH
Romans 6:23

XIII

LAID THEIR CAPS
Apparently a variation on the phrase *to set one's cap*, as used by Jane Austen (1775 – 1817) in *Sense and Sensibility* (1811):

"Aye, aye, I see how it will be," said Sir John, "I see how it will be. You will be setting your cap at him now, and never think of poor Brandon."

"That is an expression, Sir John," said Marianne, warmly, "which I particularly dislike. I abhor every common-place phrase by which wit is intended; and 'setting one's cap at a man,' or 'making a conquest,' are the most odious of all. Their tendency is gross and illiberal; and if their construction could ever be deemed clever, time has long ago destroyed all its ingenuity."

Sir John did not much understand this reproof; but he laughed as heartily as if he did, and then replied—

"Ay, you will make conquests enough, I dare say, one way or other. Poor Brandon! he is quite smitten already, and he is very well worth setting your cap at, I can tell you, in spite of all this tumbling about and spraining of ankles."

XIV

IT WILL GO FROM FORTY TO FIFTY BUSHELS
At the time of this volume's publication, this is a high average yield for non-irrigated wheat in the western U.S.

XV

FULSOME
Excessively complimentary.

XVI

CARLIA DAVIS
Anderson used this name for Carlia at earlier stages of the novel's creation.

THE CARMINE LIPS

Carmine is a deep, almost purplish red, although lighter shades may be made with the pigment—carminic acid—which is derived from certain insects, especially cochineals, who use it as a predator deterrent. It is still used in lipsticks today.

XVII

HAD HE FOUND HER DEAD, IN HER VIRGINAL PURITY

The question of whether it is better to be murdered or raped has been a constant in Latter-day Saint discourse. While Brigham Young said, "Any man who humbles a daughter of Eve to rob her of her virtue, and cast her off dishonored and defiled, is her destroyer, and is responsible to God for the deed. If the refined Christian society of the nineteenth century will tolerate such a crime, God will not; but he will call the perpetrator to an account. He will be damned; in hell he will lift up his eyes, being in torment, until he has paid the uttermost farthing, and made a full atonement for his sins" (JD 11:268), Anderson's contemporary (and Young's fifth-removed replacement as president of the Church) Heber J. Grant said, "There is no true Latter-day Saint who would not rather bury a son or a daughter than to have him or her lose his or her chastity—realizing that chastity is of more value than anything else in all the world" (qtd. *Gospel Standards: Selections from the Sermons and Writings of Heber J. Grant*, 1941). The tension of blame—and between the relative values of potential losses—remains uncertain, though the idea has largely disappeared from LDS discourse.

HIS CHUMMY COMPANION

Chummy suggests a particularly intimate friendship.

FOR THE SON OF MAN IS COME

Matthew 18:11 – 13

IF I SIN AGAINST THAT LIGHT
D&C 82:3 reads, "For of him unto whom much is given much is required; and he who sins against the greater light shall receive the greater condemnation."

"DRUGGED" WAS THE WORD MRS. WHITMAN USED.
As evidenced by earlier versions of the text, Anderson did not always plan to give Carlia this out. Whether the decision to lessen her culpability was based in aesthetics or marketing (or, differently phrased, if it was his own decision or his publisher's) remains unproven.

XVIII

OLD-TIME ROSES
According to "Old-Time Roses: Early Friends which Still Deserve a Place in the Garden," written by H. G. Pratt (as published in the January 1893 issue of *American Gardening*), old-time roses include "single white Cherokee, double white Cherokee, sweetbrier or eglantine, Gloire de Rosomanes, Beauty of Glazenwood or Fortune's double yellow, white and yellow Banksias, and last, but not least, the Castilian." These roses seem to have had little in common besides the presence of a variety of imperfections bred out of newer roses, and their very oldness and familiarity. Pratt was a farmer from Fruitvale, California, who would go on to propose in August 1895 to the State Floral Society to undertake an improvement in the classification of roses as the taxonomic "superstructure is built to a great extent on chaos" (see the article "Classifying our Roses" in the *San Francisco Call*'s August 10 issue for more information on this proposal). It's not clear that Anderson intended any allusion to these old favorites of gardeners

XIX

XX

DRAUGHT
Draft.

THE WAGES OF SIN IS DEATH ...
Romans 6:23

THOUGH YOUR SINS BE AS SCARLET ...
Isaiah 1:18

SUPINELY
Lying on the back, face upward.

XXI

CHOKE-CHERRY BLOSSOMS
Prunus virginiana is a small tree or shrub that flowers in late spring. It grows widely in the Northern Plains and Rockies of the United States.

UP THROUGH GREAT TRIBULATION
This phrase is used occasionally by Joseph Smith (1805 – 1844) and other religious figures of the era (such as Charles G. Finney [1792 – 1875] who wrote an entire sermon so titled). Ultimately it is derived from Revelation 7:14:

> These are they which came out of great tribulation, and have washed their robes, and made them white in the blood of the Lamb.

BLESSED ARE THE PURE IN HEART
Matthew 5:8

WHAT WOULD IT PROFIT ...

A concept drawn from the Synoptic Gospels:

> For what is a man profited, if he shall gain the whole world, and lose his own soul? or what shall a man give in exchange for his soul? (Matthew 16:26)

> For what shall it profit a man, if he shall gain the whole world, and lose his own soul? (Mark 8:36)

> For what is a man advantaged, if he gain the whole world, and lose himself, or be cast away? (Luke 9:25)

KNOWLEDGE IS POWER

Commonly attributed to Francis Bacon (1561 – 1626), though his phrasing (in Latin) may actually be intended to suggest that knowledge is God's power.

SCRIPTURE WHICH SAYS THAT THE WORLDS WERE FRAMED ...

Through faith we understand that the worlds were framed by the word of God, so that things which are seen were not made of things which do appear (Hebrews 11:3).

KNOWLEDGE HAS ALWAYS EXISTED ...

Latter-day Saint theologian B.H. Roberts (1857 – 1933) citing Cicero (106 – 43 BCE) citing Plato (c. 427 – 347 BCE):

> It is interesting to note that this truth, at least in part, seemed to impress itself upon the great minds of the antique world. Cicero says, in speaking of the spirit of man: "I might add that the facility with which youth are taught to acquire numberless very difficult arts, is a strong presumption that the soul (spirit) possessed a considerable portion of knowledge before it entered into the human form, and what seems to be received from instruction is, in fact, no other than a reminiscence or recollection of its ideas. This at least," he adds, "is the opinion of Plato."

THE SUM OF TRUTH IS ETERNAL.

Mormon historian and hymnist John Jacques (1827 – 1900) wrote these lines still popular with the Latter-day Saints:

Then say, what is truth? 'Tis the last and the first,
For the limits of time it steps o'er.
Tho the heavens depart and the earth's fountains burst,
Truth, the sum of existence, will weather the worst,
Eternal, unchanged, evermore.

HE COMPREHENDS ALL TRUTH ...

This is a phrase used by early Church leaders:

> The Gospel of life and salvation that we have embraced in our faith, and
> that we profess to carry out in our lives, incorporates all truth ... The Gos-
> pel that I have embraced comprehends all truth. "How much of it is true?"
> All of it. "How much does it embrace?" All the truth that there is in the
> heavens, on the earth, under the earth; and if there is any truth in hell, this
> doctrine claims it. It is all the truth of heaven, the truth of God, the life of
> those that live forever, the law by which worlds were, are, and will be
> brought into existence, and pass from one degree or one state of being to
> another, pertaining to the exaltation of intelligence from the lowest to the
> highest state. This is the doctrine that the Latter-day Saints believe, whether
> they realize it or not. (Brigham Young, 1873, JD 16:160)

> It has often been remarked respecting our meetings in this Tabernacle, by
> persons who have not been accustomed to our form of worship and our
> method of instruction, that we very frequently dwell upon a great many sub-
> jects that other people do not deem appropriate to the Sabbath. There is a
> reason for this; it is found in the fact which I have stated—that the Gospel
> of Jesus Christ comprehends all truth; and therefore everything necessary for
> the promotion of a man's happiness, for the enlargement of his views and
> his mind, and for the development of all his being, physical and mental, eve-
> rything of this kind should be treated upon at the time and the season when
> it is needed. I do not, myself, value a religion that confines its teachings to
> the Sabbath, that does not enter into the everyday life of those who profess
> it. (George Q. Cannon, 1879, JD 20:288)

The phrase is significantly older than Mormonism, however.

> I thus argue: That Being which Comprehends all Truth is Omnifcent.
> But God Comprehends all Truth.
> Therefore God is Omnifcient.
> The firft Propofition is plain from the Definition of Knowledge. The Con-
> clufion therefore depends wholly upon the proof of the Second; namely,
> that God comprehends all Truth.
> (*Treatises upon Several Subjects* by John Norris, 1698)

ALL POWER AND ALL GLORY IS FOUND IN HIM
This idea is found in the Lord's Prayer.

> Our Father which art in heaven, Hallowed be thy name. Thy kingdom
> come. Thy will be done in earth, as it is in heaven. Give us this day our daily
> bread. And forgive us our debts, as we forgive our debtors. And lead us not
> into temptation, but deliver us from evil: For thine is the kingdom, and the
> power, and the glory, for ever. Amen. (Matthew 6:9 – 13)

WE SHOULD SEEK THE TRUTH FROM THE FOUNTAIN HEAD
Dorian is making a distinctly Mormon reworking of the argument made by
Protestant reformer and close associate of John Calvin, William Farel (1489 –
1565):

> And if we doubt whether anything we are told by men is really what Christ
> has said and commanded, we are to turn to the Holy Scriptures, which are
> the fountain-head from which God intends we should draw forth *all* truth.
> (*William Farel* by Emma Frances Bevan, 1883, 20 – 21)

WHEN THE SON OF MAN COMETH ...
Luke 18:8

EDISON IS BRINGING FORTH ...
Thomas Alva Edison (1847 – 1931), inventor, businessman, and, to some even
in his own lifetime, folk hero.

BURBANK IS DOING MARVELOUS THINGS ...
Luther Burbank (1849 – 1926) was an American botanist and horticulturist.
Among the over 800 strains and varieties of plants he developed are many food
and ornamental crops still popular.

SIR OLIVER LODGE
Lodge (1851 – 1940) was one of the most respected physicists of his day, and
an inventor who made important contributions to the telegraph and automobiles. He is also remembered for investigations into such fields as telepathy and
departed spirits. Lodge's words were read by Dorian under Uncle Zed's direction in chapter twelve.

LORD KELVIN

William Thomson (1824 – 1907) was made the first Baron Kelvin in 1892 by Queen Victoria (1819 – 1901). He first came to public attention with his theoretical work related to the transatlantic cable. He had previously significant work in thermodynamics, and would go on to be a major contributor in other scientific fields. His theories of geology were influenced by his Christian faith. He felt the Earth was 20 to 40 million years old, which would not allow for Darwin's imagining of evolution. He proposed a theistic variation on evolution to explain both the evidence and his understanding of a solar system too young to allow for Darwin's theory. The keystone of Thomson's argument was based on then-current understanding of the source of solar energy; not until the description of thermonuclear fusion in the 1930s would this difficulty be resolved.

KEY OF KNOWLEDGE

This phrase appears in Luke 11:52, but its appearance in the D&C seems more intended here.

> And this greater priesthood administereth the gospel and holdeth the key of the mysteries of the kingdom, even the key of the knowledge of God. (D&C 84:19; see also D&C 128:14)

The phrase was also used by Eliza R. Snow (1804 – 1887) in her hymn "Invocation, or The Eternal Father and Mother":

> I had learned to call thee Father,
> Through thy Spirit from on high,
> But until the key of knowledge
> Was restored, I knew not why.

DOWN INTO THE VALLEY OF SUNSHINE AND SHADOW

A reworking of Psalm 23:

> Yea, though I walk through the valley of the shadow of death, I will fear no evil: for thou art with me …

CRITICAL ANALYSIS
OF *DORIAN*

NEPHI ANDERSON'S *DORIAN* AND THE PROJECT OF
TWENTIETH-CENTURY MORMONISM

SCOTT HALES

At the time of his 6 January 1923 death, Nephi Anderson was the premier man of letters in The Church of Jesus Christ of Latter-day Saints. His friend, Church President Heber J. Grant, credited his writing for making "a financial success" of one of the Church's official magazines, the *Improvement Era*, which had published Anderson's fiction, nonfiction, and poetry for more than twenty years. Indeed, three months before his death, Anderson received an admiring letter from Grant telling him "that there are few, if any, of the writers to *the Improvement Era* that I feel more grateful to than your dear self for the many contributions which you have made to our splendid little magazine" (Grant). This praise was echoed in Anderson's two-page obituary in *the Improvement Era* which called him "a gifted writer of fiction" who "always provided clean stories permeated by the spirit of the gospel" ("Nephi Anderson" 373 – 375). Another obituary, published on the front page of the *Box Elder News*, claimed that Anderson's novel *Added Upon* had been "read by almost every person in the state" of Utah ("Called by Death" 1).

Sadly, the popularity of Anderson's work did not last, and his reputation diminished as the twentieth century progressed and literary tastes changed. By 1974 most of his ten novels were out of print and his fiction had become the object of nearly universal scorn among the rising generation of Mormon literary critics. Karl Keller, a Mormon professor of American literature at California State University, San Diego, called Anderson's most enduring and commercially successful novel, *Added Upon* (1898), "a tract-like novel" that was "ultimately insulting to the mystery of the Resurrection," citing "its lack of love of the worldly concrete and its sentimentalized guesswork" as its primary sins. Dismissing it as "didactic" and "escape fiction," Keller insisted that it had "no faith in the real" and was "incapable of stirring the minds of real people." In short: Anderson, by writing *Added Upon*, had committed an affront to Mormonism. Rather than illuminating "the philosophical foundations of the gospel," he had dabbled around with "unfleshed ideas and emotion" as he "[tried] to make that which is good without giving enough consideration to the good of that which [was] made" (63).

Keller's low opinion was shared by others. In their introduction to Mormon fiction in the anthology *A Believing People: Literature of the Latter-day Saints* (1974), Richard H. Cracroft and Neal E. Lambert described the work of Anderson and his contemporaries as "long on plot and short on artistry and character development" (257). A few years later (1978), Edward A. Geary characterized the works of Anderson's generation of writers—known collectively as Mormonism's "Home Literature" writers—as neither "powerful" nor "pure." In these works, he reasoned, "distinctive Mormon characteristics [were] only skin deep, masking an underlying vision which is as foreign to the gospel as it is to real life" (15). Likewise, Eugene England dismissed the same body of work as "essentially devoid of genuine conflict" (196). As with Keller, these critics had limited patience for Nephi Anderson and writers like him; for them, his brand of sentimental, moralistic fiction was merely an embarrassing steppingstone in the development of more sophisticated Mormon literature. And while they acknowledged its contribution to Mormons letters, they did so quietly and with the suggestion that it had little meaningful to say about Mormonism and its people.

To be sure, critical antagonism toward Anderson's work has not gone unchecked. Norwegian critic Ole Podhorny submitted his graduate thesis on Anderson to the English Department in the University of Oslo in 1980. In lt, he suggested that while Anderson's works were "poor in literary artistry," they "should definitely be better known to students of 'Mormon' social history" because they pioneered Mormon literature and serve today as "a record of what large numbers of his readers believed about their history, their doctrine, and their destiny" (81). Five years later, *A Believing People* editor Richard H.

Cracroft followed Podhorny with a sympathetic reassessment of Anderson's work, "Nephi, Seer of Modern Times: The Home Literature Novels of Nephi Anderson" (1985). Published in *BYU Studies*, the essay continued the critical tradition of denigrating *Added Upon* as an "ambitious failure" and a "wooden *tour de force*," yet it also worked against the critical consensus, praising Anderson for possessing "a fine narrative gift, a rich imagination, and a keen sense of appreciation for literary style." Furthermore, the essay also lamented that much of Anderson's reputation among "modern Mormon critics" was based on *Added Upon*, rather than his subsequent nine novels, leaving students of Mormon literature with the misleading impression that Anderson was "a one-novel, one-failure author." Cracroft believed that Anderson's prodigious body of work, which also included some forty-eight short stories, made him "a vital and positive force in turn-of-the-century Mormon letters" and a Mormon author worthy of serious scholarly attention (3). Unfortunately, copies of Anderson's novels and short stories—with the exception of *Added Upon*—were rare and sometimes inaccessible in the mid-1980s, particularly for scholars working outside of Utah, so Cracroft's plea for more Anderson scholarship went largely unheeded.

Things have since changed. Thanks to digitization technology and websites like Google Books (books.google.com) and the Internet Archive (archive.org), computer scans of Anderson's novels are now easily accessible—for free—on the Internet. Likewise, many of his essays, articles, and short stories—if not all of them—are also available in digital formats, either on the web or on CD-ROM. With these developments, the time seems right for the kind of Anderson scholarship Cracroft envisioned in 1985, yet scholars still seem largely unaware of it and its potential. Accordingly, Anderson and his work need to be brought out of obscurity and returned—as much as possible—to their former place in the Mormon consciousness. Moreover, a new generation of literary scholars needs to salvage Anderson's reputation from the writings of Mormon critics in the 1970s and 1980s, who, in retrospect, were far too zealous in their efforts to distance contemporary Mormon fiction from predecessors that seemed by their standards old fashioned, sentimental, didactic, or overly pious. Such an effort, no doubt, will reveal the hitherto untapped rewards of Anderson scholarship. Few of his contemporaries came close to being as ambitious and prolific as he was in the pursuit of a distinctive Mormon literature, and none was more widely respected. A study of his writings promises, among other things, insight into the very beginnings of Mormon fiction.

BEGINNING AT THE END: A CASE FOR *DORIAN*

For readers and scholars with interests in learning more about Anderson and his work, it may prove beneficial to become familiar first with *Dorian* (1921), Anderson's last novel, which Cracroft called the "best, and certainly his boldest" (13). *Dorian* is a coming-of-age story about the spiritual, intellectual, and moral awakening of Dorian Trent, a young Mormon man in a Modern age of science, atheism, and automobiles. According to Cracroft, the novel is "generally a success" in its realism and handling of "serious human dilemmas and problems," and marks a pronounced change in the way Anderson uses his trademark doctrinal discussions between characters to resolve conflict and develop plot. As Cracroft points out, the doctrinal discussion in *Dorian* tend to serve not as Mormon propaganda, but as "a counterpoint" to "the ongoing life in the valley" and as "obstacles to Dorian's real understanding" of life and the human condition. *Dorian* is a "real" novel that "underscores a maturity not only in Anderson, but in his readers." In it, Cracroft sees the beginnings of "a more sophisticated" Mormon literature that tragically went undeveloped following Anderson's 1923 death and the emergence of "enervating policies" that limited the extent to which Mormon writers could realistically portray their world in "Church magazines" (13 – 14).

Cracroft's positive appraisal of *Dorian* is a welcome reprieve from the criticisms of Anderson's detractors, yet his lamentation for what might have been distracts in some ways from what the novel *was* and *continues to be* for Latter-day Saints and their fiction. Reading it today, nearly one hundred years later, it is easy to see that *Dorian* was not only a generally successful aesthetic production and a milestone in Mormon literary realism, but also a statement of identity for Mormons in the early twentieth century, particularly young Mormons whose task it was to take the Church into the future. As one reviewer pointed out in the January 1922 issue of *the Improvement Era*, the novel provided "boys and girls" with "a class of reading which [aimed] to teach the way of righteousness in attractive story form" ("Editor's Table" 361). Its Horatian mixture of entertainment and instruction, in other words, could serve as a vehicle for shaping Mormon character, clarifying cultural boundaries, and teaching correct gospel principles. To a Mormon community still in the process of steadying itself from the institutional trauma of the Woodruff Manifesto, the 1890 edict that signaled the beginning of the end of the group-defining practice of Mormon polygamy, *Dorian* served as a kind of guidebook for performing twentieth-century Mormon identity.

Dorian, to be sure, was only one of many efforts to stabilize Mormon identity in the early twentieth century. As Armand Mauss notes, Mormons in the nineteenth century "had self-consciously cultivated institutions, both religious and secular, that were uniquely their own." These institutions—particularly polygamy—did much to rouse the suspicions of mainstream Americans with their Protestant values, leading them to see Mormons as "an un-American, even anti-American, insurgent counterculture" (21). Following the Manifesto, and the intense persecution preceding it, Mormons sought to develop what Jan Shipps describes as "patterns of behavior" that were not only socially acceptable to a nation wary of powerful institutions, but also unique enough to cultivate an identity that set them apart and kept them "unspotted from the world" (116). These patterns unfolded with the help of official and unofficial Church discourse in sermons, Church magazines and other influential forms of communication, including fiction (see de Schweinitz 27 – 54; Hoyt 72 – 74). As the twentieth century dawned, for example, Church leaders placed more emphasis on performance-based practices that stressed clean living and personal righteousness, such as the Word of Wisdom and law of tithing (Shipps 128). Moreover, they also embraced capitalism, participated more in national politics, and began to de-emphasize the nineteenth-century practice of gathering newly-converted Latter-day Saints to Utah (see Flake 1 – 2; Yorgason 5 – 6, 130 – 134; Arrington 139 – 140). According to Mauss, these efforts were the product of "deliberate church policy," which was carried out well into the century to be "conspicuously assimilationist in most respects" (22). In fact, by 1921, when *Dorian* was published, these efforts were beginning to bear fruits. Not only were Mormons more assimilated into the American mainstream, but they were also becoming more comfortable with their new post-Manifesto identity.

Born in Norway in 1865, Nephi Anderson's life spanned the most critical years of this time of upheaval and transition. After he and his family emigrated to the Utah Territory in 1871—two years after the completion of the transcontinental railroad put an end to the Mormon pioneer era (1847 – 1869)—they settled in Coalville and Ogden, where Anderson received his education against the turbulent backdrop of the 1880s and the federal government's aggressive crackdown on polygamy. Like other prominent Mormon men of his generation—most notably J. Reuben Clark, David O. McKay, Reed Smoot, James E. Talmage, and John A. Widtsoe—Anderson remained an observer of polygamy only, never practicing the "principle" even though he married four years before the Manifesto. Consequently, he belonged to a generation of Mormons whose task, in many ways, was to carry out the project of defining post-polygamy Mormon identity for a world that had a hard time separating the Church from the practice. Smoot, as senator from Utah, carried out these efforts as a nationally-prominent Mormon in Washington DC. Widtsoe and Talmage, in turn, pioneered a new kind of Mormon intellectualism that sought to reconcile science and religion—and downplay the centrality of polygamy in Mormon thought. Clark and McKay, while dissimilar in many ways, embodied the rising generation of monogamous Mormon leaders and teachers, shaping new Church policies along the way. Nephi Anderson, for his part, carried out this work on a literary front. Along with artists and writers like Susa Young Gates, Josephine Spencer, Alfred Lambourne, and others, Anderson wrote articles, essays, short stories, poems, and novels that downplayed polygamy's central role in nineteenth-century Mormonism and offered young Latter-day Saints literary models to help them through the difficult transitional period. With novels like *Dorian* and essays like "The Pilgrims: The Pioneers" (*Improvement Era*, July 1900) and "Are We Americans?" (*Improvement Era*, Oct. 1900), he showed young Mormons how to find space within (rather than against) American society.

To be sure, the significance of *Dorian*'s role in this process of transition is uncertain. Unlike *Added Upon*, which remained continuously in print for a little more than one hundred years, *Dorian* has enjoyed neither generations of readers, nor much recognition as a culturally significant work of Mormon literature. Still, as a product of its time, *Dorian* says much about the state of Mormonism in the early twentieth century and the path it would take as the century progressed. Dorian Trent, after all, is a transitional figure—much like Anderson himself—and his coming of age is marked with episodes that try to work out a twentieth-century Mormon's ambivalence toward the pioneer past and the seemingly uncertain present. Frequently, these episodes involve his friend and mentor, Uncle Zed, "a little frail old man with clean white hair and beard" who functions in the novel as a kind of embodiment of Mormonism's first generation (46). Through Zed and his interactions with Dorian, Anderson assesses both the value of the Church's nineteenth-century legacy and its relevance to twentieth-century Mormons. Uncle Zed, for example, reads voraciously from the writings of Orson Pratt and other early Mormon leaders, and his discussions with Dorian read like homilies of pioneer wisdom. Importantly, however, these discussions also reflect Zed's familiarity with the writings of such thinkers as Scottish theologian Henry Drummond and English scientist Oliver Lodge, suggesting a kind of intellectual ecumenism that approaches Truth broadly

(49). Dorian, as Uncle Zed's student, follows a similar track, drawing from "the doctrinal articles of these first elders" and benefiting from "their plain bluntness" and "charm," but also keeping an open mind to ideas that seem at first to fall outside of a Mormon framework of belief (143). For Dorian, this pioneer wisdom, as introduced to him by Uncle Zed, establishes both the beginnings of his faith and his first line of defense against secular challenges to it:

> By his reading that winter Dorian obtained an enlarged view of his religion. It gave him vision to see and to comprehend better the whole and thus to more fully understand the details. Besides, he was laying a broad and firm foundation for his faith in God and the restored gospel of Jesus Christ, a faith which would stand him well in need when he came to delve into a faithless and a Godless science. (143)

Significantly, though, while Dorian certainly views his education in pioneer-era theology as a check on his secular education, neither he nor Uncle Zed considers it to be a rival form of knowledge or learning. Rather, as the above passage suggests, Dorian views spiritual knowledge as a medium through which he can "comprehend better" and "fully understand" secular learning without embracing "faithless" or "Godless" perspectives. In a sense, Dorian's education in the teachings of his pioneer forbears is meant to cooperate with and complement all other forms of learning, thus eliminating a dualistic view of learning that sets knowledge up as something either secular or spiritual.

Dorian's desire to find common ground between Mormonism and other systems of knowledge is consistent with the efforts of post-Manifesto Mormons and their twentieth-century project of assimilation. Like them, he seems open-minded in his dealings with those who differ ideologically from him— although, to be sure, he is not without a belief in the superiority of Mormonism to the ideas of "Sir Oliver Lodge and Lord Kelvin" or any other non-Mormon thinker (221). Indeed, in outlining his academic goals, he grandly states:

> I must be greater than either of them [i.e. Lodge and Kelvin]. I must know all they know, and more; and that is possible, for I have the "Key of Knowledge" which even the most learned scholar cannot get without obedience to the laws and ordinances of the gospel. (222)

The "apparent egotism of [this] proposition" notwithstanding (221), Dorian's approach to knowledge and learning is mostly one of determination and openness to new and challenging ideas, including those that seem to contradict his understanding of Truth. When he studies Charles Darwin's *On the Origin of Species*, he initially finds the book "rather heavy," but ultimately comes to "[learn] what the scientist [is] 'driving at'" through diligence and "close application." Moreover, he discovers that the book has "much truth in it" even though it contains "some things which [do] not agree with what he [has] been taught to be true." "[D]isturbed," but not deterred, by Darwin's theories, Dorian finds value in them; rather than retreat into his established notions of Truth, he "[realizes] his lack of knowledge" and resolves to learn more, since "[more] knowledge must clear up any seeming contradiction" between his understanding of Truth and Darwin's (72).

Again, Dorian's complementary approach to the study of science and religion is inspired and encouraged by Uncle Zed, who, aside from fostering Dorian's faith, also encourages him to "make it his life's mission to work to learn the truths of science and harmonize them where necessary with the revealed truth" (119). In this regard, Uncle Zed is instrumental in helping Dorian become a new kind of Mormon—one who is defined by his respect for his pioneer heritage and rural upbringing, but also not limited by the isolationist tendencies that often characterized them. Such ambivalence toward the pioneer legacy is consistent with trends in "the assimilation process," which, as Mauss points out, show that "the upward social mobility and growing affluence" of a rising generation of a religious community makes them "begin to find the religious zeal of their ancestors primitive and unsophisticated" (6 – 7). Indeed, by the end of the novel, Dorian is doing just that as he makes preparations to leave the farm and enter East coast academia, where he hopes to become a kind of intellectual ambassador for the Church and its doctrines.

Uncle Zed's influence over Dorian has its limitations, however, and part of Dorian's maturation involves recognizing the theological shortcomings of his mentor. For example, before his death, Uncle Zed teaches Dorian about "the law of eternal progress," which states that "there always have been intelligences evolving from lower to higher life, which in the eternity of the past would inevitably lead to the perfection of Gods" (122). From this, Uncle Zed infers that God's work necessarily involves aiding His children—the lower intelligences—in their individual processes of eternal progression; His work, in a sense, is

> to labor for those who are yet on the lower rungs of the ladder, to institute laws whereby those below may climb up higher; [...] to use His greater experience, knowledge, and power for others, to pass down to those in lower or primary stages that which they cannot get by self-effort alone. (123)

Furthermore, Uncle Zed believes that God's "sons and daughters" must "follow His example as far as possible in [their] sphere of action" by "[helping] along the road those who are lower down, those who are more ignorant and are weaker than [they]" (125). By doing so, he believes, all "men and families and races and worlds [will] be linked together in chains of love, which cannot be broken, worlds without end" (126).

To a certain extent, Uncle Zed's understanding of the law of eternal progression, as well as of the work of God and His children, seems to promote such virtues as love, compassion, generosity, charity, and friendship. What is more, it solicits from Dorian an overwhelming appreciation for God and a sense of the "tremendous responsibility" he, Dorian, carries "because of the knowledge he already [has]" about God's laws and expectations for His children (126 – 127). At the same time, however, it leads Dorian to set himself apart—quite inadvertently—from others whom he deems to be on a lower rung of the ladder than he. Throughout the novel, for instance, his relationship with Carlia Duke is strained, despite their close friendship, because he is subtly repulsed by her seemingly crude, impoverished, and unenlightened surroundings:

> There was the same lack of books or music or anything pretty or refined [in Carlia's home]; and as Dorian stood and looked about, there came to him more forcibly than ever the barrenness of the room and of the house in general. […] The Duke home had always impressed him as being cold and cheerless and ugly. There were no protecting porches, no lawn, no flowers, and the barn yard had crept close up to the house. It was a place to work. […] The father and the mother and the daughter were slaves to work. Only in work did the parents companion with the daughter. The visitors to the house were mostly those who came to talk about cattle and crops and irrigation. (86)

In noticing the homeliness of Carlia's life, Dorian has only a "dim conception" of how "her sordid environment seemed to be crushing her" and leading her to grow not only "resentful and sarcastic," but also scornful and angry "in wild and undirected ways" (86 – 87). Indeed, as Dorian begins to share Uncle Zed's views on the law of eternal progress, his narrow pursuit of that which is higher and nobler causes him to overlook even more Carlia's struggle to endure her difficult life. Yet Carlia notices it. "You," she says to Dorian in a "hard voice," "you're altogether too good and too wise for such as I. You're so high up that I can't touch you. You live in the clouds, I live among the clods. What have we two in common?" (148).

Uncle Zed's lofty teachings and ideals present other obstacles in Dorian's "real understanding" of life. Upon Uncle Zed's death, for example, he leaves Dorian a letter in which he argues that "Man belongs to an order of beings whose goal is perfection," that "[t]he way to that perfection is long and hard, narrow and straight," and "[a]ny deviation from that path is sin" (137). He also outlines the consequences of sin in no uncertain terms, drawing a bleak picture of the existence—mortal and post-mortal—of those who fail to follow God's laws with exactness:

> Banishment from the place where God lives is death. By the operations of a natural law, a person who fails to correspond with a celestial environment dies to that environment and must go or be placed in some other, where he can function with that which is about him. God's presence is exalted, holy, glorified. He who is not pure, holy, glorified cannot possibly live there, is dead to that higher world. [...] This is inevitable—it cannot be otherwise. Immutable law decrees it, and not simply the ruling of an allwise power. The soul who fails to attain to the celestial glory, fails to walk in the straight and narrow path which leads to it. Such a person wanders in the by-paths called sin, and no power in the universe can arbitrarily put him in an environment with which he cannot function. 'To be carnally minded is death', said Paul. 'The wages of sin is death', or in other words, he who persistently avoids the Celestial Highway will never arrive at the Celestial Gate. He who works evilly will obtain evil wages. (139 – 140)

Such a bleak view reflects, in some ways, Uncle Zed's upbringing in an era of Mormon history steeped in a belief that a life of strict obedience to God's law—or good works—was more important than one dependent on repentance and faith in Christ's grace. As a student of the JD, Uncle Zed is certainly familiar with the sermons of the "Mormon Reformation" of 1856 – 1857. While not well remembered by most Mormons today, the Reformation was a period of Mormon history marked by the pervasive "notion that wickedness had penetrated the cordon of purity that was supposed to protect" Latter-day Saints from the evils of the world. Consequently, it was a time when a widespread "process of purging the evil elements in their midst" was seen as a solution for bringing about the "purification of every Mormon" and renewing their commitment to righteous living (Taysom 176). According to Stephen Prothero, it was also a time when Mormon temple rites for the salvation of the living and the dead, which were centered on commitments to personal righteousness, seemed to "[edge] out Jesus as the mediator between God and humanity" (183). In a sense, these Reformation-era pioneers viewed salvation through Christ as only "a step (and a relatively minor one) along the road to exaltation to godhood," an eternal "pilgrimage" in which "rites were more important than words, works more important than faith, and (for all practical purposes) the church more important than Jesus" (184). Redemption through Christ, while important to them, "was [then] understood as one scene in the broader drama of the Plan of Salvation." Christ was best viewed not as an intermediary figure on the cross, but "as an example of obedience to God" in the Garden of Gethsemane (185). As a pioneer likely influenced by these teachings, Uncle Zed's call for a life of undeviating righteousness and severe, mortal consequences for the "person [who] wanders in the by-paths called sin" is unsurprising. Nor is it surprising that Dorian, having heard "Uncle Zed [paint] the terrors of sin," has "a dreadful fear of moral wrong doing" and wishes to "live so that he might always be alive to the good and be dead to sin" (203, 140).

While Dorian initially accepts Uncle Zed's views on the "wages of sin," he is forced to re-evaluate them after Carlia runs away from home when she becomes pregnant by Jack Lamont, a local non-Mormon who drugs and rapes her. Without knowing the cause for Carlia's disappearance, Dorian searches for her in sordid, unfamiliar places that cause him to "[sink] to gloomy depths" (167). When he finally discovers a clue to Carlia's whereabouts, it comes with the shocking news of her pregnancy and a subsequent stillbirth (170). Assuming the pregnancy to be the result of consensual sex, Dorian becomes "benumbed" into inactivity (171). His notion of the "wages of sin," nurtured through long discussions with Uncle Zed, renders him incapable of thinking of Carlia as a person. For him, her apparent sexual sin transforms her almost into the embodiment of the sin itself:

> Dorian had not found Carlia Duke; instead, he had found something which appeared to him to be the end of all things. Had he found her dead, in her virginal purity, he could have placed her [...] safely away in his heart and his hopes; but this! ... What more could he now do? (173)

Dorian finds himself in a theological and moral quandary. On the one hand, "[a]s far back in his boyhood as he could remember, he had been taught the enormity of sexual sin," so that the very thought of what Carlia seems to have done "stand[s] as a repellent specter between them." On the other hand, Dorian recognizes his own role in what befell Carlia:

> He remembered how she used to run from him, and then at other times how she would cling to him as if she pleaded for a protection which he had

not given. The weak had reached out to the strong, and the stronger one had failed. If 'remorse of conscience' is hell, Dorian tasted of its bitter depths, for it came to him now that perhaps because of his neglect, Carlia had been led to her fall. (173 – 174)

In recalling his prior rejections of Carlia—motivated, as they were, by his pursuit of higher things—Dorian recognizes that he has grossly misapplied Uncle Zed's teachings and failed to live up to his own ideals. Even with this recognition of error, however, Dorian remains horrified at the thought of loving and marrying Carlia without "her virginal purity."

Gradually, Dorian's horror at Carlia's apparent sin subsides as he earnestly reassesses Uncle Zed's instruction and modifies his personal understanding of Mormon doctrine. After passing a "long night" that seems to be one long "hideous nightmare," Dorian awakes on a Sunday morning only to be unsettled by a "vision" of Uncle Zed raising a hand "in warning against sin." Immediately, though, Dorian "[seems] to hear a voice read" Christ's parable of the lost sheep (175). The parable has an instant effect on Dorian, countering the rigidity of Uncle Zed's teachings and permitting him to recognize Carlia as an individual, not a sin. Dorian's change is not immediate, to be sure, and he continues to doubt, even after he learns of the rape, whether "his love for [Carlia]" will be able to counteract the "repulsion" he feels over the ordeal (190). Carlia, likewise, aware of Uncle Zed's teachings about the "wages of sin," feels unworthy of Dorian's love and compassion. It is only after Dorian admits his own imperfections and asks that they "forget everything else but the fact that [they] love each other" that they begin to find their way out of Uncle Zed's long shadow (197, 215).

In his ambivalence toward Uncle Zed's pioneer-era theology, Dorian looks upon the Mormon past with new eyes. While he continues to affirm the core principles of righteous living, including the reality of sin and the need for repentance, he nevertheless rejects Uncle Zed's Reformation-style dogma that would leave someone like Carlia convinced that she was spiritually dead and hopelessly damned. Interestingly, in the original manuscript of *Dorian*, Dorian's epiphany about the lost sheep happens in a Protestant church, and the voice that speaks the parable is that of a minister. Carlia's pregnancy, likewise, is the result of a consensual affair, rather than rape, which, aside from explaining the inconsistency of the novel's problematic suggestion that Carlia is accountable for her rape, forces Dorian to confront with more immediacy his response to an individual's willful violation of the community's moral boundaries. In both cases, Anderson's original version questions the established boundaries of the Mormon community, raising the possibility that a Protestant "sectarian" could prove an earnest vessel of Christian Truth, and one once guilty of sexual sin—particularly a woman—could be worthy of respect and admiration. Unfortunately, Anderson left no clues for why he rewrote these passages. Perhaps his personal prejudices against Protestants, acquired through his interactions with them as a missionary, got the better of him, or he felt the Protestant setting of Dorian's epiphany pushed his careful critique of Mormon culture and pioneer-era dogma too far and suggested too much. Perhaps he worried that Carlia's consensual relationship with Jack Lamont would make her an unsympathetic character in the puritanical eyes of his Mormon readers, and thus turn them against her. Perhaps the changes were simply the result of a cautious publisher's or editor's request.

Whatever the case may be, one thing Anderson retains in the revised version is Dorian's crucial turn from the dogmatic image of Uncle Zed's raised hand, the symbol of a theology best left in the nineteenth century. By having this critique come through Dorian, a faithful twentieth-century Mormon, Anderson is able to suggest that Mormonism is an adaptive system that has within itself the capacity for its own course corrections. Furthermore, in acquiring this different perspective on sin and its consequences, Dorian rediscovers Jesus and the doctrines of grace and mercy—a rediscovery that parallels Mormonism's own rediscovery of Jesus during the period of transition and assimilation (see Prothero 187). Indeed, as Prothero points out, it was during these years that "Mormons began to consolidate their theology" about Jesus with works like James E. Talmage's *Jesus the Christ* (1915) and LDS First Presidency's statement on "The Father and the Son" (1916), which quietly sifted from Mormon theology radical Reformation-era ideas about Christ, including those that suggested he was a polygamist and father (189 – 190). In its emphasis on Christ's love and compassion, *Dorian* reflects and participates in Mormonism's twentieth-century movement toward an understanding of a salvation and exaltation that relies as much on grace and mercy as it does on good works (see Prothero 191).

CONCLUSION: A DARKLY SENTIMENTAL ALLEY

Nephi Anderson's detractors, of course, never bothered much with *Dorian* and its sophisticated critique of pioneer-era theology. By making *Added Upon* the target of their attacks, they were better able to set Anderson up as a straw man for everything that was supposedly wrong with Mormon fiction. Ironically, the kind of fiction they called for—Karl Keller, for instance, sought a Mormon fiction that could "excitedly and convincingly […] represent [Mormon] theology in both form and content," depict characters whose "faith is not detached from the natural world," and create "a fictional world in which [the writer's] beliefs are shown to be true"—already existed in *Dorian* (64). Indeed, *Dorian* is so similar thematically (and, to a certain extent, stylistically) to many of the best contemporary Mormon novels—Levi S. Peterson's *The Backslider*, Margaret Blair Young's *Salvador*, Jack Harrell's *Vernal Promises*, Douglas H. Thayer's *The Tree House*, and Todd Robert Petersen's *Rift*—that it would not be altogether inappropriate to honor it with the distinction of being the first modern Mormon novel.

With that possibility in mind, it is tempting to end with a scene from *Dorian,* altered slightly to imagine what would happen if Dorian Trent met his creator's chief detractor in a darkly sentimental alley of "unfleshed ideas and emotions." The scene is gritty and visceral, not "vague," "maudlin," or very "tract-like" (see Keller 63). Sweet Brother Anderson, I'm sure, would not approve:

> The accusing mouth closed there, closed by the mighty impact of Dorian's fist. The blood spurted from a gashed lip, and Mr. [Keller] tried to defend himself. Again Dorian's stinging blow fell upon the other's face. [Keller] was lighter than Dorian, but he had some skill as a boxer which he tried to bring into service; but Dorian, mad in his desire to punish, with unskilled strength fought off all attacks. They grappled, struggled, and fell, to arise again and give blow for blow. It was all done so suddenly, and the fighting was so fierce, that Dorian's fellow travelers did not get to the scene before [Karl Keller] lay prone on the ground from Dorian's finishing knockout blow.
>
> "Damn him!" said Dorian, as he shook himself back into a somewhat normal condition and spat red on the ground. "He's got just a little of what's been coming to him for a long time. Let him alone. He's not seriously hurt. Let's go." (205)

WORKS CITED

Anderson, Nephi. *Dorian*. Salt Lake City: Bikuben Publishing Company, 1921. Print.

Arrington, Leonard J. and Davis Bitton. *The Mormon Experience: A History of the Latter-day Saints*. New York: Alfred A. Knopf, 1979. Print.

Cracroft, Richard H. "Nephi, Seer of Modern Times: The Home Literature Novels of Nephi Anderson." *BYU Studies* 25.2 (1985): 1 – 13. Print.

Cracroft, Richard H. and Neal E. Lambert. "Introduction." *A Believing People: Literature of the Latter-day Saints*. eds. Cracroft and Lambert. Provo: Brigham Young UP, 1974. Print.

de Schweinitz, Rebecca. "Preaching the Gospel of Church and Sex: Mormon Women's Fiction in the LDS *Young Woman's Journal*, 1889 – 1910." *Dialogue: A Journal of Mormon Thought* 33.4 (Winter 2000): 27 – 54. Print.

"Editor's Table." Rev. of *Dorian*, by Nephi Anderson. *Improvement Era* Jan. 1922: 361. Print.

England, Eugene. "Faithful Fiction." Rev. of *Greening Wheat: Fifteen Mormon Stories*, ed. by Levi S. Peterson; *Summer Fire*, by Douglas H. Thayer; and *Zinnie Stokes, Zinne Stokes*. *Dialogue: A Journal of Mormon Thought*. 18.4 (1985): 196 – 200. Print.

Flake, Kathleen. *The Politics of American Religious Identity: The Seating of Senator Reed Smoot, Mormon Apostle*. Chapel Hill: The U of North Carolina P, 2004. Print.

Geary, Edward A. "The Poetics of Provincialism: Mormon Regional Fiction." *Dialogue: A Journal of Mormon Thought*. 11.2 (1978): 15 – 24. Print.

Grant, Heber J. "To Elder Nephi Anderson." 26 October 1922. MS. Nephi Anderson Collection. Chuch History Lib., Salt Lake City.

Hoyt, Amy and Sara M. Patterson. "Mormon Masculinity: Changing Gender Expectations in the Era of Transition from Polygamy to Monogamy, 1890 – 1920." *Gender & History*, 23.1 (2011): 72 – 91. Print.

Keller, Karl. "The Example of Flannery O'Connor." *Dialogue: A Journal of Mormon Thought*. 9.4 (1975): 62 – 71. Print.

Mauss, Armand. *The Angel and the Beehive: The Mormon Struggle with Assimilation.* Urbana, IL: U of Illinois P, 1994. Print.

"Nephi Anderson" (obituary). *Improvement Era* 26.4 (1923): 372 – 375. Print.

"Nephi Anderson Called by Death" (obituary). *Box Elder News* 28.79 (1923): 1. Print.

Podhorny, Ole. *Christian Nephi Anderson: Popular "Mormon" Author of Norwegian Origin.* Diss. U of Oslo, 1980. Print.

Prothero, Stephen. *American Jesus: How the Son of God Became a National Icon.* New York: Farrar, Straus and Giroux, 2003. Print.

Shipps, Jan. *Mormonism: The Story of a New Religious Tradition.* Urbana: U of Illinois P, 1985. Print.

Taysom, Stephen C. *Shakers, Mormons, and Religious Worlds: Conflicting Visions, Contested Boundaries.* Bloomington: Indiana UP, 2010. Print.

Yorgason, Ethan R. *Transformation of the Mormon Cultural Region.* Urbana: U of Illinois P, 2003. Print.

INTEGRATING THE "BEST BOOKS"

INTERWAR INTELLECTUALISM AND EXTRATEXTUALITY IN
NEPHI ANDERSON'S *DORIAN*

MASON ALLRED

The twentieth century began with Mormonism being forced into the limelight. With the problematic appointment of Reed Smoot as the first Mormon senator, the stage was set for a reexamination of "this most strange and peculiar faith" (qtd. in Flake 100). How, if at all, did Mormons fit into the nation and world at large? As if striking the tuning fork of assimilation and listening for resonance in Mormon thought, a generation of academically trained leaders of the Church also set their minds to work out the place of Mormon thought within a wider intellectual framework. The first few decades of the twentieth century bear this significant trend of intellectually and culturally locating Mormonism within a broader context. Major figures forming a constellation around this drive to integrate, or even circumscribe, Mormonism include John A. Widtsoe, James E. Talmage, and B.H. Roberts, among others. Their influential work engendered a new rationality in Mormon intellectual history, which can be characterized by an increased awareness of secular knowledge and a sustained effort to reconcile such with Mormon faith-based knowledge.

Their work seemed the inevitable outcome of following the admonition of the D&C to seek wisdom "out of the best books" and to "seek learning, even by study and also by faith" (D&C 88:118). Widtsoe, Talmage, and Roberts loom large in the phase of Mormon intellectual history labeled "the stage of creative adaptation" by Leonard Arrington, and characterized by "the adaptation of the doctrines and practices of the Mormons to the secular world in which they live[d]" (20 – 21). This experimental stage of acculturation also gave birth to a series of sincere attempts at a Mormon "Home Literature."

The drive to intellectualize and historicize the Mormon worldview was emblematic of the historical context, within which Nephi Anderson's final novel, *Dorian* (1921), was published. Reading the refraction of this cultural milieu through the formal attributes of Anderson's novel attests to the embedded location of the novel in its historical moment. Indeed, this essay will serve to highlight the structural and narratological ways in which *Dorian* stages this cultural moment of (con)textualizing Mormon thought and life. The *Bildungsroman* account of Dorian's development allows for a sense of exploring and integrating new knowledge as an individual journey. This is partly due to the plasticity of the novel as a modern form. In a Bakhtinian sense, *Dorian* exploits the very quality that is distinctive of the novel: its capacity to incorporate a diversity of forms and texts within the narrative (7). This feature is repeated throughout *Dorian* and parallels the textual citation and integration in the intellectual writings of Widtsoe, Talmage, and Roberts.

In light of the burgeoning new Mormon rationality, the precarious Mormon navigation of identity and culture at large is staged, in *Dorian*, as deeply intertwined with doctrine and as a series of textual integrations. This provides an overarching project of intermingling without losing core identity in faith and remaining, like the protagonist, "proud to be Mormon." However, instead of a mere sustaining of Mormon culture, the novel insists on reaching outside itself, displaying a robust citationality. Much like Dorian, who will need to leave his home and rely on outlying villagers for help in recovering Carlia, the novel relies on a web of extratextual references. On both narrative and formal levels, the novel offers lessons in navigating and exploring the thorny space between Dorian's familiar countryside Mormon life and a series of "others." These others surface in the binaries of mind/body (in books/shoes), Mormon/non-Mormon, faith/science, country/city, and male/female, to name but a few. It is particularly interesting how the novel bridges the borderlands between such binaries through textual citation.

Surprisingly, for a representative work of Home Literature, *Dorian* is incessantly about this space between. Like Uncle Zed, who attempts to filter outside knowledge through the gospel, the novel constantly reaches out to outside texts and spaces of experience. This reflects a contextual milieu of an interwar

Mormonism, which was distinct, yet increasingly aware of its connection to a broader national/world culture.

FITTING MORMON THOUGHT

Shortly after the Great War, Reed Smoot was still busy defending the Church publicly (*New York Times* 12). This was a continuance of the national scandal surrounding his appointment and hearings from 1903 – 1907. Nephi Anderson had even outlined the events of the Smoot affair in the 1916 edition of his historical primer, *A Young Folks' History of The Church of Jesus Christ of Latter-day Saints*. The Smoot hearings served to make concerns about Mormonism public. Indeed, as Kathleen Flake has observed, "The public participated actively in the proceedings. In the Capitol, spectators lined the halls, waiting for the limited seats in the committee room, and filled the galleries to hear floor debates. For those who could not see for themselves, journalists and cartoonists depicted each day's admission and outrage" (5). The Smoot affair, followed by Senator Smoot's subsequent actions as a senator, provided a political impetus to consider Mormonism, once again, *vis-à-vis* the nation at large.

However, Mormonism was not only being reexamined from the outside. The writings of Widtsoe, Roberts, and Talmage navigated this political wave in an intellectual vein. Widtsoe had already written *Joseph Smith as Scientist* in 1908 and *Rational Theology* in 1915. The former offered itself as an aid for those who were struggling with the "opposition between man-made knowledge and God-made knowledge," the "reconciliation" of which was not "an easy one" (Widtsoe 1). The latter was explicitly based on "fundamental principles that harmonize with the knowledge and reason of man" (iii). B.H. Roberts, the only one of these three to be a "self-taught scholar," (Bitton) vacillated between doctrinal treatises and an expansive historicizing of Mormonism. Roberts's *Book of Mormon Study* and *The Truth, the Way and the Life* (never published in his lifetime), capture the spirit of the times in their rigorous attempts at reconciling Mormon scripture with historical-critical methodology (Madsen). James E. Talmage, after publishing *The Philosophy of Mormonism* (1914), contributed to a delineation of Mormon doctrine against the backdrop of a larger conception of Christology with his seminal work *Jesus the Christ* (1915). The cultural and intellectual work of these men provided various attempts to fit Mormonism into established paradigms, whether theological, historicist, or scientific.

From 1918 – 1919, Talmage also ran columns in the *San Francisco Chronicle* on a diversity of Mormon topics. He compiled and published the essays in book form under the title *The Vitality of Mormonism*. A review in the *Los Angeles Times* quoted Talmage in stating the importance of Mormonism as the necessary supplement to worldly knowledge. "Man can no more be saved by ethics than he can live by bread alone." Talmage saw the contemporary conceptions of moral and ethical conduct as insufficient for the salvation of man. The book was to make the necessary complements to worldly knowledge available. The author of the review also picked up on Talmage's assertion that "the message of Mormonism was of summoning interest in the world today." A later review in the *San Francisco Chronicle* highlighted Talmage's own designation of the "vitality of Mormonism" in its impeccable track record and ability to constantly grow.

Anderson's novel seems to realize this growing awareness of the vitality of the Church. In Talmage's book, the vitality was evidenced by the continuous expansion of church membership at home and abroad. This plasticity of the Church to incorporate disparate peoples into one body is paralleled in the novel form of *Dorian*. The constant incorporation of non-Mormon sources into a distinctly Mormon worldview carries the narrative. The dramatic events between the characters coming into contact with each other and outsiders are the narrative counterparts to Dorian's life mission to integrate faith and science. His wish is to continue the work of the novel itself in marrying texts outside the faith with those within.

ENCOUNTERING THE OTHER

Anderson was no stranger to such integration. He was involved in multiple ecclesiastical missions abroad and worked in Utah's education system. His life was an intertwining of the gospel and higher learning, the sacred and the secular. Far from the first to investigate such integration, Anderson duly recognized a lineage of learned Mormons by tipping his hat to Orson Pratt and Orson Spencer in the novel. These and others had already made advances in fusing scientific and rational thought into Mormon understanding. With mentions of Drummond's *Natural Law in the Spiritual World*, he also indicates important milestones in this project outside the faith, at once entertaining and educating his audience. Anderson explored this integrative tendency in his writing with didactic force. Literature provided a medium of hope for the further intellectual development of his co-religionists.

This project of a Mormon *Bildung* is encapsulated in the figure of Dorian, who must learn to navigate the city, the opposite sex, love, education, and sin, all while maintaining his religion. By venturing into these realms,

Dorian is faced with the difficult task of modernity: situating one's own identity within society at large. It was the same hallmark of modernity, in the collapsing of geographic space, which brought the isolated Utah so close to the rest of the nation in the political and cultural arenas. Necessitating examinations of faith and assimilation, modernity thrust itself upon the Mormons. Dorian's proximity to and reliance on the city is likewise evident in the construction of his identity, and this relationship provides the first textual citations in the story.

This modern notion of navigating the world outside oneself is evidenced in Dorian's consumer trips to the city. It is perhaps appropriate that the novel opens with Dorian strolling the city streets, as a flaneur of sorts. Dorian is flaneur-like in his consumption of books and candy and in his detached stance to the city and its pleasures. However, unlike the flaneur roaming the city in Baudelaire, Benjamin, or Poe (Benjamin 79), Dorian's experience with the material reality of modernity often underscores his ignorance and asserts his solitude. Yet, despite his lack of knowledge about automobiles and moving picture shows, Dorian is connected to a broader world through the "imagined communities" of established readership (Anderson, B. 25). Selectively partaking of the city, yet remaining distinctly separate is the modus operandi of Dorian and *Dorian*. They both pick and choose of the best texts to "use" in their construction of self.

During the shopping trip, Dorian enthusiastically peruses the available books. "Here were books he had read about, but had not read—and the prices!" (5). At this point the literature of the world is named and encapsulated in the actual tangible books themselves. Charles Dickens, William M. Thackeray, Humphrey Ward, Margaret Deland, Daniel Defoe, and William H. Prescott; they all stand there, at Dorian's disposal. The books mentioned in the opening scene carry out this didactic function of putting a country kid into contact with the stories and ideas of the world. It is through familiarity with the great works of the world that Dorian is metaphorically brought out of the country.

These citations are equally placed at the reader's disposal. We, as readers, are also invited to recognize and/or become curious about the references throughout the novel, for these texts might also enlarge our understanding and allow for our own integration. In order to achieve this double objective, the novel continues with the constant reaching out to extratextual citation. This seems symptomatic of a Mormon literature, which, in the hands of Nephi Anderson, ventures outside the Mormon countryside into the literature and knowledge of the world through citation.

Operating equally as a flaneur of available sources, of which he makes his personal selections, Anderson's experience as an editor is evidenced in his ability to compile, include, and reference a myriad of texts. This tendency to cite provides the novel's extratextual gesturing and continually highlights a heavy reliance on texts to make sense of the novel's characters. Rather than a disjointed montage of colliding texts, Anderson's awareness of world literature, as well as Mormon scripture, is tactfully presented as harmony. Anderson's erudition is also evidenced in the life ambition of Zed, which is bequeathed upon Dorian. This aim is nothing short of the complete integration of science and faith.

Integration becomes increasingly necessary in the novel as Dorian is exposed to the various "others" mentioned earlier. The element of the other in the dichotomies of the text is generally introduced through not-so-subtle characterization. Mildred exposes Dorian to art, high school offers secular knowledge, and Jack Lamont presents the dark underworld of gentile city life. From within the country, Zed lectures on a faithful approach to science and Carlia presents the immediate concerns of practical and emotional life. In other words, if Zed were the books, Carlia would definitely be the shoes in Dorian's initial dilemma of consumption and attention. Each of these exposures can be jarring and requires cognitive integration, a certain bridging into Dorian's worldview.

Dorian's mother "mildly resented" his formal education, as it "seemed to intrude on her old-established ideas" (53). Such discomfort necessitated assuaging by Dorian, yet provided release from insulated provinciality. Paralleling the early scene of Dorian saving Carlia, who ventured across the stream on a rickety stick, the bridges spanning science and faith, or any of the above-mentioned binaries, are much broader, yet equally treacherous. The real task for Zed and Dorian is textually fitting their Mormon worldview in relation to new knowledge and experience.

A real credit of the novel is its refusal to exclusively deal with integration on either the intellectual or dramatic level alone. Both realms are problematized and receive explanatory integration through extratextuality. We witness this as Dorian attempts to integrate new intellectual and emotional experiences into his field of understanding. When he begins to feel something akin to Lois Lowry's "stirrings," his inner passions are integrated into a larger scheme of loving all the creations of God. Dorian could love Mildred "as he loved his mother, or as he loved the flowers, the clear-flowing water, the warm sun and the blue sky. He could at least cast adoring eyes up to her as he did to the stars at night" (41 – 42). As a sublimation of his feelings, this passage not only serves to naturalize his surfacing emotions, but simultaneously integrates the city-girl and unfamiliar sexuality into a broad synthesis of accepted expressions of love. However, it is William Wordsworth's "trailing clouds of glory," later set off in quotation marks (40), that is employed to semantically integrate the innocent youthful brand of love, which Anderson's readers might otherwise "scoff" at. The bridges of integration that are of interest here are not those that force Dorian into an isolated interiority, but those that, like the Wordsworth quote, reach outside the novel to create meaning through other texts.

By placing cited texts in *Dorian*, the novel is able to forge its own identity among the extra texts yet not entirely detached from them. Reaching outside the novel are numerous citations, which at times can even come across as superfluous, like Ralph Waldo Emerson's "hitch your wagon to a star," quoted by Zed while lecturing Dorian (61). Of course, the name of Dorian, appearing even in the sentence "where should we hang Dorian's picture?" points to Oscar Wilde's work (42). This wording (although it does not refer to a picture depicting Dorian himself), along with the discussion of Dorian being both young and old in his boy/manhood, creates a possible intertextuality with *The Picture of Dorian Gray*. The appearances of other texts in *Dorian* multiply the literary experience of the novel by leading the reader and providing the nourishment for Dorian's intellectual growth.

MODELING INTEGRATION

At the very least, these citations always carry the function of getting the reader out of the otherwise enclosed diegesis by tapping other archives of textual experience. All this extratextuality also requires merging and narrative incorporation. In a dialectical way, the texts become objects that the subject (Dorian, reader, novel itself) must synthesize or, as I have chosen to call it here, integrate. A standing objective of the novel is precisely such gelling of texts. Moments of free indirect speech and interior monologue also serve to integrate speech itself into one reported experience for the reader. The union of distinct voices into one interiorized stream of information for the reader supports integration on the level of form.

For instance, as Dorian speaks with Mrs. Brown, their conversation gels into one block of freely reproduced speech. "Yes, Mildred was very ill. Mrs. Brown was plainly worried. Could he or his mother do anything to help? No; only to lend their faith and prayers. Would he come into the sick room to see her for a few minutes? Yes, if she desired it" (63). Quotation marks and enunciation are elided in this merged body of expression. It is the same way with disparate texts that are continually juxtaposed. The use and positioning of these texts allows meaning to run across the edges into the next text. While speaking of love stories and literature, Zed then states "here's the most wonderful love story ever written" and retrieves a copy of the D&C. This genre-bending and cross-stitching brings textual realms into conversation with each other in a unifying way.

The same bleeding between discursive realms occurs when Dorian is described as reading "Howell's [*sic*] easy-going novels" (71), and at other times captivated by *Lorna Doone* or *Ben Hur*. The novel's following paragraph outlines Dorian's relationship to Darwin, Huxley, Ingersoll, and Paine. It describes his increased study of Ingersoll and Darwin, which he "read carefully." In these few lines, the reading practices of a young Dorian are delineated. Dorian's consumption of texts is shown to require careful integration. For Dorian, any disturbance or lack of reconciliation between his worldview and these works must be due to a mere "lack of knowledge" (73). This is an important detail underpinning Dorian's reading strategies and informing his subsequent integration. While he certainly reads for leisure, he explicitly situates himself in relation to serious or threatening works. Dorian feels his need for increased knowledge through reading Darwin. When reading Robert Ingersoll, Dorian immediately begins mentally refuting Ingersoll's claims.

Dorian's strategy of consuming and synthesizing various texts is verbally expressed by Zed, who wants to "harmonize the great body of truth coming from any and every source" (74). The subsequent scene, depicting Dorian and Uncle Zed discussing Dorian's future, provides an important narrative turning point in this regard. After Uncle Zed extends the challenge to Dorian to complete this great work, Zed immediately begins marshaling texts into their discussion through skillful citation. By quoting Alexander Pope, Alfred Tennyson, Psalms 139:7, Acts 17:38, and Ecclesiastes 12:1, Zed arrives at a textual confluence that endows his conversation with meaning through textual relations. He has also just simulated for Dorian the work of textual *bricolage*, taking what he needs from an archive of texts to arrive at a functioning integration. He has introduced "other" texts and integrated them into his own explanation.

Zed navigates these various texts as a compiler—a keen editor who can call on texts of the world to nuance, substantiate, or even shape his arguments. A key function of Zed's character is to break Dorian and the reader out of the parochial worldview of small-town, insulated Mormonism into a broader panoramic view. In the novel, this rhetorical strategy never cuts ties with representation of the inherently beautiful and privileged attributes of Mormonism or country life. This attachment can be, like the character of Dorian, a bit tiresome in its "short-sightedness" (Cracroft 11). Largely a work of its time, in its reaching outside and positioning Mormon literature and thought within a wider view of the world, *Dorian* maintains a distinct quality of being for Mormons and by a Mormon. However, the implicit notion that coming up against "others" and seeking for proper integration can lead to enlightened living is a striking feature in *Dorian*. Additionally, the impression that individuals might make sense of themselves and the world through texts hints at an awareness of the force and ubiquity of textuality, prefiguring the linguistic turn.

Could, however, a plurality of readers, like the multiplicity of texts referenced in *Dorian*, be sutured into such a work? Could the novel conceivably contribute to an imagined community beyond Mormons? Rather than a work inviting the outsider in, Dorian often slips into a Home-Literature stance of integrating Mormon reading subjects into a broader realm of textual understanding. Similarly, although Talmage, Roberts, and Widtsoe extended their work to the outside through proselytizing efforts, the bulk of their influence lies in repositioning Mormon understanding from within. All these authors knew their audience well and constructed their integrations accordingly.

Part and parcel with Anderson's project of textual integration is the familiarization of his audience with such texts in an entertaining way. This literary education would hopefully lead to a literature that was not only "home" as "a credit to you and to the land and people that produced you, but likewise a boon and benefaction to mankind" (Whitney). Rather than adept integration of texts into Mormon narratives, perhaps a plasticity appealing to the integration of a wider gamut of readers is the missed opportunity of such a textual strategy.

WORKS CITED

Anderson, Benedict. *Imagined Communities: Reflections on the Origin and Spread of Nationalism*. New York: Verso, 2006.

Arrington, Leonard. "The Intellectual Tradition of the Latter-day Saints." *Dialogue* 4 (Spring 1969): 13 – 26.

Bachtin, Michail. *The Dialogic Imagination*. Ed. Michael Holquist. Trans. Caryl Emerson and Michael Holquist. Austin: University of Texas, 1983.

Benjamin, Walter. *The Writer of Modern Life: Essays on Charles Baudelaire*. Ed. Michael W. Jennings. Trans. Howard Eiland, et al. Cambridge, Mass.: Harvard University Press, 2006.

Bitton, Davis. "B.H. Roberts and Book of Mormon Scholarship: Early Twentieth Century: Age of Transition." *Journal of Book of Mormon Studies* 8:2 (Fall 1999): 60 – 69.

Cracroft, Richard H. "Nephi, Seer of Modern Times: The Home Literature Novels of Nephi Anderson," *BYU Studies*, 1985: 10 – 11.

Flake, Kathleen. *The Politics of American Religious Identity: the Seating of Senator Reed Smoot, Mormon Apostle*. Chapel Hill: University of Carolina Press, 2004.

The *Los Angeles Times*. Oct. 12, 1919: III34

Madsen, Truman G. "B.H. Roberts and the Book of Mormon." *In Book of Mormon Authorship: New Light on Ancient Origins*, ed. Noel B. Reynolds (Provo, UT: Religious Studies Center, Brigham Young University, 1982): 7–32.

The *New York Times*. "Defends Mormon Church." Nov. 12, 1919: 12.

The *San Francisco Chronicle*. "Saturday Book Reviews." Sep. 20, 1919: 9

Sherlock, Richard. "'We Can See No Advantage to a Continuation of the Discussion:' The Roberts/Smith/Talmage Affair." *Dialogue* 13, (Fall 1980): 63 – 78.

Whitney, Orson. "Home Literature." *The Contributor*. July, 1888. Retrieved December 20, 2013, from mldb.byu.edu/homelit.htm.

Widtsoe, John A. *Joseph Smith as Scientist: A Contribution to Mormon Philosophy.* Salt Lake City: The General Board of the Young Men's Mutual Improvement Association, 1908.

Widtsoe, John A. "Rational Theology as Taught by The Church of Jesus Christ of Latter-day Saints." Utah: Deseret News, 1915.

THIS IS NOT A PHOTOGRAPH

NEPHI ANDERSON'S *DORIAN* AS A SORT OF LDS *SONS AND LOVERS*;
OR A PORTRAIT OF THE MORMON SOLIPSIST AS A YOUNG MAN

JACOB BENDER

The wonder of Nephi Anderson's *Dorian* is that it isn't called *Carlia*, who is arguably the far more interesting character. In Carlia we have someone straight out of a Thomas Hardy novel, a Mormon *Tess of the d'Urbervilles*: She is a poor, rural, working-class farm girl forced by poverty and circumstance to forsake any chance of higher learning and a better life, instead to toil obscurely for her broken and indifferent family. She is ignored by her would-be lover and her spirit cracks under the constant grind and toil. In a moment of weakness she is seduced, violated, and disgraced by an unscrupulous interloper. Ashamed, she runs away into even greater penury and misery, her child dies soon after birth, and she is left alone to suffer in the dead of winter. As compared to Dorian, she is the more fascinating, pathos-ridden character, but Anderson didn't give us *Carlia*. He gave us *Dorian*, and hovering around the peripheries of *Dorian* is a more interesting novel wherein Carlia's suffering resonates more profoundly and speaks to the human condition more deeply than golden boy Dorian's good fortune ever does.

For Dorian *is* the golden child; everything works out for him. In school, as the novel reports, "Boys came to him for help in problems, and the younger girls chattered about him with laughing eyes and tossing curls" (53). His mother is more bemused and indulgent than angered at his self-focus. The wise-old-wizard archetype Uncle Zed takes him under his wing, bequeaths him his massive library at his death, and hand-picks him to carry on his work ("You are the man to do this, Dorian—you, not I," he says [74]) under his "mantle" ("The mantle of Brother Zed seems to have fallen on Dorian Trent," says the Bishop [133]). Dorian's first love appears at his home without any sort of activity or agency on his part and, what's more, she reciprocates his love without condition. All good things flow unto him, an individual who is showered with gifts and powers less due to his abilities than because he is the protagonist.

To take a more high-literary example, Dorian can be compared to Paul Morel, the protagonist in D.H. Lawrence's *Sons and Lovers*.[1] Consider the broad strokes both protagonists are painted in: Both Paul and Dorian are hard-working working-class sons of mothers with whom they have an almost uncomfortably close relationship.[2] Both are treated as prodigiously gifted; both become entangled in relationships with not one, but two different girls; and both are unconscious solipsists. That is, Paul and Dorian are men who are only sure of their own existence, and therefore relate to the world only as it relates directly back to them. For example, the original working title of *Sons and Lovers* was *Paul Morel* (just as Anderson's novel is simply *Dorian*), emphasizing how the novel's world focuses solely around how it relates solely to Paul—just as *Dorian*'s world relates solely to Dorian.

Sons and Lovers is somewhat disquieting because of this lack of sympathy and understanding in Paul's worldview: when he breaks up with his first lover to move on to his next, the discussion is rarely on how *she* feels or deals with the breakup, only on how the breakup affects Paul. Paul hates his father, an imperfect man who nonetheless has suffered and sacrificed more for his family than Paul ever will. When Paul's mother dies in the novel's finale, the ending focuses on how *Paul* changes and moves on as a result of this event, not on what her death may mean to herself or anyone else. The narcissism in Paul's worldview is solipsistic in nature, and all the more insidious because his solipsism is evidently unconscious. Lawrence, by all evidence, *intends* for us to identify with and root for Paul Morel, not critique him for no more profound reason than because Paul is the protagonist.

---

1.   Given how Anderson and Lawrence are contemporaries, it behooves us to compare the two.

2.   Dorian even compares his first romantic love to his mother's maternal affection, musing, "But there could be no harm in loving [Meredith] as he loved his mother" (40).

Similarly, Anderson apparently wants us to root for Dorian and be happy when he succeeds simply because the novel is entitled *Dorian*. Consider the novel's near-relentless Dorian-centric worldview: right from the first chapter, his inclination is to spend his mother's money on his leisure activities, not for his necessities, as she had directed. Dorian ignores her instructions to spend the money *on himself*, for *his own good*, specifically on a nice new pair of dress shoes. But, to follow those instructions, Dorian would first have to imagine that others view his relationship with the world differently from how he views it himself, and that perhaps they can see benefits that he cannot. This is a leap he is not ready to make at this point in the novel. Thus, even when it's for his own good, Dorian has no room for non-Dorian-centric viewpoints.

Likewise, Dorian's desire for Prescott's *Conquest of Peru* is based not on a feeling for an oppressed people, but "vaguely as a dim fairy tale … the whole story, beautifully and minutely told"; that is, he wants to learn from Pizarro only how that "bad, bold Spaniard" can affect *him*, not how Pizarro affected the Incas (7). As for his first love Mildred, Dorian "placed … Mildred, safely away in his heart and his hopes" (173), as though Mildred were a possession for him to keep. Dorian enacts this possession when he hangs in his room one of her paintings, replacing an earlier painting that represented his ideal woman. Mildred has become Dorian's new ideal in this exchange, but Dorian is still only engaging with her as she relates to *him* and *his* ideals, not with who she is as an autonomous, separate human being.

Now, to be fair, Dorian also displays selfless tendencies from the first chapter, as when he first saves young Carlia from drowning; however, after saving her, his focus is on the loss of his new books to the river. There is hope from the beginning that Dorian will overcome his solipsism, but he is a work in progress.

Still, let's not pick on Dorian too harshly. Anderson is presenting to us a common type: an aspiring professional destined to become highly educated and well versed in Church doctrine. He is a charming, amiable, athletic fellow groomed from a young age to be a missionary assistant to the president, an elders quorum president, and bishop. He is expected to marry young and well, and is successful at everything he does because he enjoys the approbation of God.

For much of the novel, Dorian is the rural 1920s version of this type. He is faithful, he studies his scriptures, and he is a true believer—but he is focused on himself. And perhaps Anderson's genius in *Dorian* is how he suggests this type is not yet a true Christian, a sort of Pip figure. Like the protagonist from *Great Expectations*, Dorian is a fundamentally good and agreeable man who receives fortune without merit. By novel's end, he recognizes that he is a short-sighted fool, one who in his self-focus has failed to notice how others are living their lives. Hence, Pip is surprised at the novel's end when, once he at last decides to propose to Biddy, he finds that she has become engaged to Joe on her own. Dorian's arc ends more happily than Pip's, but Dorian must still follow the same trajectory. He must learn to abandon his own solipsism if he is to become a true Christian. For this abandonment to occur, Dorian must learn to follow someone else's story instead of his own. That someone else is Carlia.

Anderson, then, does what apparently never occurred to Lawrence to do: namely, Anderson shakes his protagonist awake from his own solipsism. *Dorian* is certainly a *bildungsroman*,[3] but the manner by which Dorian must come of age is distinctly different from Carlia's. Carlia learns to find a core sense of self, breaking free of the crushing expectations placed upon her by always thinking of others and not herself. Dorian is the inverse: he already *has* a stable sense of self and must now learn to think of others.

Carlia could have been more interesting than *Dorian*, though perhaps too voyeuristic, too far removed from us for us to understand our own complicity in her destiny. But as Dorian learns to read *Carlia*, he *does* learn of both his complicity and responsibility toward her. Anderson, by showing us how Dorian breaks out of his solipsism, shows us how to break free of our own as well.

But Dorian's preparation for reading Carlia's novel begins far earlier. Meredith is the first to try to break Dorian out of his self-focus; in the middle of chapter three, early in their relationship, she and Dorian have the following fascinating exchange while she is painting a landscape scene of a sunset:

> "Tell me which is redder, the real or the picture?" she asked.
> Dorian looked critically back and forth. "The sky is redder," he decided.
> "And yet if I make my picture as red as the sky naturally is, many people would say that it is too red to be true. I'll risk it anyway."
> Then she carefully laid on a little more color.
> "Nature itself, our teacher told us, is always more intense than any representation of nature." (29 – 30)

That final line is a lesson Dorian has yet to learn, that nature is more intense than representation. We must remember that Dorian's relationship with

---

3. The repeated references to *David Copperfield*, that arch-*bildungsroman* of the Victorians, certainly telegraphs that message.

Conquest of Peru isn't one of encountering the historical intensity of brutal colonization, but rather as "a dim fairy tale," distant, ephemeral, unreal. The gravity of the Spanish conquest hasn't struck him—but then, if we understand Meredith right, *nothing* has struck Dorian quite yet. He will continue to deal in much more safe, containable, and un-intense representations for chapters to come, from the books in Uncle Zed's library to Meredith's painting, which will take precedence over Meredith herself in Dorian's imagination.

What Meredith wants Dorian to do is look closer at what is *being* represented, not just the representation itself. Consider the following exchange between them:

> "What—what is an artist?"
> "An artist is one who has learned to see more than other people can in the common things about them." (32)

For Meredith, what sets an artist apart is not skill but perception; to be a true artist, one must learn to see more than others see. This deeper perception is a lesson Dorian learns when, in his search for Carlia, he follows her trail more closely than her own father does. For example, when Dorian, in search of missing Carlia, reads from the hotel register "Carlia Davis," he is able to determine that Carlia, "unexperienced in the art of subterfuge, had started to write her name, and had gotten to the D in Duke, when the thought of disguise had come to her. Yes; there was an unusual break between that first letter and the rest of the name" (166). This seemingly innocuous moment of detective work is important in the evolution of Dorian; he is trying to understand Carlia—how she thinks and why. He looks beyond the mere signature to see what the signature *means*. She is no longer simply one of the supporting characters in his life; Dorian is now following her story, not his own. We are reading Dorian reading Carlia.

This conception of artistic perception as character growth makes Meredith positively Joycean; consider that *other* twentieth-century *bildungsroman*, James Joyce's *A Portrait of the Artist as a Young Man*. In *Portrait* too, a solipsistic young man must learn to see outside himself; throughout the first four of the novel's five chapters, protagonist Stephen Daedalus is firmly entrenched in his own worldview, engaging with the world only as it relates to him. For example, while it is revealed that Stephen's father has fallen into financial troubles, the troubles' sources are never mentioned, only acknowledged, in a side conversation Stephen overhears; for Stephen, what's relevant is not what the problems are, only that they exist. He isn't interested in his father's narrative, except in how it affects his own. At the end of the second chapter, Stephen is visiting prostitutes to satisfy his own urges, and at the end of chapter three, Stephen is thinking of becoming a priest to satisfy his need for repentance. But whether Stephen's focus is on his urges or his sins, his focus remains primarily on himself.

Then at the end of chapter four, something remarkable happens: While Stephen ponders whether to become a priest, he stumbles upon a girl walking along the surf of the beach. She barely acknowledges him. This becomes an epiphanic moment in Stephen's life, for he has beheld the intensity of someone else's experience—someone living an entire life outside of his own. "Heavenly God!" he cries. He decides to become an artist so as to see, like Meredith, more than is commonly seen. Near the novel's close, Stephen writes, "Welcome, O life! I go to encounter for the millionth time the reality of experience." For Joyce, an artist recognizes the intensity of life and experience. Meredith also recognizes life's intensity through artistic perception. She is in fact training Dorian to look more closely, to experience life more intensely, that is, to think more like an artist—like Stephen Daedalus before him.

But Dorian, by chapter three, has still not learned to look more closely. For example, he protests of Meredith's painting:

> "You haven't put that tree in the right place," he objected! "and you have left out that house altogether."
>
> "This is not a photograph," she answered. "I put in my picture only that which I want there. The tree isn't in the right place, so I moved it. The house has no business in the picture because I want it to represent a scene of wild, open lonesomeness. I want to make the people who look at it feel so lonesome that they want to cry!" (33)

Dorian protests that the painting is not a correct representation, for surface-level representations—the world through his eyes—are still the only level upon which Dorian operates. She counters that her painting is representing not the landscape, but *loneliness itself.* Dorian cannot see the loneliness in the painting, which foreshadows the loneliness he will later fail to recognize in Carlia. Meredith, then, with her statement, "This is not a photograph," is calling upon Dorian to take a more active role in examining the intensity of the "wild, open lonesomeness" before him instead of passively waiting for things to be represented for him. For Dorian to become a better Christian, Meredith must first make Dorian a better artist.

Meredith begins the process, but it is Carlia who expedites it. In contrast to Meredith's gentle prodding, Carlia throws cold water on Dorian's self-perception when she declares:

> " ... I—hate you!" ...
> "What have I done that you should hate me?" he asked as quietly as his trembling voice would allow.
> "Done? nothing. It's what you haven't done. What have you done to re-pay—my—Oh, God, I can't stand it—I can't stand it!"
> [...]
> She hated him. He had not thought that possible. (148 – 149)

And why *would* Dorian have thought that possible? He has been, up to this point, a thorough solipsist, one who only engages with the world as it directly affirms his own existence; for the solipsist, if there's no self, then there's no existence, so therefore how can Carlia hate the foundation of all existence?

It takes Carlia running away to make Dorian suddenly and painfully aware that there is a narrative outside himself. He engages with her now not on his terms, but on hers—he goes out in search of her, tracing her steps, reading her clues, piecing together her narrative. He has switched genres, from some self-involved *bildungsroman* to a romance; Dorian's focus has shifted from himself onto Carlia. So perhaps, in a sense, we *do* get Carlia's novel—but we are reading Dorian reading it. Anderson via Dorian trains us to get outside our own narrow tales and into others', to de-privilege our centrality in our own narrow novel, and instead join the far larger and more interesting novel taking place all around us. This transformation in Dorian's reading abilities reaches its apotheosis when he helps the poor family who had sheltered Carlia to have a real Christmas; he has helped fulfill *their* Christmas story, not just his own.

To give Anderson credit where credit's due: Even today (let alone in rural 1920s Utah), there is a stigma in certain LDS circles against marrying a woman impregnated outside of marriage. A "fallen woman" does not normally bring with her the happy ending promised to the golden boy. But Dorian has left that type behind for a happy ending available only to the passionate, the suffering, the redeemed—for Carlia. *Carlia*, finally, is the more engaging novel. And Dorian's shift in focus from himself to others brings him to the more important book. He is thinking more like the true artist as he reads those around him; he is losing himself to find himself; he is behaving more like a true Christian.

THE DEAD VIRGIN AND THE ACCIDENTAL WHORE

A. ARWEN TAYLOR

The history of men writing women shows an established tendency to corral female characters to one side of a sexual dichotomy, such that they embody one of two tropes, the angel or the whore. These polarized figures represent men's response to the masculine perception of women's sexuality, which means that women are defined according to their (apparent) sexual availability, both to the male from whose perspective we're currently gazing, and to men in general.[1] Thus we have Eve and Mary (the seductress who lures man into sexual knowingness, and the virgin so pure she gives birth without having sex); Veronica and Betty (the sexy shopaholic who dates widely, and the wholesome, loyal girl next door); the White Swan and the Black Swan; Arabella Donn and Sue Bridehead; Helen Ramirez and Amy Fowler; the list goes on. The angelic woman is pure, good, modest, faithful, and, most critically, sexually restrained, while the whore

---

1.   This dichotomy, which is now widely accepted, has been overtly a concern of feminist thought at least since Sherry Orter's essay "Is Female to Male as Nature Is to Culture?" (reprinted in *Woman, Culture, and Society*, ed. Michelle Zimbalist Rosaldo and Louise Lamphere, Stanford: Stanford UP, 1974) made the argument that patriarchy tends to place women simultaneously above and below culture. Women are imagined as spiritually and morally superior (angelic) beings who must be protected from the corruption of culture, but also as polluted, fallen, degraded and degrading figures.

character tends to be voluptuous, exotic, irresistible, and sexually flagrant. The male protagonist's desire is fraught as he navigates between these two types: the sexually available woman can never belong exclusively to him, and the woman who can be his exclusively is by nature non-sexual—or worse, if she is convinced to have sex, then she will no longer be the virginal ideal worthy of his desire.[2] Stories that rely on the tension between angel and whore tend most often to show the male protagonist seduced by the latter but desiring the former; the allure of the whore is only a distraction from his pursuit and eventual conquest of the angel.

Nephi Anderson's *Dorian* turns out a few compelling variations on the angel/whore binary, although it remains nonetheless thoroughly invested in its dichotomous logic. Its eponymous protagonist Dorian Trent escapes the dilemma of choosing between the two types of women because the two characters barely overlap as love interests; the story dispatches the angelic Mildred Brown less than a third of the way through the book, leaving the field to the younger, earthier Carlia Duke, who has the space to fall, reform, and eventually be worthy of the male character's affections. Anderson thus makes the "whore" character not only desirable but sympathetic, though he accomplishes this only by consigning her to be restrained, controlled, and domesticated—her lot is to learn to stand in for the dead angel, inadequate though she will always be to the role. Mildred, meanwhile, is frozen in her idealized, pure virginity, always out of reach, to be held forever in a love that will never be sullied with consummation. *Dorian* is a paragon of male wish fulfillment, as its upstanding young male protagonist is able to have it all, enjoying all of his symptoms at once: a virgin to adulate but never touch, and a sexually available wife to have and desire, but to pity rather than admire.

---

2. Freud, in his essay "The Most Prevalent Form of Degradation in Erotic Life," discusses this dichotomous trope as a paradox in the psychology of male desire: a [dysfunctional] man is unable to reconcile desire and love, as his desire is for a sexually debased woman, and his love for a respectable Madonna-figure; he cannot be sexually interested in the woman worthy of his love. Thus Freud reports treating men who were impotent with their spouses, but perfectly virile with their mistresses. ("Über die allgemeinste Erniedrigung des Liebeslebens," *Jahrbuch für psychoanalytische und psychopathologische Forschungen* 4 [1912]: 40 – 50. For discussion, see Irving Singer, *Philosophy of Love: A Partial Summing-Up*, MIT Press 2009, 73 – 75.)

Dorian's feeling for Mildred is perhaps better described as piety than romantic love. It is wholly chaste, and inspired more by her unobtainability than by her attractiveness. The narrator depicts their affection in pre-lapsarian terms, the love felt by two people still young and innocent enough to retain a glimmer of the "glory" of their heavenly home; it is "clean and pure and undefiled by the many worldly elements which often enter into the more mature lovemaking" (40). Knowing her to be "far above him in every way" (40), Dorian does not imagine he will marry her—he does not even dream of any physical manifestation of his love—but he loves her "as he loved his mother, or as he loved the flowers, the clear-flowing water, the warm sun and the blue sky. He could at least cast adoring eyes up to her as he did to the stars at night" (40 – 41). He looks at the stars and thinks of Mildred the way other religious imaginations might look at them and think of God.

The interchangeability in Dorian's affections of mother, lover, and nature might suggest an eroticism to Dorian's love for his mother, except that his love for Mildred is marked specifically by its *a*sexuality; a more apt reading is that both filial and romantic love have taken on the intense but impersonal affect of the natural world. Dorian enjoys the "quiet longing happiness of [Mildred's] absence" just as well as he does the "nervous happiness" he feels in her presence (40); the idea of her, the ache of dwelling on her in her absence, is as pleasurable as her actual company. His desire for her is not one that motivates him toward her, but only toward himself, or rather, an improved self; her (perceived) superiority to him makes him want to "strive to rise to her level" (41). Mildred's person—her body, her presence, her individual being—matters less to her barely-a-romance with Dorian than does his consciousness of her.[3]

---

3. All of this falls comfortably within the Victorian ideal of the "angel in the house," which itself recalls the tradition of courtly love wherein the lover's devotion to his beloved, his worship of her beauty, virtue, and distance, are more meaningful and arguably more pleasurable than it would be to actually achieve and enjoy a relationship with the woman. In courtly love structures, the woman is more fascinating, more admirable and even more womanly, as a distant and abstract ideal for the man to fixate on than as an attainable, individual person with whom he might have, in every sense of the word, intercourse. The trope of the angel in the house grounds the distant beloved in the domestic sphere, where she attends to her male companion's every need with innocence and mildness, and lends some of her sublimity to the house which she elevates into a home. Mrs. Trent fits into the scheme of things Dorian loves precisely because she is able to fulfill this latter role, as a comfort and support and most importantly as the designer of a home with an "air of comfort and refinement about it" (86). It is perhaps disappointing that Dorian's love for his mother is not more personal, that it is of a kind with the way he feels about flowing water or about a girl whose chief attraction is in her distance from him. (For foundational criticism of the "Angel in the House," see Virginia Woolf's "Professions for Women," in *Women and Writing* [San Diego: Mariner Books], 2003.)

After Mildred's death, a grieving Dorian happens upon the summer's first patch of sego lily blossoms and thinks, appreciating their beauty, "How like Mildred they were!" (68). Neither he nor the narrator elaborates on what makes this flower particularly like Mildred; is it their fragility, whiteness, transience, or perhaps the fact that they, like Mildred, are stuck in the dirt, that causes Dorian to draw this connection? But the details of the association are immaterial; Mildred is on Dorian's mind, and it is his habit to mediate his feelings for her through natural imagery. Yet in important ways, she is never herself a part of nature. She transcends nature rather than participating in it as Carlia and Dorian do; she represents *culture*, as opposed to *nature*, particularly in the sense that she comes into Dorian's rustic life from a sophisticated urban environment—she is wealthy, educated, and travelled. She paints landscapes which improve upon the scene they depict, moving trees to the "right place" and telling Dorian that a house visible in the real landscape but not in her painting "has no business being there because I want it to represent a scene of wild, open lonesomeness. I want to make the people who look at it feel so lonesome that they want to cry!" (33). Painting is thus an act of affective interpretation for Mildred, a way of reading a scene for the meanings, especially the emotional meanings, buried therein, waiting for an artist to come draw them out. By Mildred's definition, an artist both "is one who has learned to see more than other people can in the common things about them" (32) and "wants to make people feel like laughing or crying, for then he knows he has reached their soul" (33). The natural scene itself might not have this effect; Mildred defines her artistry as a superiority of perception, rather than creativity, which allows her to find the affect latent in the image, and mediate the natural scene into something sensible to human feeling.

Mildred's early expiration, by some vague, feminine, wasting-away disease, is an appropriate end to a character who seemed barely embodied to begin with; of course an earthly existence would exhaust her. It moreover extends her artistic mediation of nature to humanity and culture, as she transforms from artist to artistry. Susan Gubar and Sandra Gilbert have described a similar process by which Snow White is "killed into art" by her lethal mouthful:

> [D]ead and self-less in her glass coffin, she is an object, to be displayed and desired, patriarchy's marble "opus," the decorative and decorous Galatea with whom every ruler would like to grace his parlor. Thus, when the Prince first sees Snow White in her coffin, he begs the dwarves to give "it" to him as a gift, "for I cannot live without seeing Snow White. I will honor and prize her as my dearest possession." An "it," a possession, Snow White has

become an idealized image of herself, a woman in a portrait like Aurora Leigh's mother, and as such she has definitively proven herself to be patriarchy's ideal woman, the perfect candidate for Queen."[4]

Mildred's fate reverberates remarkably with Snow White's. As she is dying, her room is evacuated of books and artistic materials, and her speech is reduced to a single sentence; the last time Dorian sees her, he finds her "thinner and paler than ever, eyes bigger, hair heavier and more golden," and Dorian is able to enjoy looking on her "angel-face," now "marble-like" (63 – 64). Stripped of her trappings of culture, she is reduced to a body to be admired. Dorian does not visit her again, not even when he learns that the crisis has come and she is on the verge of death. Instead he lingers outside her home until someone comes out and tells him that she has died. Then, "He felt the night wind blow cold down the street, and he saw the storm clouds scuttling along the distant sky. In the deep blue directly above him a star shone brightly, but it only reminded him of what Uncle Zed had said about hitching to a star; yes, but what if the star had suddenly been taken from the sky!" (66). At the critical moment of pathos, Mildred, who has been curiously absent from her own death scene, is projected as a star—beautiful but utterly out of reach, high above the world; incorporeal for all intents and purposes, and even more so now that she is "taken from the sky."

The telling difference between Mildred and Snow White is in the way the latter is fetishized as a body and an object, while the former's disembodiment is central to her idealization. Rather than the boxed-up corpse of the woman herself, as the Prince wanted, Dorian is left with the marshland painting Mildred gave him. He removes a picture of the Blackmore character Lorna Doone (an artwork of an artwork, as the fictional character is herself a work of art), whom he had previously jokingly referred to as his "best girl," and gives the space instead to this painting (42); eventually he will add a photograph of Mildred as well. Mildred displaces Lorna spatially, via art and image, just as she has displaced her in Dorian's affections. Her physical absence, "safe in the world of spirits" (144), makes her all the more compelling as a spirit and an idea: perfectly unobtainable, but also unimpeachable, frozen like Snow White in her beauty and purity. Death is perhaps just as well; embodiment is dangerous, as Carlia's experiences witness.

---

4. Sandra M. Gilbert and Susan Gubar, *The Madwoman in the Attic: The Woman Writer and the Nineteenth-Century Literary Imagination* (Princeton: Yale UP, 2000), 41.

Carlia is introduced in the first chapter of the novel as a child who falls into a canal because of her own headstrong character and attraction to danger. Dorian rescues her from the swift water, dropping his precious cargo of newly purchased books in the process. One of her friends declares to Carlia, as the episode draws to a close, that "I know who you are going to marry ... You're going to marry Dorian" (14). In this vignette, which has little to do with the action of the novel otherwise, Anderson has cleverly laid out an allegorical set-piece for the rest of the plot: Carlia's recklessness and lack of governing authority will lead to her descent into the treacherous rapids of erotic entanglement, but Dorian will rescue her and, thereafter, marry her. From the outset, Carlia is given as imperiled, already figured as falling and in danger, in need of a farmer-scholar in shining armor as much because of her natural/material environment as because of her choices.

In contrast to Mildred, Carlia is rosy-cheeked, plump and round, "full of health and life and color" (35). She is emphatically alive, fulgently embodied and grounded in the material world, and her livingness is contrasted with Mildred's deadness by both her and Dorian at different moments. She is "not a very wise girl" (66), insufficiently religious, attracted to the wrong sort of men, and damaged by her environment; as the girl next door with a longstanding crush on Dorian, she's as romantically available to him as he wants, though for this she lacks the almost mystical allure that Mildred had (and has). If anything, Carlia views Dorian as above and inaccessible to her, telling him in a moment of high temper, "you're altogether too good and too wise for such as I. You're so high up that I can't touch you. You live in the clouds, I among the clods" (148). His increasing interest in books and scholarship contrast painfully with her constriction in a life of menial labor, and when that distance is exacerbated by Dorian's romantic neglect of her, she makes herself available to the man who eventually rapes her. Material excess beleaguers her, and Dorian's role as rescuer is to not only retrieve her physically, but to save her from the weight of too much materiality.

Mildred's transcending relationship to the fallen material world allowed her to avoid being corrupted by it; on the other hand, Dorian, at least according to Uncle Zed, is improved by his years of farming, having "laid away ... a generous store of nature's riches; for you have been in close touch with the earth, and

the life which teems in soil and air and the waters" (59). Dorian's scholarly career ambitions, to become a theologian-naturalist and resolve the laws of science
with LDS theological precepts, are in part drawn from his agricultural background. Carlia, however, is not given any particular ambitions or interests, and
so for her the labor of the farm is "drudgery" (157, 194), a way for the material
to smother the intellectual, spiritual, and social. Her natural cheerfulness is
crushed into pessimism, sarcasm, and resentment, not only by her work but by
the failings of her home. Whereas Dorian's mother keeps a home that imbues
its humbleness with "a sense of comfort and refinement," Carlia's mother is
evidently a failure in this regard; their home is hot and uncomfortable, lacking
in books and music, in sum, "cold and cheerless and ugly … It was a place to
work" (86). Feminine shortcomings are evidently cross-generational, as Carlia's
mother's domestic inadequacies set Carlia up for her fall into sexual error.

The corruption of Carlia's personality that accompanies the crushing of her
intellectual and cultural interests paves the way for her fall into the prototypical-
ly material danger of illicit sexuality. After she runs away from home, her re-
pentant father mourns that Carlia's natural vivacity and curiosity "were
suppressed so long that this is the way it has broken loose" (157), but he is not
quite right. Her interest in Mr. Lamont is certainly motivated at least in part by
her sense that nobody else cares about her (114 – 115)—but then, he is also an
urban fellow with an automobile who brings roses and takes her to the movies,
and might have commanded the interest of a curious and lively farm girl in any
case. What has *broken loose* is Carlia herself, literally in that she has left her parents' home and her constricting life there, but also in that, her virginity lost to a
man she is unlikely to marry, she has broken out—or been broken out—of the
sexual contract. An awareness of exactly this "loss" torments Dorian when he
learns what has happened to Carlia:

> Dorian had not found Carlia Duke; instead, he had found something which
> appeared to him to be the end of all things. Had he found her dead, in her
> virginal purity, he could have placed her, with Mildred, safely away in his
> heart and his hopes; but this! … What more could he now do?
> […]
> But what could he now do? Find her. And then, what? Marry her? He re-
> fused to consider that for a moment. He drove the thought fiercely away.
> That would be impossible now. The horror of what had been would always
> stand a repellent specter between them … Yes, he had loved her—he knew
> that now more assuredly than ever; and he tried to place that love away from
> him by a play upon words in the past tense; but deep down in his heart he

knew that he was merely trying to deceive himself. He loved her still; the fact that he loved her but could not marry her added fuel to the flames of his torment. (173 – 174)

Because she can no longer offer a potential husband exclusive sexual access to her, Carlia can no longer participate in the patriarchal marriage exchange. Without her virginity intact, and the attendant control over her sexuality that it symbolizes, Dorian's love for Carlia is inadequate to make her marriageable.[5] This is indicative of how the sexual contract, especially in a first marriage, works retroactively: the woman is not only the sexual property of her husband going forward, but is known, by virtue of her virginity, to have always already been her husband's sexual property. Carlia's loss of virginity does not make Dorian love her any less; it merely exposes the reality that sexual exchange is more fundamental to the marriage contract than is love. If only she were a dead virgin, like Mildred, then she could remain his *in potentia* at least (and given LDS theology about the eternity of marriage and the probability of post-mortem polygamy, eventually more concretely as well).

Learning that Carlia was drugged and raped does not seem to change Dorian's mind. While it is probably this that enables him to "forgive" her, he is still unsure that he can "close his eyes" to the "grim skeleton" (190) of her having a sexual past with anyone but himself. He, Carlia, and the narrator all still understand this as a sin. Carlia's anxiety that because "the wages of sin is death," she has therefore "already died," is relieved by the assurance that Christ makes repentance possible (215); no one suggests that being drugged and raped simply isn't a sin to begin with. Carlia is allowed to slip out of the "whore" role opposite Mildred's angel not because she, Dorian, Zed, or anyone else is interested in challenging this dichotomy, or this essentializing view of women's sexuality, but because even whores can repent through "the gift of God ... eternal life through Jesus Christ our Lord" (215).

The *felix culpa* of Carlia's fall is that it solidifies Dorian in a position of moral superiority that he never would have been able to occupy if he had married Mildred. The pairing of Dorian and Carlia rather than Dorian and Mildred makes for a more normative patriarchal relationship, in which Dorian,

---

5.   See Carol Pateman's *The Sexual Contract* (Stanford UP, 1988) for the argument that the social contract is built on the patriarchal sexual contract, which encodes the male desire to control and access female bodies, and that marriage is naturally the clearest instantiation of this contract.

with his superior wisdom, strength, learning, age, ambition, spirituality, and sexual purity, is able to truly preside. Carlia herself is, on the one hand, terribly aware of this, accusing him of being "unable to love me for my sake, but you are doing this for fear of not doing your duty" (197). On the other hand, it is in this imbalance that her love for him is rooted: "Yes, I have always, even as a child, looked up to you as someone big and strong and good—Yes, I have always worshipped you, always loved you!" (197). The final chapter portrays Dorian sermonizing in much the way that Uncle Zed used to, rhapsodizing about his mission to develop a grand unified theory of the natural sciences in harmony with LDS theology; "Carlia silently worshiped" (222).

In one of Zed's many impromptu sermons, he suggests to Mildred that the D&C actually contains "the most wonderful love story ever written" because it includes "the revelation on the eternity of the marriage covenant ... the endlessness of life and love under this new and everlasting covenant of marriage" (48). Presumably he is thinking of D&C 132, in which it is revealed that the new and everlasting covenant of marriage will allow marriage contracts made on earth, if done so according to God's law and "sealed ... by the Holy Spirit of promise," to persist into the eternities and allow their participants to become "gods, because they have all power, and the angels are subject unto them" (v. 19 – 20). This section of scripture also explains that David and Abraham were justified in having multiple wives and concubines "because they were given unto [them], and [they] abode in my law" (v. 37). Likewise, if a man has "ten virgins given unto him by this law, he cannot commit adultery, for they belong to him, and they are given unto him; therefore is he justified" (v. 62). God not only allows but requires the practice of polygamy, and reproves Emma Smith for resistance to it. Zed's "love story" entails the promise that women who do not abide by the commandment to practice polygamous marriage will be destroyed (v. 54).

It's no surprise that, writing thirty years after the first Manifesto declaring the end of the Mormon practice of polygamy, Anderson makes no explicit reference to this element of Mormon history and practice, which had been a political embarrassment not so long before, and continued as an object of cultural suspicion. Nonetheless, the promise seems to be of a polygamous heaven for Dorian, Carlia, and Mildred. Carlia has not replaced Mildred in Dorian's interests, nor do she and Mildred seem to be in competition for Dorian's affections.

Other than one early moment in which Carlia awkwardly assures Dorian that Mildred "just loves" him (57), she never seems insecure about her comparison to his first, dead, perfectly angelic love. And Dorian, in thinking about them both, finds that "Carlia's image persisted even as Mildred's did. Mildred, away from the entanglements of the world, was safe to him; but Carlia had her life to live and the trials and difficulties of mortality to encounter and to overcome" (153). With one dead and the other living, they easily co-inhabit his romantic imagination, but if, as Zed reminds the reader early on, marriage is to persist for eternity, then what will happen when Dorian and Carlia, as a married couple, meet Mildred again in the next life? What will be her relationship to them then? D&C 132 seems to provide an answer to this as well.[6]

An obvious narrative wrinkle of redeeming the whore in the angel/whore dichotomy, not only morally but romantically, is that the main character is given competing romantic possibilities without an obvious better choice. Killing off the angel is one tidy solution, since angels are only barely in the mortal world to begin with; as Gilbert and Gubar note, "the surrender of her self ... that is the beautiful angel-woman's key act" also "dooms her both to death and to heaven. For to be selfless is not only to be noble, it is to be dead."[7] But Anderson, via the only semi-defunct Mormon doctrine of polygamy, is able to do one even better: Dorian can enjoy his redeemed wife while he lingers on earth, and be rewarded with an untouched virgin in heaven.

---

6. Maia McAleavey ("Soul-mates: David Copperfield's Angelic Bigamy," *Victorian Studies* 52.2 [2010], 191 – 218) argues that in *David Copperfield*, the two women David marries sequentially, Dora and Agnes, sets the three of them up for an eventual situation of heavenly bigamy. David's marriage to Agnes, who is described throughout the novel in angelic terms, "unifies the past and future, refining rather than erasing [his first wife] Dora in a perfect (re)union" (204). Because his second marriage takes on a transtemporal element that allows it to co-exist with his first, the afterlife for all of them can be imagined as a bigamist triangle. Not only is this a parallel case to that of Dorian, Carlia, and Mildred, but it is alluded to when Carlia gives Dorian *David Copperfield* as a gift. By the novel's end they are still promising to read it; the reader familiar with the Dickens novel is thus able to interpret Dorian and Carlia's relationship as implicitly a second marriage, although the characters themselves may not.

7. Gilbert and Gubar, *Madwoman*, 25.

"WHY ARE THERE CLASSES AMONG MEMBERS OF OUR CHURCH?"

ANDERSON'S ECONOMICS OF MORMONISM IN TRANSITION

SARAH C. REED

The publication of Nephi Anderson's last novel, *Dorian*, in 1921, came near the end of an era of Mormon history marked by a number of dramatic changes. During the 50 years from 1880 to 1930, the Mormon Church abandoned many of its idiosyncratic practices: polygamy was officially ended, the LDS political party disbanded, communitarian economics de-emphasized. At the same time, it increasingly participated in American politics and culture: Mormons sent a delegation to the 1893 World's Fair, Utah gained statehood in 1896, Reed Smoot weathered the congressional hearings regarding his election and was finally seated in the Senate in 1907. This process has been called "Americanization" or even "assimilation" because of the way the Mormon cultural region (to borrow Ethan Yorgason's term) came to conform to hegemonic economic, political, and social norms; nevertheless, the integration of the region into America was not an unequivocal development. Mormonism's doctrines and narrative had to be reinterpreted to harmonize the change from a separatist society to one accommodating the dominant cultural conventions.

One of the major features of this transformation was the acceptance of American capitalism and its attendant consequences. Mormon life in Utah had relied on a communal economic system, achieved with varying success over the years in various forms, from the United Order movement in individual communities to the regional project Zion's Central Board of Trade. The Law of Consecration, instituted by Joseph Smith, provided the spiritual motivation in asking Saints to consecrate or share their wealth, time, and labor with the Church for the care of the poor and the growth of the kingdom. The communitarian system gave way to capitalism after the anti-polygamy legislation allowed the confiscation of Church property, limiting the Church's economic influence as well as the social changes that accompanied the increasing numbers of non-Mormons in the region and a rapid urbanization around the turn of the century. As president and prophet, Joseph F. Smith took the Church out of a number of businesses, including sugar, mining, utilities, and resorts, between 1901 and 1906. Leonard Arrington believed that with regard to these changes, "the self-sufficient Kingdom may be said to have been brought to an end [...] Individualism, speculation, and inequality—once thought to be characteristic of Babylon—were woven into the fabric of Mormon life" (409). While this was undoubtedly the result, the compromise of Mormon communalism with American capitalism was not without debate, reservations, or competing reinterpretations of Mormon life in the accommodation of the dominant economic system.

Anderson includes one scene in *Dorian* which explicitly takes up the result of the Mormon adoption of capitalism. Dorian finds out from his neighbor Carlia that Mildred, their mutual acquaintance from the city, loves him. The feeling is mutual, yet this troubles our hero. He visits Uncle Zed, an older member of the ward and a mentor to Dorian, and asks, "Uncle Zed, how can I become something else than a farmer?" (59). Uncle Zed wonders what's wrong with being farmer and Dorian replies, "Well, a farmer doesn't usually amount to much, I mean in the eyes of the world. Farmers seem to be in a different class from merchants, for example, or from bankers or other more genteel workers" (59). Uncle Zed replies with a vigorous defense of farming, praising its closeness to nature in contrast to life in the city:

> Listen to me, Dorian Trent [...] Let me tell you something. If you haven't done so before, begin now and thank the Lord that you began life on this globe of ours as a farmer's child and boy. Whatever you do or become in the future, you have made a good beginning. You have already laid away in the way of concepts, we may say, a generous store of nature's riches, for you

have been in close touch with the earth, and the life which teems in soil and air and the waters. Pity the man whose childish eyes looked out on nothing but paved streets and brick walls or whose young ears heard nothing but the harsh rumble of the city, for his early conceptions from which to interpret his later life is artificial and therefore largely untrue. (58 – 60)

Dorian isn't satisfied, but pushes the question further, asking, "Uncle Zed, why are there classes among members of our Church?" and clarifies, "the rich do not associate with the poor nor the learned with the unlearned. I know, of course, that this is the general rule in the world, but I think it should be different in the Church" (60). Uncle Zed is forced to admit that there is evidence of class divisions in the Church even as he defends it: "Yes; it ought to be and is different. There are no classes such as you have in mind in the Church, even though a few unthinking members seem to imply it by their actions; but there is no real class distinction in The Church of Jesus Christ of Latter-day Saints, only such that are based on the doing of the right and the wrong. Character alone is the standard of classification" (60). He adds to the defense by citing the lack of inherited authority, the case of a blacksmith presiding over a banker, and a shoemaker teaching a theological class made up of "merchants, lawyers, doctors, and the like" (61).

This brings Dorian to the point of his visit: "So you think—that a young fellow might—that it would not be wrong—or foolish for a poor man to think a lot of—of a rich girl, for instance" (61). Uncle Zed responds positively, while insisting on Dorian's potential and equality: "My boy, Emerson said, 'Hitch your wagon to a star,' and I will add, never let go, although the rocks in the road may bump you badly. Why, there's nothing impossible for a young man like you. You may be rich, if you want to; I expect to see you learned; and the Priesthood which you have is your assurance, through your diligence and faithfulness, to any heights. Yes, my boy; go ahead—love Mildred Brown all you want to; she's fine, but not a bit finer than you" (61 – 62). While embarrassed by the praise, Dorian is pleased with Uncle Zed's words.

In this exchange, the older Uncle Zed reaffirms Mormonism's historical socioeconomic communal project based on the nobility of farming, while Dorian voices the reality of an increasingly capitalist economy and accompanying class structure. This minor scene provides the economic logic underlying the novel, which informs the characters' material condition, motivations, and actions. An examination of the novel's economics reveals the laborer's plight, the pathology of class distinctions, and the resulting problematic gender roles. This focus makes clear Anderson's distrust of Mormonism's collusion with capitalism and what he saw as that economic system's dissonance with Christian values; Anderson mourns the passing of the old system of cooperative agriculture and worries about the new model of individual wage earners, but fails to provide a solution to this problem. To show this, I will give an economic portrait of the major characters and how they reflect the historical conditions.

Zedekiah Manning, in his late seventies, is the oldest character in the novel. Although without any relations in Utah, he is known as "Uncle Zed" to the inhabitants of Greenstreet. An immigrant, he converted to Mormonism in England after his wife and children died. In Utah, he became a farmer and an "uncle" to his ward, where he is also a noted theologian. Much of Uncle Zed's discourse in the novel consists of theological arguments drawn on his extensive reading. He owns shelves of Mormon classics, including JD, *Millennial Star*, *The Contributor*, and the *Improvement Era* as well as works by Orson Pratt, Parley P. Pratt, and Orson Spencer. Through his biography and interests, Uncle Zed represents an older strain of Mormonism.

His lifestyle and beliefs reflect the passing communalism. Although hampered by his age, he is invested in his community. He is described as having been "a ministering angel" to poor souls in need. He takes an interest in the widow Mrs. Trent and the fatherless Dorian as well as the vulnerable Carlia. In fact, he foresees Carlia's troubles and tries to warn Dorian to pay more attention to her. Indeed, he acts as a father figure and mentor to Dorian in all sorts of matters. Mrs. Trent reciprocates by celebrating his birthday and taking care of him when he is sick. Carlia, we find out, also visits him and brings him homemade bread and butter. In his will, Uncle Zed leaves his property to the ward for any "worthy poor" as determined by the bishop (minus his library, intended for Dorian).

As Mormonism shifted from communalism to capitalism, the individual began to displace the community in the building of Zion. The emphasis on self-sufficiency moved from a community effort to the onus of individuals. Even so, vestiges of the older model remained in the discourse. For example, apostle Anthon H. Lund was himself a Danish immigrant and was sympathetic to the difficulties that other immigrant converts faced. In various conference talks he reminded the saints of their responsibilities in helping these new members integrate into the community. Similarly, Andrew Jenson, assistant church historian and also a Danish immigrant, continued to speak about the gathering and praised the Mormon communities and warned against their dissolution, even as other leaders de-emphasized this model. Uncle Zed's immigrant background fits in with this perspective; for him, communitarianism wasn't just an economic model, but had a theological implication. In one of their theological talks, Uncle Zed explains to Dorian his idea of salvation, blending together science, religion, and economy. Christ works for those of us below him who can't get there "by self-effort alone," that "the great error" of evolutionists is that "higher forms evolve from the initial and unaided movements of the lower," which "is as impossible as that a man can lift himself to the skies by his boot-straps" (122 – 123). In working out individual salvation, Uncle Zed gives three principles: 1) the individual must be willing to progress; 2) he must be willing to accept help; and 3) he must be willing to "share all good with others" (125). Uncle Zed goes on to expound on the third principle: "Coming back now to the application I mentioned. If it is God's work and glory to labor for those below Him, why should not we, His sons and daughters, follow His example as far as possible in our sphere of action? If we are ever to become like Him we must follow in His steps and do the things which He has done. Our work, also must be to help along the road to salvation those who are lower down, those who are more ignorant and are weaker than we" (124 – 125).

Uncle Zed's model of salvation resonates with the contemporaneous social gospel ideas in America. While Mormonism was removed from this primarily Protestant movement, there were nonetheless some intersections. The most radical is perhaps the United Order, which attempted to establish egalitarian and self-sufficient communities. One of the most successful of these was in Brigham City, Utah, where Anderson spent a number of years as a teacher. Edward Bellamy visited the community and spent time with resident Lorenzo Snow in preparation for writing his (socialist) utopian novel *Looking Backward*. That volume in turn influenced Anderson's first novel, the plan-of-salvation romance *Added Upon*. Anderson's descriptions of Christ's millennial kingdom focus on the economic and social equality achieved by the members working together to share their wealth. With the conceit of a visit of the King of Poland, Anderson's language is explicit in addressing questions of property, class, and labor in his conception of a millennial utopia.

In many ways Uncle Zed's lifestyle prefigures the eschaton just as it represents Mormonism's past; in either case, Uncle Zed is out of his time. In contrast are the Trent and Duke parents' embodiment of present troubles. Uncle Zed represented the Jeffersonian, yeoman farmer that was the basis of early Mormon economy, so that by 1878 most Mormons "owned property or realistically saw themselves as potential property owners" and "depended on more than wages for maintenance" (Yorgason 84). Between then and 1920, Utah became more urban and more non-Mormon. In 1880, Mormons made up 80% of the population in the state, compared to 55% in 1920. In 1890, Utah was 65% rural and 35% urban; by 1910 there was an even divide. There was a corresponding shift from the regional communal economy based in agriculture to a capitalist economy based in wage labor. While Church hierarchy rarely challenged the inevitability of this arrangement, some authorities endorsed the "Back to the Farm" movement that had gained support across the nation in the years around 1910. The plea to return to the farm must have had special resonance for Mormons. In General Conference, John Henry Smith warned against the allure of city life and then made the case for returning to the land as a way of becoming self-sufficient, especially to the sons who had drifted away: "The man who lays his foundation upon the basis of the soil, builds his home, increases its comforts, enlarges his acres, and increases the cattle, horses, and sheep necessary to stock his homestead properly, soon finds himself among the independent ones in the world" (36).

We learn early in the novel that Dorian's father answered this call to return to the land. A schoolteacher evidently in the city, Mr. Trent had always had "a longing to be a farmer" and eventually purchased twenty acres in Greenstreet. But the water situation made the farming difficult and when he died nine years previous to the opening of the novel, "the result of his failure was a part of the legacy which descended to his wife and son" (19). The idealized situation envisioned by John Henry Smith in his talk was a long process for the Trent family and not without untoward consequences. The work, which had ostensibly contributed to Mr. Trent's death, also takes its toll on mother and son. Anderson describes Mrs. Trent as looking older than she was, with wrinkles and hair "white at the temples," and that "hard work had bent her back and roughened her hands" (17). The precariousness of their economic situation is emphasized by the scandal of Dorian using the money to buy books rather than his much-needed shoes. We discover that Dorian had previously wanted to give up and move to the city, but Mrs. Trent had hope in the new canal and believed that Dorian "would be better off working for himself on the farm than drudging for others in the town" (20). The narrator informs us that the "summit of their difficulties seemed now to have passed, and better times were ahead" even as "they struggled along, making their payments on the land and later on the canal stock" (21).

The Trents deal with the difficulties of farm life as best they can, investing in canals for irrigation and experimenting with dry-farming. Dry-farming was supported during this time by extension programs administered by the Utah Agricultural College (now Utah State University) and by John A. Widtsoe's efforts to bring the science of arid farming to the farmer. Even so, during the 1910s, Utah's crops suffered failures from drought. More broadly, the American agricultural market fell into a depression following the outbreak of WWI and the closing of the European markets. The combination of events created massive farming failure in Utah, with a census taker in 1920 traveling through 300 miles of Utah's dry farms only to find "that nearly 90 percent of the people he expected to find were no longer living on the land" (Bowen 1). This failure shows the disconnect between the ideal of the "Back to the Farm" movement and the lived reality, or the contrast between Uncle Zed's praises of farming and the Trents' material condition. Thomas Alexander points to the divide between the urban and rural conceptions of farming: "Though settlers faced the reality of a harsh life in these rural areas, the mythology to those on the urbanizing Wasatch Front had it quite otherwise" (197). *Dorian* diverges from themes in other Anderson works in this regard. In *Piney Ridge Cottage*, for example, Anderson paints a picture of farm life in rural Utah as idyllic; farm success in *Added Upon* is achieved through hard work. In contrast, *The Castle Builder*, set in Norway, shows the impossibility of living on the land in that country. (Similarly exoticized, Anderson looks at the consequences of industrial labor in the foreign context of England in *Romance of a Missionary*.) *Dorian* brings these economic concerns home to Utah and challenges the myth of the universal good of agricultural labor.

The situation of the other Greenstreet farmers in the novel reflects the struggle of living off the land. The neighboring Duke family also has difficulties making ends meet; their troubles worsen as the son abandons the family and farm. The narrator provides a curt description of this character who appears only once: "Will Duke should have been a hard-working farmer's boy, but he was somewhat a failure, especially regarding the hard work part" (44). The "hard work" of farming extends far beyond the fields into every aspect of their lives. The description of the Dukes' house shows how it pervades their lives:

> The front room was very hot and uncomfortable [...] There were the same straight-backed chairs, the same homemade carpet, more faded and threadbare than ever, the same ugly enlarged photographs within their massive frames which the enterprising agent had sold to Mrs. Duke. There was the same lack of books or music or anything pretty or refined; and as Dorian stood and looked about, there came to him more forcibly than ever the

barrenness of the room and of the house in general. True, his own home was very humble, and yet there was an air of comfort and refinement about it. The Duke home had always impressed him as being cold and cheerless and ugly. There were no protecting porches, no lawn, no flowers, and the barn yard had crept close up to the house. It was a place to work. The eating and the sleeping were provided, so that work could be done, farm and kitchen work with their dirt and litter. The father and the mother and the daughter were slaves to work. Only in work did the parents companion with the daughter. The visitors to the house were mostly those who came to talk about cattle and crops and irrigation. (85 – 86)

Their house is deformed by their labor: the Dukes are "slaves to work," which prohibits them from adding any refinements to their utilitarian dwelling. The Trents are able to maintain more cultural artifacts, like paintings and books, but their lives, too, are defined by the work they must do simply to survive.

The poverty of the farmers is contrasted with the middle-class characters from the nearby town, the most prominent of whom is Mildred Brown. Mildred's mother is an old friend of Mrs. Trent, presumably from before the Trents moved to Greenstreet. Before the Browns come to visit, Mrs. Trent tells Dorian "They are dear, good people. They know we are simple farmers" (24). Mildred's poor health prompts their visit and she stays for some time with the Trents, as she seems to improve in the country air. She brings with her hallmarks of civilized society. We first meet her painting a landscape in the Trents' fields. Her conversation with Dorian reveals some of her superior qualities: she's well traveled, she studied painting in Boston, and she has attended high school. Later we learn she plays the violin—and she doesn't like it called a fiddle! The violin/fiddle divide parallels the contrast between Dorian's talents as a carver and Mildred's painting. Where Dorian is unconscious of his ability, Mildred waxes philosophical about her role as an artist. The difference is reminiscent of Kant's (classist) distinction between arts and crafts.

Dorian's thoughts in this first scene emphasize the distance between them: "He had met no other girl just like her, so young and so beautiful, and yet so talented and so well-informed; so rich, and yet so simple in manner of her life; so high born and bred, and yet so companionable with those of humbler station" (29). As Dorian falls in love with Mildred, he becomes increasingly concerned with her higher status. This is not a manifestation of the "eternal feminine," but an anxiety born of real class difference. Orson Pratt had already commented on the problem of class among Latter-day Saints in 1873 in regard to gender relations: "A rich man can educate his daughters, and have them

taught music and everything calculated to make them refined, polite, and genteel. This enables these daughters to fascinate the rich, and should a poor man
come along, and knock at the rich man's door and tell him he desires to keep
company with his daughters, he is told that he has no business there" (JD
15:357). Mildred dies before Dorian gets the chance to court her, but the conversation with Uncle Zed quoted earlier reveals his intentions, even with their
acknowledged differing classes and his accompanying trepidations. After she
dies, Dorian replaces his prized picture of Lorna Doone with a picture of Mildred's. The comparison drawn between the two female characters points also to
the class structure underlying the two romances: like Dorian, the farmer Jon
Ridd pines for a noble woman (Lorna Doone).

Despite her many advantages, Mildred is in a delicate and precarious situation. She is sickly and depends on the poverty-stricken Trents' kindness to re-
gain her health. While culturally refined, she lacks basic practical skills; she
doesn't know how to milk a cow, for example, nor is she shown doing any sort
of manual labor. In this way, she resembles Dora, the impractical first wife from
David Copperfield, which novel serves as a motif in Anderson's story. Mildred's
relationship with the Trents also highlights the reliance of the upper classes on
the labor of the lower classes. The end of the painting scene illustrates her vul-
nerability. A few escaped cows charge at her and she cowers behind her easel.
She is saved from being stampeded by Carlia Duke on horseback. Carlia down-
plays her heroics, but it is clear that the world Mildred has carefully controlled
in her painting poses a danger that Carlia, with her practical knowledge, can
mediate. Despite this dramatic rescue, all the fresh air and simple farm life fails
in the end to save Mildred, who succumbs to her illness and dies.

The other major bourgeois character is Carlia's boyfriend, Mr. Jack Lamont.
While Mildred's relationships with the lower classes are benevolent, Lamont's
are exploitative. Like Mildred, Lamont lives in the city and he is the only character who earns a wage. Even worse, he is a salesman: he contributes to the al-
ienation of the workers from their products and the means of production, and
to their commodification while profiting directly from the surplus value. His
identification with capitalism is mirrored by his identification with modernity.
He is the only character in the novel to drive an automobile, he smokes and
swears, and he often goes to the movies. He uses his wealth and position to gain
control over Carlia and Dorian. Unlike Dorian, he has the leisure and the funds
to take Carlia out. When Dorian runs into them at the movies, Lamont exerts
his position over him instead of treating him like a rival for Carlia's affections.

He insists that Dorian accompany them to the ice cream parlor, where he pays for the ice cream, and then drives them all home. Although puzzled why Lamont would want a "third-wheel," Dorian is helpless to find a way out of the awkward situation. Anderson puts it laconically: "This Mr. Lamont had not only captured Carlia but Dorian also" (113).

Carlia's capture has more consequences than Dorian's hurt feelings. Lamont's sexually abusive behavior is foreshadowed early, both from his secretive meetings with Carlia and Carlia's fear of him. Later, we find out that he drugged and raped her and then abandons her pregnant. Carlia has no choice but to leave her community: with her virginity Lamont has taken her social capital, and the difference in their social classes legitimizes his behavior and prevents any retribution on her part. When Dorian initially confronts Lamont after Carlia disappears, Lamont intimates that he gave up on Carlia when he learned that Dorian was his rival. He refuses to offer any other information, and Anderson ends the exchange with "Dorian was dismissed" (160). The passive construction removing the agent highlights the system that has forced Dorian into this role as subordinate to Lamont and others of his class.

After Dorian finds Carlia and brings her back to Greenstreet, Lamont attempts to reassert his claim on her. He drives his automobile down to the Dukes' farm, but runs into Dorian on the way. Dorian, who knows the full circumstances of Carlia's flight and stillbirth, takes control of the situation and reacts with the only means available to him: violence. He stands in the middle of the road, forcing Lamont to stop and then walks to the side of the car and, "looking steadily into Mr. Lamont's face," tells him, "I'm going to Mr. Duke's also. If I find you there, I'll thrash you within an inch of your life. Drive on" (202). The threat of physical harm has its desired effect and Lamont retreats.

Some months later, Dorian has been dry-farming with some fellow ward members and they stop at a small hotel in the canyon while it rains. Lamont comes in and begins taunting Dorian. Dorian objects and a fight nearly breaks out when Lamont raises his riding whip. Dorian composes himself, but once outside he challenges Lamont on his treatment of Carlia. Lamont tries to place the blame on Dorian, implying he was also intimate with her. Dorian punches him and a fight ensues: "Lamont was lighter than Dorian, but he had some skill as a boxer which he tried to bring into service; but Dorian, mad in his desire to punish, with unskilled strength fought off all attacks. They grappled, struggled, and fell, to arise again and give blow for blow. It was all done so suddenly, and the fighting was so fierce, that Dorian's fellow travelers did not get to the scene before Jack Lamont lay prone on the ground from Dorian's finishing knockout blow" (205). Despite Lamont's advantages—riding whip and training—Dorian wins with "his desire to punish" and his "unskilled strength." Dorian tells his companion that Lamont "got just a little of what's been coming to him for a long time" (205).

Dorian's blow is one for chivalry, but also an instance of class warfare as Dorian rises up successfully against his oppressor. The era leading up to the novel's publication was the heyday of radicalism in America, which was strongly linked with violence, beginning with the iconic Haymarket Affair in 1886. While American socialism and anarchism are often associated with the labor movements in the Midwest and the East, these movements were also active in the Western United States. The Western Federation of Miners (WFM) was formed in 1893 in response to the poor mining conditions in the region. A founding member of the International Workers of the World (IWW), the WFM became one of the most radical and militant labor organizations in the country. It was a part of a number of mining strikes marked by violent altercations with the owners or the government, including the Coeur d'Alene confrontation in Idaho and the Colorado Labor Wars of 1903 – 1904. The WFM also organized the labor federation the Western Labor Union (WLU) in 1897 in Salt Lake City. The WLU represented miners and several other trades, including railway workers, cooks, clerks, typographers, butchers, carpenters, laundry workers, etc. Utah's connections to the movements include labor organizer "Big Bill" Heywood, who was born in Salt Lake City, and Joe Hill, the Swedish-American labor activist who was executed in Salt Lake City in 1915.

For the most part, the official LDS position was against these radical movements. Ephraim Ericksen, writing in 1922, sums it up well, noting the irony of abandoning the United Order:

> There is a growing tendency to take sides with the capitalist class and with large corporations against the laboring classes. The philosophy of the church leaders was at one time radical and socialistic; it is now conservative and capitalistic. They do not hesitate in their sermons and in the editorial columns of the official papers to denounce socialism and trade unionism as anarchism when those become active in opposing the interests of business corporations. The present economic order is accepted by them as right and proper. In fact their philosophy seems to have completely changed in this respect from that held forty years ago. The United Order is as far from their minds as is socialism from the minds of the owners of large corporations. (72)

Ericksen sees the connections between the contemporaneous labor and socialist movements and the abandoned forms of communitarianism in the Mormon cultural region. But even at the time of the United Order, Church leaders would distinguish between what they saw as God's order and the worldly counterfeit of socialism. Nonetheless, leaders were aware of the increasing class divisions. Orson Pratt noted in 1873 that "[t]here are certainly existing now among us distinctions of classes which if not checked, may prove the overthrow of many" (JD 16:7). George Q. Cannon made a similar warning in 1882: "I dread the increase of luxury; I dread the increase of class distinctions which I see growing up. The disintegrating influences of wealth are far more to be dreaded than any outside pressure of this character" (JD 24:46).

These sentiments endured with a certain segment of the Mormon population even as the majority of members and leaders no longer challenged capitalism. According to John S. McCormick and John R. Sillito, during this period 40% of the official Socialist Party in Utah were Mormons. These authors document many cases of faithful socialists as faithful Church members. For example, the mining town of Eureka had a socialist Mormon bishop and a Mormon socialist mayor. George W. Williamson, Jr. included this statement in the time capsule of the Gila Stake Academy in Arizona: "I am a member in good standing in The Church of Jesus Christ of Latter-day Saints and among the few workers in that organization who comprehend the class struggle, and are fighting and working for the education of our people along these lines. But so effective [have] the great money kings done the work of deception among the people that even the Church of Christ is permeated with its pernicious doctrines" (qtd. in McCormick and Sillito 113). A.L. Porter expressed a similar sentiment when he included Socialist Party and labor paraphernalia along with this statement in the cornerstone of the Springville High gym: "Our political faith is Socialism, our religious faith is (Mormon) the Latter-day Saints. We are living under Capitalism and the wealth of the world is privately owned by individuals ... but this building is collectively owned by the community and is to be used for high school gymnasium purposes. It is built by wage slavery as all labor at this point in history is" (qtd. in McCormick and Sillito 110).

Scandinavian immigrants, including Mormon converts, were also important members of the socialist movement in Utah. The Scandinavian socialist organizations, particularly in the Midwest, played a significant role in the greater Socialist coalition, and similar Scandinavian groups were formed in several places in Utah, including Salt Lake City and Eureka (McCormick and Sillito 109).

One Swedish-American socialist in Murray carried in his store a Swedish-language socialist newspaper from Minneapolis (*Forskaren*), indicating that there was an interested reading audience. Scandinavian immigrants in Utah had been enthusiastic adopters of the progressive economic communitarian programs, like the United Order and cooperative merchandising, such as Zion's Cooperative Mercantile Institution (ZCMI). Nephi Anderson, a Norwegian immigrant himself, was more open about his contact with progressive ideals in the Scandinavian context. The journal of his mission in Norway indicates that he frequently rented labor halls (*Arbeiderforening*) to hold meetings and he records at least once of attending a political meeting of the Liberal Party. Anderson's Norwegian novels, particularly *The Castle Builder*, thematize the problems of class distinctions. In this rags-to-riches story, the protagonist Harald suffers from harsh poverty and class prejudice in childhood, and as an adult he is involved with progressive politics in Norway before converting to Mormonism and setting his sights on emigrating.

While it would be wrong to call Anderson a socialist, he was class conscious and did not "take sides with the capitalist class and with large corporations" as Ephraim Ericksen accused contemporaneous Church leaders. Dorian's violent triumph over Lamont comes near the end of the novel and acts as a climax to a number of tensions—economic, sexual, and moral. These are resolved further in the very next chapter when some time later, Dorian and a friend happen upon Lamont's car crashed in the river. Dorian manages to pull Lamont from the wreckage and out of the river, but they fail to revive him. Lamont's ignorance of his natural surroundings and his reliance on modern technology have killed him and not even the lower class could save him. In contrast to Lamont's recklessness, Dorian's rescue attempt is calm and measured. The three Dorian and Lamont episodes—the confrontation, the fight, and the accident—take place over a series of months in the narrated time, but with the time ellipses they follow each other directly in the narrative structure. The close succession of these events emphasizes Dorian's eventual triumph in their class conflict and Lamont's fatal concessions: 1) Lamont obeys Dorian's order to leave; 2) Dorian physically beats Lamont when Lamont tries to reassert his dominance; 3) Lamont's negligence leaves his life in Dorian's merciful hands. Rather than allowing Lamont to live, Anderson underscores how unsustainable the current class structure is. Not only does Lamont self-destruct, but he was also apparently genetically unfit, as his baby is stillborn. To add to the pathology of the middle and upper classes, both major bourgeois characters (Mildred and Lamont) are dead by the end of the novel.

Lamont's death (and to a certain extent Mildred's) provides the necessary catharsis for Dorian and Carlia to come to an understanding about her past and their future together. Only with the removal of the upper classes are the lower-class characters able to progress.

Lamont's fall in the river parallels Carlia's fall into the same river in the opening chapter—except that Dorian was able to save her. More often, Carlia is compared with Mildred. The contrasts between the two are outwardly manifested. Carlia is healthy, tall, tanned, dark-haired, with features rough from work; Mildred is sickly, short, pale, golden-haired, and delicate. Mildred has had all the advantages of her class, including extensive education, music and art lessons, etc.; Carlia has had all the disadvantages of her class, with education, other luxuries, and even church worship falling second to the constant burden of domestic and agricultural labor. But even with these differences Carlia and Mildred become fast friends and Carlia mourns Mildred's death as much as Dorian does. Carlia's thoughtful friendship and loyalty are described by the recipients of her kindness, like bringing Uncle Zed home-churned butter and homemade bread when his cow is dry, or gifting Dorian with *David Copperfield* for his birthday to replace the copy lost when he saved her from drowning.

Carlia's life is completely dominated by her work; one early description emphasizes this: "Carlia, though so young, was already a hardworking farmer girl, with no chance of escape, as far as she could see, from the hard-working part" (44). In a conversation with Dorian she admits to being tired and when he says she's working too hard, she counters, "Hard work won't kill anybody—but it's the other things [...] The grind, the eternal grind—the dreary sameness of every day" (89). She explains that in addition to her normal chores, she has taken over more since her father started dry-farming. She complains that her father is blind to the labor she and her mother do and that he believes "the only real work is the plowing and the watering and the harvesting" (89). Her description in this instance shows the intersection of labor and gender. The rise of capitalism shifted the discourse about gender and labor as it posited wage labor as masculine, progressive, and civilized, and non-wage labor as feminine, timeless, and uncultured. Life in the early Mormon cultural region meant an agrarian model that relied on a family economy based on active cooperation of parents and children. The shift to wage labor "shunted women to increasingly narrow forms of participation" and "was regarded as morally acceptable, because it provided opportunity for male advancement and fluid labor roles" (Yorgason 86). Work was increasingly gendered and in particular "women who worked at home were marginalized from the 'progress' the wage labor system seemed to embody" (86). The effects of this can be seen in Mr. Duke's blindness to the women's domestic labor as work. Similarly, characters will mention that Carlia does too much men's work on the farm, even though she's obviously physically capable of doing it. Dorian convinces her to return home after she's run away by promising that her father won't give her "so much work—man's work, to do" (194).

Carlia's life of drudgery has negatively shaped her character. Anderson describes how the constant labor simply to exist has affected her:

> As a child, Carlia was naturally cheerful and loving; but her sordid environment seemed to be crushing her. At times she struggled to get out from under; but there seemed no way, so she gradually gave in to the inevitable. She became resentful and sarcastic. Her black eyes frequently flashed in scorn and anger. As she grew in physical strength and beauty, these unfortunate traits of character became more pronounced. The budding womanhood which should have been carefully nurtured by the right kind of home and neighborhood was often left to develop in wild and undirected ways. (86 – 87)

The all-encompassing work of farming leaves no time for self-improvement or even rest. This has left her vulnerable to Lamont's advances. When Dorian asks her why she goes out with Lamont, her explanation expresses the connection between her labor and his courtship: "I sometimes have thought that you cared for me—but I'm through with that now. Nobody really cares for me. I'm only a rough farm hand. I know how to milk and scrub and churn and clean the stable—an' that's what I do day in and day out. There's no change, no rest for me, save when he takes me away from it for a little while. He understands, he's the only one who does" (147 – 148). Lamont's attentions appear to provide a rest for her, but the power imbalance between the two, based on class and gender, breeds an abusive relationship. When Dorian finds Carlia irrigating their crops late at night, she hides from him at first, thinking Dorian is Lamont, and then begs Dorian "don't let him hurt me!" (105). Lamont's intimidation of Carlia continues until his death frees her.

The adversarial relationship between the Lamont and Carlia reproduces the economic relationship of market capitalists and farmers. While there had been many agricultural movements in the United States in the nineteenth century, the volatile market of the early twentieth century and politics of the Progressive Era began to convince the public that farmers were not being fairly compensated for their products via capitalism. The post-WWI era would see the beginning of attempts by the federal government to support farm prices: the Packers and Stockyards Act of 1921, regulating the meat-packing industry; the Capper-Volstead Act of 1922, protecting farm co-ops from anti-trust suits; and the Grain Futures Act of 1922, regulating grain futures trading. This began a process of farm legislation that would lead to the price and income supports of the Depression Era.

While socialism is associated with urban industrial labor, its principles appealed to many rural farmers as well. Attempts were made during the Progressive Era to bring together these two groups. One of the most successful third parties in American political history was the Farm-Labor Party, which did bring together the interests of farmers and laborers. Both groups saw themselves as casualties of the capitalist system. Although the Farm-Labor Party was most successful in the Midwest (and even still exists in Minnesota as the Democratic-Farm-Labor Party), its first presidential candidate in 1920 was Parley P. Christensen from Utah. Christensen was the son of Danish Mormon converts, who became disillusioned with the Church after emigration. Christensen had been a prominent Republican politician in Salt Lake before joining Theodore Roosevelt's Bull Moose Progressive Party and serving in the Utah legislature, advocating labor rights. When that party became defunct, he joined the Farm-Labor Party. One biographer connects his childhood in the Intermountain West directly to his politics: "Mr. Christensen as a boy pioneered with his parents in Idaho and Utah where his father drove wagons of freight from the railway terminus in Utah up cross country into Idaho, Montana, and the Dakotas. This background gave [him] an insight into the struggles of those who labor and those who wrest their living from the soil" (Goddard).

Carlia's community is overworked with "wresting a living from the soil" and leaves Carlia prey to Lamont. Her father admits blame, commenting that "[t]he poor girl has been confined too much to the work here" and that "all work and no play [...] doesn't always make Jack a dull boy: sometimes, it makes dissatisfaction and rebellion—and it seems it has done that here" (157). Blame is also partially laid at Dorian's feet, as he had begun a romantic relationship with Carlia, but with his time so preoccupied with his farm, he is unable to give much attention to this developing relationship. At the height of their budding romance, Dorian promises to take her to the movies someday and that when they get more time, they will read *David Copperfield* together. But even their first kiss is overshadowed by their work obligations: "That goodnight's kiss should have brought Dorian back to Carlia sooner than it did;

but it was nearly a month before he saw her again. The fact that it was the busiest time of the year was surely no adequate excuse for this neglect. Harvest was on again, and the dry-farm called for much of his attention. Dorian prospered, and he had no time to devote to the girls" (109). Dorian's neglect helps drive Carlia to Lamont. When Dorian asks Carlia about why she goes with Lamont and why she hates him, she tells him it's not anything he's done, but what he hasn't done (148).

When Carlia runs away, Mr. Duke makes an effort to find her, but cannot abandon his farm for long. Some months later, Dorian is reading some of Uncle Zed's papers on his social gospel ideas, starting with "[t]he acquisition of wealth brings with it the obligation of helping the poor; the acquisition of knowledge brings with it the obligation of teaching others; the acquisition of strength and power brings with it the obligation of helping the weak" (162). He comments to his mother he has failed in his duty to Carlia and decides to take up the search for her. Initially, he looks for her in nearby mining towns, but realizes she probably offered her skills at the farms close by. He soon finds the farm where she found employment and the mistress comments on the rarity of Carlia's choice: "it was strange, this girl comin' from the city a' wanting to work in the country. It's usually the other way" (169).

Carlia's flight to the country is in part because her skills are better suited there, but it also represents a rejection of wage labor. Dorian similarly rejects the wage labor that once appealed to him. We learn of Dorian's life trajectory when Uncle Zed challenges him to synthesize religion and science:

> He had wanted to become a successful farmer, then his vision had gone on to the teaching profession; but beyond that he had not ventured. He was already well on the way to make a success of his farms. He liked the work. He could with pleasure be a farmer all his life. But should a man's business be all of life? Dorian realized, not of course in its fuller meaning, that the accumulating of worldly riches was only a means to the accomplishing of other and greater ends of life; and here was before him something worthy of any man's best endeavors. (81)

Dorian's initial plan—to become a teacher rather than a farmer—reverses his father's decision and follows the trend to abandon farming in favor of wage labor. Church leaders at this time were encouraging men to become skilled laborers. A contemporaneous manual for the Young Men's Mutual Improvement Association (YMMIA) "argued that a man's vocation ought to ensure not self-sufficiency or independence but adequate income. It claimed that since unskilled laborers' incomes were usually not sufficient (and implied that this state of affairs was entirely appropriate), young LDS men should become specialists" (Yorgason 88). Becoming a teacher would fit this profile of skilled labor. But Dorian comes to reject this and chooses instead to retreat into academia. They plan to rent out the farm while Dorian is in school and Mrs. Trent will live with Dorian and Carlia in the city. Even though Dorian intends to do the dry-farming, he warns Carlia of the hard life she has ahead of her: "do you realize what you are doing when you say you will be my wife and put up with all the eccentricities of such a man as I am planning to be? Are you willing to be a poor man's wife, for I cannot get money and this knowledge I am after at the same time? Are you willing to go without the latest in dresses and shoes and hats—if necessary?" (222). Dorian's quest for knowledge prohibits an income that will propel them into the middle class with the latest fashions, but Anderson privileges "the greatness" and "the glory" of this intellectual work as a higher, nobler endeavor (81).

Dorian sees himself doing graduate work at an institution back east. The naturalness of this assumption shows how far Mormonism had come in its assimilation into the dominate American society. While Anderson seems to appreciate this greater commerce of ideas, he seems to be disappointed with its economic consequences. The communal system that strove for community well-being has been replaced by individual self-interest. The negative consequences are manifested in *Dorian*. Despite being a widow and orphan, we never see the Trents receive any physical help from the community. The aged Uncle Zed appears to be the only character actively committed to the economic (and to a certain extent spiritual) principles of Zion-building. The other characters have segregated into classes, with the lower class struggling with subsistence farming and the middle class enjoying money and recreation at the expense of the farmers, whom they exploit in material and sexual ways. Dorian breaks out of this system by following Uncle Zed's view of the gospel, which empowers Dorian to save Carlia and challenge Lamont (even though he resorts to violence). Rather than replacing Lamont in a position of dominance, Dorian refuses to participate in the capitalist system and opts out by entering the ivory tower. The economics underlying the novel reveal a distrust of American capitalism and a nostalgia for Mormon communalism. Anderson doesn't provide any easy solutions—Dorian's exit strategy doesn't work on the macro scale. But it provides an alternate view of the Church-sanctioned adoption of capitalism by showing its effects on the micro level.

WORKS CITED

Alexander, Thomas G. *Mormonism in Transition: A History of the Latter-day Saints, 1890 – 1930*. Urbana, IL: U of Illinois P, 1986.

Anderson, Nephi. *Added Upon*. Salt Lake City: Deseret News Press, 1912.

———. *The Castle Builder*. Salt Lake City: Deseret News Press, 1909.

———. *Dorian*.

———. *Piney Ridge Cottage*. Salt Lake City: Deseret News Press, 1912.

———. *Romance of a Missionary*. Independence, MO: Zion's Printing and Publishing, 1919.

Arrington, Leonard J. *Great Basin Kingdom*. Cambridge, MA: Harvard UP, 1959.

Bellamy, Edward. *Looking Backward: 2000 – 1887*. Boston: Ticknor, 1888.

Blackmore, Richard Doddridge. *Lorna Doone: A Romance of Exmoor*. London: Sampson Low, Son, & Marston, 1869.

Bowen, Marshall E. "Crops, Critters, and Calamity: The Failure of Dry Farming in Utah's Escalante Desert, 1913 – 1918" *Agricultural History* 73.1 (1999): 1 – 26.

Dickens, Charles. *David Copperfield*. London: Bradbury & Evans, 1850.

Erickson, Ephraim Edward. *The Psychological and Ethical Aspects of Mormon Group Life*. Chicago: U of Chicago P, 1922.

Goddard, Florence H. "Parley P. Christensen." *Local History Collection*. Los Angeles: Los Angeles Public Library, 1937.

JD. 26 vols. Liverpool and London: various publishers, 1854 – 1886.

McCormick, John S. and John R. Sillito. *A History of Utah Radicalism: Startling, Socialistic, and Decidedly Revolutionary*. Logan, UT: Utah State UP, 2011.

Mulder, William. *Homeward to Zion: The Mormon Migration from Scandinavia*. Minneapolis: U of Minnesota P, 1957.

Sillito, John R. "A Utahn Abroad: Parley P. Christensen's World Tour, 1921–23." *Utah Historical Quarterly* 54.4 (1986): 345–357.

Smith, John Henry. Address. *Conference Reports*. Salt Lake City: Deseret News, 1899. 32–36.

Yorgason, Ethan R. *Transformation of the Mormon Cultural Region*. Urbana, IL: U of Illinois P, 2003.

HARMONIZING MORMONISM AND SCIENCE

"IN THE VALLEY OF SUNSHINE AND SHADOW"

BLAIR DEE HODGES

INTRODUCTION

The turn of the twentieth century marked a period of intense cultural shifts, not least of all regarding widespread views about the relationship between the natural sciences and religion. John William Draper's massively influential *History of the Conflict between Religion and Science* (1874) promoted the view that these were irreconcilable foes fighting to the death. Draper's book is one of the chief disseminators of "the greatest myth in the history of science and religion … that they have been in a state of constant conflict."[1] True, Enlightenment-inspired confidence in human reason and technological advances challenged religious beliefs as the nineteenth century closed. Darwin's *Origin of the Species* (1859) contributed to larger concerns about humanity's place in an apparently

---

1. Ronald L. Numbers, *Galileo Goes to Jail: And Other Myths About Science and Religion* (Cambridge, MA: Harvard University Press, 2010), 1 – 3. Mormons who bought into Draper's thesis attributed the warfare to apostasy, arguing that Mormonism provides the key to true religion *and* science—a major theme in Nephi Anderson's *Dorian*. See B.H. Roberts, *The Truth, the Way, and the Life: An Elementary Treatise on Theology*, ed. Stan Larson (Salt Lake City: Smith Research Associates, 1994), xxxviii.

indifferent universe. The Bible lost credibility due to developments in geology, biology, and textual criticism. Charles Taylor, who traces prehistories of skepticism, naturalism and humanism, identifies the nineteenth century as the period in which "unbelief comes of age," but argues that science and religion have had a more interesting relationship than simple "subtraction stories" suggest.[2]

Most historical accounts of these culture wars gather evidence from newspapers, sermons, and scientific publications. The literary responses are often overlooked, but fiction contains some of the most fascinating reactions to these cultural changes. Pre-Darwinian novels like Mary Shelley's *Frankenstein* (1818) warned of the dangers of modern science, while Charles Kingsley's *Water Babies* (1863) drew on Darwinism to explore the social implications of natural selection.[3] In contrast to these more fantastical works, a number of realist novels— inspired in part by Darwinism but also by the general cultural shift toward a more secular age—appeared around the turn of the twentieth century. Mrs. Humphrey Ward's *Robert Elsmere* (1888) and Harold Frederic's *The Damnation of Theron Ware* (1896) depict religious figures whose icy faith melts in the face of human reason's sunlight. Thomas Carlyle and Matthew Arnold poetically mourn the loss of childhood/child-like faith, hoping that humanity can ascend to greater heights through the arts and education.[4]

This is the literary lineage of Nephi Anderson's 1921 novel, *Dorian*, which focused on tensions between science and religion at greater length than any Mormon novel to that point. This essay situates *Dorian* within Mormonism's cultural landscape dating back to the mid-nineteenth century. This extended

---

2.   Charles Taylor, *A Secular Age* (Cambridge, MA: Belknap Press of Harvard University Press, 2007), 22, 374.

3.   See Gillian Beer, *Darwin's Plots: Evolutionary Narrative in Darwin, George Eliot and Nineteenth-Century Fiction* (Cambridge, MA: Cambridge University Press, 2009). Nephi Anderson quoted one of Charles Kingsley's poems ("A Farewell") at the beginning of his serially published story "Piney Ridge Cottage," *The Juvenile Instructor* 46, no. 2 (February 1911): 72. Some of the issues haunting *Frankenstein* show up in a discussion about the "Law of Biogensis," on pp. 120 – 121.

4.   Harold Frederic, *The Damnation of Theron Ware* (Chicago: Stone & Kimball, 1896); Mrs. Humphrey Ward, *Robert Elsmere* (London: Smith, Elder & Co., 1888). Anderson depicts Dorian as being drawn to "books by Mrs. Humphrey Ward" among other books in the opening chapter (5). My inclusion of Carlyle and Arnold follows Charles Taylor, *A Secular Age* (Cambridge, MA: Belknap Press, 2007), 377–419.

backdrop enables us to highlight anxieties which Mormons like Anderson were dealing with.[5]

MORMONIZING SCIENCE

The earliest Latter-day Saints constructed a restorationist self-identity largely at odds with their surrounding culture while simultaneously drawing from and appealing to its views. Joseph Smith proclaimed his was the "only true and living church," but also encouraged his disciples to gather up all the truths they could find in the world because they all belonged to "pure" Mormonism.[6] Leading Mormon thinkers freely mingled theological visions with emerging scientific proposals, as when Parley P. Pratt systematized Joseph Smith's striking revelations about God's innumerable inhabited planets in *Key to the Science of Theology* (1855).[7]

Mormons in Britain had to reckon with Darwin's *Origin of the Species* when the book first appeared in 1859, and they had a number of uniquely Mormon cosmological ideas to draw upon. The first editorial response largely dismissed Darwin by describing earth's "pre-Adamite ages" when a "'Royal Planter' sows the primordial seeds" that evolved into plants fit to host other species. As opposed to emerging from some primordial soup, reptiles and mammals were "transferred from another sphere ... each kind being reproductive of itself"—but nevertheless evolving: "Progression marked every age of this planet's existence—eternal progression which has stamped in indelible characters its future destiny."[8]

Other editorials followed as more prestigious Church leaders like Orson Pratt and Erastus Snow decried Darwinism from the pulpit while simultaneously cashing in on the theory's cultural prestige by asserting a Mormon variant:

---

5.   For representative samples of an extensive literature, see Gene A. Sessions and Craig J. Oberg, eds., *The Search for Harmony: Essays on Science and Mormonism* (Salt Lake City: Signature Books, 1993).

6.   See D&C 1:30; Scott H. Faulring, *An American Prophet's Record: The Diaries and Journals of Joseph Smith* (Salt Lake City: Signature Books, 1989), 399.

7.   See Moses 1:35; 7:30; D&C 76:24. Erich Robert Paul describes Pratt's cosmological and eschatological fusion in the massively underrated book *Science, Religion, and Mormon Cosmology* (Urbana: University of Illinois Press, 1992), 110 – 112.

8.   n.a., "Creation," *Millennial Star* 8, vol. 22 (February 25, 1860), 113 – 115.

Humans were God's offspring, evolving into gods themselves.[9] Thus, Mormon leaders weren't entirely dismissive of Darwin. Charles W. Penrose said evolution was "true in some respects," maintaining individualized speciation.[10] James E. Talmage—the faith's first PhD recipient and eventual apostle—discussed evolution with cautious optimism.[11] There was no settled Mormon doctrine with regard to the theory, but critics and sympathizers alike affirmed that Mormonism's religious tenets offered something truer.

Rather than understanding Darwinism as a paradigmatic example of how science threatens religious faith, Mormon leaders confidently affirmed that true science and true religion were one and the same (while reserving first right of refusal to any given theory in the form of revelation). Mormonism, wrote one enthusiastic elder, "comprehends UNIVERSAL TRUTH!—all truth, of every kind and degree" whether in Mormonism or out of it. Distinctions like "religious and secular," "theological and scientific," "spiritual and natural," were meaningless because "Truth is *one*," including astronomy, geology, chemistry, natural philosophy, physiology, mathematics, geometry, and the gospel. As for Mormonism's motto? The poet had it right: "Seize upon truth where'er 'tis found, / On Christian or on heathen ground; / The flower's *divine,* where'er it grows."[12] Rather than being a religious tradition fading in the face of Enlightenment's bright dawn, Mormonism enthusiastically imbibed the spirit of progress as part of its divine mission.

Mormons tempered this optimism with warnings that the theories of men should be carefully adapted to the imperatives of their faith. A month after Darwin's death in 1882, Orson F. Whitney lamented that "even Christian churchmen are beginning to regard [Darwin's] once flagrant heresy with lenience." He either didn't know or glossed over the fact that Mormons like Talmage regarded the "heresy" with the sort of "cautious ambiguity" he

---

9.   Erastus Snow, "There is a God, Etc.," (March 3, 1878) JD 19:266 – 279; Orson Pratt, "The Book of Mormon, Etc." (August 25, 1878) JD 20:62 – 77. Other editorials include George Q. Cannon, ed., "Origin of Man," *Millennial Star* 23, no. 41 (October 12, 1861): 651 – 654.

10. Charles W. Penrose, "The Personality of God, Etc.," (November 16, 1884) JD 26:18 – 29.

11. James E. Talmage, *The Theory of Evolution* (Provo, UT: Utah County Teachers' Association, 1890); Matthew Bowman, *The Mormon People: The Making of an American Faith* (New York: Random House, 2012), 161.

12. Henry Whittall, "What is 'Mormonism'?," *Millennial Star* 23, no. 17 (April 27, 1861): 257 – 259; an unattributed and truncated stanza often attributed to Isaac Watts.

opposed.[13] Whitney was one of the strongest proponents of Mormonism's growing "Home Literature" movement, which encouraged authors to convey the spirit of Mormonism to youth via home-grown fiction. He might have been alarmed had he known that Nephi Anderson, Mormonism's most successful Home Literature author, was not entirely dismissive of Darwin. Anderson's first and last novels were published during a liminal period in Mormonism before Darwinism was banished from orthodox consideration. They offer a glimpse of the tensions present in Mormonism between optimism about human progress and science on one hand, and the threat of religious disenchantment on the other.

NEPHI ANDERSON

Turn-of-the-century Mormons are typically described as an embattled minority forced to assimilate into mainstream American society. By 1900, "polygamy lay in ruins, [the economic principles of] consecration had ended, and the theocracy of Utah was defeated."[14] At the same time, many "values, ideas, [and] habits" of Mormonism were already aligned with those of progressive America. Mormons were thus tasked with "finding ways to translate the things America demanded of them into the language and imperatives of their own faith."[15] Fiction was one of the best avenues for this. Nephi Anderson's first novel, *Added Upon*, appeared at this crucial transition point in Mormon history.

Added Upon is a narrative fictionalization of Mormonism's "plan of salvation"—the overarching worldview behind Mormon salvation. Anderson introduces readers to literal spirit children of God living in a pre-mortal world. Two of them fall in love and are reconnected during mortality on earth. By keeping the faith they jointly receive heavenly rewards after death and resurrection. The

---

13. Orson F. Whitney, "Man's Origin and Destiny," *The Contributor* 3, no. 9 (June 1882): 268 – 270. Ambivalence about Darwin's work was not unusual at this point. Real scientific uncertainties still existed; the mechanism for inheritance not understood until Thomas Morgan combined Mendelian genetics with his chromosomal theory of inheritance in 1915 (see Robin Marantz Henig, *The Monk in the Garden: The Lost and Found Genius of Gregor Mendel, the Father of Genetics* [Boston: Mariner Books, 2001]). The unsettled state of the theories help explain why Mormons who embraced aspects of evolution, including John A. Widtsoe and James E. Talmage, were careful in their acceptance.

14. Matthew Bowman, *The Mormon People: The Making of an American Faith* (New York: Random House, 2012), 152.

15. Ibid., 153.

closing chapter subtly engages Darwinism in a poetic recapitulation of the plan of salvation. Anderson employs the typical Mormon tactic of overlaying Darwinian evolution with Mormonism's eternal-progression evolution. Humans are righteous offspring of a "Celestial Father [and] Mother" who can develop the same qualities as God and return to the "celestial world, [where] *the fittest have survived.*"[16] *Added Upon* is steeped in Mormon optimism regarding human progression, inculcating progressive values like honesty, moral virtue, hard work, and the power of human rationality. In addition to its radically distinct cosmology spanning pre- and post-mortal realms, the novel's emphasis upon all-American values perfectly exemplifies the turn-of-the-century Mormon theological project of harmonizing Mormonism with the best of its host culture.

Anderson's eternal-progression evolution was not unique to him. It increasingly found expression in more sophisticated philosophical works by Mormon writers like Nels Nelson, but *Added Upon* reached more Mormon readers than more technical works could.[17] Anderson's preface presented the book's speculative nature as a benefit rather than a drawback, hoping that "the mind of the reader, illumined by the Spirit of the Lord, will be able to fill in all the details that the heart may desire, to wander at will in the garden of the Lord, and dwell in peace in the mansions of the Father."[18] Anderson affirmed the ability of human imagination guided by inspiration to flesh out nascent possibilities in Mormon thought, reflecting the Romantic side of Mormonism's "rational theology" as developed by educated Mormon leaders like apostle John A. Widtsoe and seventy B.H. Roberts, both of whom, like Anderson, emigrated from Europe to the United States after their families converted to the faith.[19]

---

16. Nephi Anderson, *Added Upon* (Salt Lake City: Deseret News Press, 1898 [1912 ed.]), 225, emphasis mine.

17. Nels Lars Nelson depicts physical evolution as a mere "husk" compared to "psychic" and "spiritual" evolution described by the Mormon system in "Heaven versus Nirvana: a brief examination of the rational sanction for immortality," *Improvement Era* 8, nos. 7 – 8 (May – June 1905): 481, 579.

18. Nephi Anderson, *Added Upon*, 3d ed. (Salt Lake City: Deseret News Press, 1912), 3.

19. See John A. Widtsoe, "Joseph Smith as Scientist, Part VI: The Law of Evolution," *Improvement Era* 7, no. 6 (April 1904): 401 – 409; *Rational Theology: As Taught by The Church of Jesus Christ of Latter-day Saints* (Salt Lake City: General Priesthood Committee of the Church of Jesus Christ of Latter-day Saints, 1915); B.H. Roberts, *The Truth, the Way, the Life: An Elementary Treatise on Theology*, ed. John W. Welch (Provo, Utah: BYU Studies, 1994).

Mormonism's rational theology was coalescing at a point when religious faith seemed to be on the wane. While many progressive Protestants articulated more rational faiths, Mormon proponents initially side-stepped religion-versus-science controversies by framing their faith as a co-evolving restoration of truth which encompassed scientific advances beyond the confines of the Church. But as Mormons became increasingly familiar with scientific theories, older theological propositions like the above-mentioned "Royal Planters" appeared increasingly far-fetched, as discussed below. Anderson seemed to sense that *Added Upon*'s creative approach might not satisfy the rising generation of Mormons who were better acquainted with scientific theories about the origin of human life. By publishing his final novel *Dorian* (1921), Anderson affirmed that fiction could still provide a garden in which faith and reason could be cultivated. But unlike *Added Upon*, the characters in *Dorian* remain firmly planted on this earth's soil.[20] Optimism about human reason is repeatedly tempered by an awareness that it could threaten religious faith.

Although *Dorian* is a faith-affirming book, it resembles some of the more pessimistic realist novels written by progressive and even lapsed Protestants struggling to keep the sinking raft of faith afloat on a rising sea of secularism. *Dorian* appeared a few decades after the most popular of these realist novels were published, as the "acids of modernity" took longer to eat through early Mormonism's protective science-affirming shell.[21] Thus, *Dorian* sheds light on the tensions Mormons felt more pressingly after 1900 and the theological means they used to alleviate the tension. Through the novel, Anderson promotes proactive engagement with emerging scientific theories, exuding confidence that religious truths could not merely remain intact in the processes, but could actually facilitate further scientific discoveries. The following overview of *Dorian* offers more reasons to suspect that simple subtraction stories fail to fully reckon with the "complex legacy of the Enlightenment."[22] Finally, a brief comparison to other turn-of-the-century novels reflecting on science and religion illuminates theological differences between Mormonism and other Christian faiths reacting to similar cultural pressures.

---

20. The topic of a premortal life is discussed, but no scenes occur there. The only postmortal encounter occurs in a dream (163).

21. Martin E. Marty, *The Public Church: Mainline – Evangelical – Catholic* (New York: Crossroad, 1981), ix.

22. Taylor, *A Secular Age*, 371.

NEPHI ANDERSON'S *DORIAN*

Dorian was written during Mormonism's most wrenching period of assimilation. Between the late 1800s and the early 1900s the LDS Church transitioned away from its communalist and polygamous practices toward an American progressivism whose underlying values already resonated with the faith. Transitional tensions peek through Anderson's narrative. When Dorian wonders aloud about class distinctions in the LDS Church he is told that while certain "unthinking members" believe themselves too educated or rich to associate with the less educated and poor, Mormonism is ideally egalitarian; "character alone is the standard of classification" (60). The shift from polygamous to monogamous marriage receives expression through Dorian's desires for his peer Mildred Brown, who dies at a young age. There are hints that Dorian anticipates an eternal union with her even after falling in love and planning marriage with Carlia Duke.[23] The need to reconcile the sciences and Mormonism intersects with these other anxieties, but ultimately transcends them as one of the book's central themes. Each of these themes—marriage, social class, and the role of the sciences—reflect some of the more salient cultural pressures facing turn-of-the-century Mormons.

MARRIAGE AND KNOWLEDGE

At its root, *Dorian* tells a double love story. Long before Dorian Trent falls in love with Carlia Duke[24] (and Mildred Brown), his heart belongs to another adored: Knowledge. Dorian is a precocious boy who excels in school and ultimately aspires to reconcile his Mormon faith with the natural sciences.

These two themes (love for knowledge and love for Carlia) seem unnaturally stacked together in Anderson's blocky narrative, but the opening scene highlights one of two connective tissues between them: The repeated deferment of educational aspirations due to more practical realities of life. Dorian and Carlia

---

23. Dorian chastises himself for pining after "the dead Mildred to the exclusion of the very much alive Carlia. Mildred was safe in the world of spirits, where he would some day meet her again ... " (103, 144). When Carlia goes missing, Dorian meets Mildred in a dream of "the heavenly land." She smiles at his arrival before asking with concern: "Where's Carlia?" This prompts Dorian to seek Carlia out (163). Anderson doesn't connect the dots, but eternal marriages to more than one wife continued after polygamy was abolished—provided only one of the wives was still alive.

24. Should we make much of the similar sounding names of Dorian/Darwin, or that Carlia Duke shares initials with Charles Darwin?

first meet when he rescues her from a canal. In the rescue's aftermath, Carlia's dark hair and white party dress can't compete with the stack of freshly purchased books Dorian drops into the canal as he pulls her from the water. Together they helplessly watch the precious package of books—which Dorian purchased with money intended for a pair of new shoes—"glide over the falls at the headgate and then go dancing over the rapids" (12). This is only the first of several interferences to Dorian's educational aspirations. Others include his own apathy, farming responsibilities, Mildred's death, caring for his single mother, and various other Carlia-related bumps. This is a common literary theme of a character torn between practical duties and aspirational desires.

Less common is the second connective tissue between his love of education and his love of Carlia. It involves shifting ideas about Mormonism's lay priesthood. An epigraph from Brigham Young appears on *Dorian's* title page: "The Keys of the Holy Priesthood unlock the Door of Knowledge and let you look into the Palace of Truth."[25] At first glance, the quotation seems to pertain more to Dorian's desire to reconcile science and Mormonism than his relationship with Carlia—odd, given that the latter theme receives more narrative attention. Dorian's mentor, the elderly Zedekiah Manning, introduces Dorian to Brigham Young's sermons (not to mention a number of other important Mormon writers[26]) in order to inspire the boy to fulfill the project he wishes he were young enough to attempt:

> I would devote all my mind, might and strength to the learning of truth, of scientific truth. I would cover every branch of science possible in the limits of one life, especially the natural sciences. Then with my knowledge of the gospel *and the lamp of inspiration which the priesthood entitles me to*, I could harmonize the great body of truth coming from any and every source. Dorian, what a life work that would be! (74)

---

25. The slightly altered quote is from Brigham Young, "Discourse delivered by President B. Young in the Tabernacle, G.S.L. City, August 15, 1852," *Millennial Star* 25, supplement (1853): 58 – 59. In context, Young explains that previous generations who passed away before Mormonism was established would return during the Millennium to assist in binding the family of God together in Mormon temples. Anderson is more likely to have seen it in "Salvation for the Dead," *The Contributor* 11, no. 3 (January 1890): 88.

26. These include Orson and Parley Pratt, Orson Spencer, W.W. Phelps, as well as sets of Mormon publications like *Millennial Star*, *Improvement Era*, *The Contributor*, and the *Journal of Discourses*.

Elsewhere, "Uncle Zed" tells Dorian, "I expect to see you learned; and the Priesthood which you have is your assurance, through your diligence and faithfulness, to any heights" (61). These heights include marriage to a girl (Mildred) beyond Dorian's socioeconomic class. Zed also introduces Dorian and Carlia to D&C 132 as "the most wonderful love story ever written ... here in the revelation on the eternity of the marriage covenant we find that men and women, under the proper conditions and by the proper authority, may be united as husbands and wives, not only for time, but for eternity" (48).

In short, what initially seem like two unrelated themes are connected through the concept of Mormonism's priesthood, which will assist Dorian in reconciling scientific truths with Mormonism, and also facilitate eternal marriage with Carlia. Young's epigraph can be read to refer to Dorian's search for a spouse as much as his search for scientific truth. Strikingly, Anderson places the culmination of both imperatives beyond the scope of the novel. It concludes with Dorian and Carlia *planning* a future wedding while Dorian is still *planning* to engage with science and Mormonism.

NATURAL THEOLOGY

Dorian's approach to the reconciliation of science and Mormonism is guided by more than the Mormon priesthood. It reflects the emphasis Mormonism placed upon the practical and applied sciences.[27] When Dorian begins coming into his own academically, his knowledge is largely of the practical, applied sort. He lectures his single mother on the virtues of good hygiene (54 – 55) and corrects Carlia's grammar (57). Uncle Zed informs Dorian that his having started out as a simple farm boy actually puts him ahead of more "genteel workers" by placing him "in close touch with the earth, and the life which teems in soil and air and the waters" (59). This practical-minded approach to science merges with Mormon theological ideas about God's creation of the earth using pre-existent matter through the application of and adherence to eternal laws. If the transcendent was moved further offstage for modern-minded folks, Mormonism radically immanentized God. By becoming acquainted with "botany, zoology, mineralogy, chemistry, and all the other sciences," one becomes acquainted with the laws under which God himself operates (118). This is just one step away from

---

27. Lester Bush argues this practical bent helped Mormons come to grips with applied medicine as the Church transitioned from greater to lesser reliance on miraculous healing in *Health and Medicine Among the Latter-day Saints: Science, Sense, and Scripture* (New York: Crossroad, 1993).

materialists who deny the transcendent by chalking mystery up to unsolved puzzles. Many believers became unbelievers when materialism combined with their conceptions of an *impersonal* cosmos, thus eliminating a place for a transcendent God. But Anderson's Mormon view accepts materialism as a reaffirmation of the fundamentally *personal* nature of God.

Mormonism's emphasis on learning about God through the laws of nature was the latest in a line of longstanding efforts at "natural theology," whereby God's will can be discerned by studying the rocks and trees as much as in the sacred scriptures. Philosophers like John Ray and William Paley allied theology with Newtonian science to discern God's purposes made evident in a mechanized universe, thereby setting the stage for the rise of Deism beginning in the seventeenth century. To become acquainted with the universe was to become acquainted with God.[28] This attitude was common enough by the nineteenth century that Darwin himself includes an epigraph from Francis Bacon on *Origin*'s title page—an epigraph which Dorian himself might have appreciated: "Let no man out of a weak conceit of sobriety, or an ill-applied moderation, think or maintain, that a man can search too far or be too well studied in the book of God's word, or in the book of God's works; divinity or philosophy; but rather let men endeavour an endless progress or proficiency in both."[29]

Much to Dorian's delight, Uncle Zed affirms a similar unfettered confidence time and again, but the young man would have felt less sanguine about the other quote Darwin included from priest/scientist William Whewell: "But with regard to the material world ... we can perceive that events are brought about not by insulated interpositions of Divine power, exerted in each particular case, but by the establishment of general laws."[30] In contrast to Deists who believed God essentially wound up the clock-universe and stepped back, Mormons like Dorian believed that God's operation according to natural laws did not prevent direct intervention in the natural order of things—by appearances in bodily form to the prophet Joseph Smith, angels miraculously transmitting golden plates, divine healings, and so forth. As James E. Talmage famously

---

28. See the entry on "Natural Theology" in the extremely useful book, *A Science and Religion Primer*, eds. Heidi A. Campbell and Heather Looy (Grand Rapids: Baker Academic Press, 2009), 155 – 157.

29. Citing "Bacon: Advancement of Learning." See Charles Darwin, *On the Origin of the Species by Means of Natural Selection, or the Preservation of Favoured Races in the Struggle For Life* (London: John Murray, 1859).

30. Darwin, *On the Origin of the Species*, citing "W. Whewell: Bridgewater Treatise."

explained in the landmark book *Articles of Faith*, there are no "supernatural miracles." Rather, God accomplishes the seemingly miraculous by "application of a higher [natural] law" of which humans remain ignorant.[31] Moreover, God desired humans to master these same laws just as He had, although ambiguity over the specific details of God's own progression is evident in Uncle Zed's description of the plan of salvation/evolution:

> God is one of a race, *the foremost and first, if you wish it,* but still one of a race of beings who inhabit the universe; that we humans are His children, begotten of Him in the pre-mortal world in His image; that we are on the upward path through eternity, following Him who has gone before and has marked out the way. (78, emphasis mine)

Uncle Zed criticizes the "metaphysical meandering" of preachers and philosophers who de-personalize God. Tennyson and Alexander Pope's affirmations that "Nature is God," makes for "beautiful poetry, but it tells only a part of the truth" (76 – 77). Zed quotes philosophical definitions of God as "the integrated harmony of all potentialities of good in every actual and possible rational agent" and "the all-controling [*sic*] consciousness of the universe ... the unfathomable, all unknowable, and unknowable abyss of being beyond." He grants that these contain "some truth," but they fall short of *the Truth* by confounding God's person with his attributes (76 – 78, 97 – 98). "I may describe the scent of the rose," Zed adds, "but that does not define the rose itself" (98). Notice Zed's objections to high-falutin' philosophies are more experientially driven—such views are wrong to the extent that they inhibit one's personal relationship with deity:

> ... for me to be able to think of God, I must have some image of Him. I cannot think of love or good, or power or glory in the abstract. These must be expressed to me by symbols at least as eminating from [sic], or inherent in, or exercised by some person. Love cannot exist alone: there must be one who loves and one who is being loved. God is love. That means to me that a person, a beautiful, glorified, allwise, benevolent being exercises that divine principle which is shed forth on you and me. (77 – 78)

---

31. James E. Talmage, *The Articles of Faith* (Salt Lake City: Deseret News, 1899), 222.

DARWIN, DORIAN, AND THE SUBLIME

Although Uncle Zed is critical of non-Mormon theologians, philosophers and scientists, he isn't entirely dismissive of them. He encourages Dorian's intellectual wrestles with some of the age's great thinkers. One of the most striking aspects of Anderson's narrative is his depiction of this young Latter-day Saint's confident engagement with difficult issues. With interesting resonances to other nineteenth-century reflections on the "sublime," Dorian must take to the wilderness to begin his ordeal. He builds himself a little one-room log house in a canyon next to a mountain stream whose "wild music sang him to sleep" (71). Like Thoreau, Dorian is deeply moved by the hills, the birds, and the wild in general; "he minded not solitude" because "the wild odorous verdure of the hills, the cool breezes, the song of the distant streams, the call of the birds, all seemed to harmonize with his own feelings" (71). Uncle Zed shares the sensibility that "nature, wild or tamed, is my schoolroom" (136). Zed even writes nature poetry. One sample reflects on the benefits of living away from cities where it is "Most peaceful here:—no city's noise obtains / And God seems reverenced more where silence reigns" (135). Another poem conceives of the wonders of nature—the humming of bees, the smell of springtime, the sunny sky—as love songs to humans (136). Dorian finds another opportunity for solitude through "a wise provision of nature that the cold of winter closes in the activity in field and garden, thus allowing time for study by the home fire" (142).

Unlike Thoreau, who is both delighted *and* disturbed by the apparently hostile and indifferent elements of the wild, Dorian takes to cultivation of the land through dry-farming, and cultivation of his mind through study. The voices tempting him in the wilderness include those "of Darwin, of Huxley, of Ingersol [sic] and of Tom Payne [sic]" (71).[32] Dorian dismisses Ingersoll as a weak polemicist, but his reaction to Darwin is strikingly nuanced, especially considering the recent firing of BYU professors over evolutionary theory and the rise of anti-Darwinist thinking within Mormonism over the next several decades:

---

32. For a fascinating turn-of-the-century response to Thomas Huxley's criticism of Mormonism, see Thos. W. Brookbank, "Professor Huxley on Mormonism," *The Contributor* 10, no. 7 (May, 1889): 249 – 253. Anderson himself critiqued Robert Ingersoll in "Wisdom of God—Agency of Man," *The Contributor* 11, no. 10 (August, 1890): 366 – 369. Such responses signal the anxiety of Mormons like Brookbank and Anderson, which is evinced by their desire to present an intellectually respectable faith. They did so in the face of charges that Mormonism appealed to deluded simpletons dating back to the archetype ignoramus, Joseph Smith.

> Darwin's book was rather heavy, but by close application, [Dorian] thought
> he learned what the scientist was "driving at." This book disturbed him
> somewhat. There seemed to be much truth in it, but also some things which
> did not agree with what he had been taught to be true. In this he realized his
> lack of knowledge. More knowledge must clear up any seeming contradic-
> tion, he reasoned. (72)

Dorian simply needs more knowledge, which he can gain as Uncle Zed's
protégé. Ward's *Robert Elsmere* and Ericson's *The Damnation of Theron Ware*
similarly ally their young male protagonists with older male mentors—only to
opposite effect. Theron loses his faith under the influence of a skeptical Catholic priest and an atheist local philosopher. Oxford fellow Mr. Grey helps Robert
trade his childish beliefs about the supernatural in for a purely human Christ
and an impersonal God of the sort decried by Uncle Zed, who hyper-
personalizes God. To Anderson, Mormonism can split the difference between
agnostic and atheistic scientists and liberal-minded clergymen who sought to
portray God as an impersonal force. Moreover, for Robert and Theron, the
score seems largely settled: science has spoken, progress is eliminating childish
faith. For Dorian, the field of knowledge is white, ready to harvest, waiting for
him to "devote [his] life to the harmonizing of science and religion" (150).[33]

HENRY DRUMMOND AND SECTARIAN SHORTCOMINGS

For some reason, Anderson doesn't acknowledge his own Mormon contemporaries who were trying to execute similar reconciliation projects, going so far as
to claim that "no one seemed to be doing it as yet" (220). Instead of pointing
Dorian toward LDS leaders like Roberts, Talmage, and Widtsoe, or other non-
hierarchical Mormons like Nels Nelson and William H. Chamberlin,[34] Uncle
Zed directs him to natural scientist and Scottish clergyman, Henry Drummond

---

33. These novels call for more comparison than I have space for. For instance, each also involves women
companions: Robert's Catherine is deeply devout and would find his loss of faith devastating, Theron's
Celia inadvertently tempts him to desire an adulterous affair, and Dorian lets Carlia know that as a
scholar's wife she'll lead a simple life.

34. Nelson explicitly declared that Mormonism was "able to organize the truths of evolution into a larger
whole and supply intelligent motive" behind God's use of evolution. See Nelson, "Theosophy and Mormonism," *The Contributor* 16, no. 10 (August 1895): 617 – 625; *Scientific Aspects of Mormonism* (New
York: G.P. Putnam & Sons, 1904), 77. William H. Chamberlin's attempt appeared in a BYU publication,
"The Theory of Evolution as an Aid to Faith in God and Belief in the Resurrection," *The White and Blue*,
14 February. 1911, n.p.

(73). Zed offers Drummond's *Natural Law in the Spiritual World* (1883) as a prototype for Dorian's project because he believes it already conforms so well to Mormon principles: "Drummond has attempted to prove that the laws which prevail in the temporal world about us also hold good in the spiritual world" (117).[35] This aligned well with Zed's interpretation of D&C 88 (100, 138), as well as Joseph Smith's assertion that "all spirit is matter" (D&C 131:7).

Zed affirms that Darwin's evolution from below is inferior to Drummond's (and Mormonism's) evolution from above because it relies on "initial and unaided movements of the lower" (124). Zed's "law of progress" demands "an exercise of the will" on the part of an evolving being who also "must be willing to receive help from a higher source," in addition to being "unselfish, willing, eager to share all good with others" (124 – 125). Drummond comes close, Zed notes, but the "weakness of his argument" stems from the fact that "much of his theology is of the perverted sectarian kind" (73). Anderson had sounded this theme in an earlier work in which a Lutheran pastor called Harald Einersen resigns from his headmaster position at a parochial school. The sanctimoniously clean-shaven Pastor Bange confronts Einersen for teaching against creation ex nihilo in a physics class. "When it came to a conflict between the catechism and the text-book on science," Einersen solemnly declares, "I decided in favor of the text-book ... I am willing to accept truth from whatever source it comes. I hope I shall be ever willing to discard all error, when my reason decides that it is error."[36]

In these instances, Anderson cashes in on longstanding anti-clerical attitudes while overlooking a tension within Mormonism regarding the priesthood and truth claims. Recall that Zed identifies the priesthood as the tool which entitles Dorian to greater truths than Drummond could attain, but he is not clear on exactly how. Is he referring to the gift of the Holy Ghost as a means of inspiration—the reception of which must occur through priesthood channels (119)?

---

35. Henry Drummond, *Natural Law in the Spiritual World* (New York: Hurst & Co., 1883).

36. Sarah Reed called my attention to Nephi Anderson, *The Castle Builder* (Salt Lake City: Deseret News Press, 1909), 122 – 124. Einersen was ultimately more offended at the evangelical Lutheran pastor's preaching against the possibility of postmortal salvation for people who never heard the gospel message than the anti-scientific fundamentalism. Notably, several Mormon professors faced similar resistance against scientific claims, resulting in loss of position at Brigham Young University two years after *The Castle Builders* was published. See James M. McLachlan, "W.H. Chamberlin and the Quest for a Mormon Theology," *Dialogue: A Journal of Mormon Thought* 29, no. 4 (Winter 1996): 151 – 167. It is significant that Anderson published his muted but positive assessment of Darwin and scientific advancement in *Dorian* just a few years after this incident.

Or does Dorian have a right to inspiration simply by virtue of holding the priesthood (61, 74, 129)? Or are additional truths confined to revelation as delivered through the Church's hierarchical authorities (78)? If the latter, couldn't Dorian be stifled by rigid beliefs as much as Drummond could? Each of these possible interpretations is present in *Dorian* without any being offered as definitive. Regardless, Uncle Zed recognizes that "the Latter-day Saints have been adversely criticized for holding out such astounding hopes for the future of the human race," but nevertheless affirms their restored truths could merge with scientific perspectives to the betterment of humanity in general (102). Zed himself wouldn't live to see that day.

TRANSPLANT THEOLOGY

"The mantle of Brother Zed seems to have fallen on Dorian Trent," the Bishop solemnly observes at Uncle Zed's funeral. "May he wear it faithfully and well" (133). To the novel's end, Dorian remains optimistic about his chances at demonstrating the compatibility of Mormonism with the natural sciences. His optimism is tempered by the understanding that the project is not without dangers. Zed had warned Dorian against missing Church meetings while reading "Ingersol [sic] and Tom Paine" because "there is danger in remaining away too long from the established sources of inspiration and uplift" (79). Dorian adds more Orson Pratt and Brigham Young to his reading itinerary in order to establish "a faith which would stand him well in need when he came to delve into a faithless and a Godless science" (143).[37] When Dorian tells his mother he plans to "go East to Yale or Harvard," she sounds a cautious note: "And all the time you'll have to keep near to God and never lose your faith in the gospel, for what doth it profit if you gain the whole world of knowledge and lose your own soul" (151). Dorian himself gives voice to the dangers while discussing his university plans with Carlia: "I know some men who have gone in for all the learning they could obtain, and in the process of getting the learning, they have lost their faith. With me, the very object of getting knowledge is to strengthen my faith. What would it profit if one gains the whole world of learning and loses his soul in the process. Knowledge is power, both for good and for ill" (220). Through Dorian, Anderson encouraged a *bridled* enthusiasm for the powers of human reason.

---

37. The stark description of a "Godless science" stands in contrast with other citations of religiously inclined scientists in the novel.

If these anxieties pressed upon Anderson's generation more than that of earlier Mormons, Dorian nevertheless countered them with Brigham Young's confident mantra: "The idea that the religion of Christ is one thing, and science is another, is a mistaken idea, for there is no true science without religion" (129 – 130).[38] As mentioned above, Mormons framed their religion as an ongoing restoration of truths which could encompass scientific advances beyond the confines of the Church. But as Mormons became increasingly familiar with scientific theories, older theological propositions fell by the wayside, including many which had been advanced as truth by leaders of the Church. Thus, scientific advances could corrode elements of Mormonism even for the most faithful. This dynamic can be seen in Anderson's pre-publication drafts of *Dorian*. One particular excerpt was removed before the book went to press. Following Uncle Zed's death, Dorian inherits the books and manuscripts Zed collected for the grand project he didn't live to complete:

> The very first paper was in the old man's own hand, and was a comment on the evolutionist's theory that life originated on this earth some millions of years ago and developed from that time to this by these long ages of growth. Uncle Zed wrote:
>
> "Life, in its various stages of progress has always existed in some place or other; therefore, life, in its so-called perfected state exists now as it always has existed. Worlds are and always have been created and endowed with life. What a waste of time and energy to have life begin on each separate world from a protoplasmic form and then have to evolve through ages of time to its present earth-stage condition! How much more reasonable to think that the germs or seeds of life in a form perfected for its environment is transplanted from a world where it exists to one ready for the planting. A gardener, having a number of plots of land would be foolish to begin with the wild rose or the crab apple from which to develop the perfect flower and fruit by long and slow process of cultivation, if that gardener already had these perfected products in one of his gardens from which he could transplant. Surely, God is as wise as any earthly husbandman."[39]

---

38. From Brigham Young, "The Things of God, Etc.," JD 17 (Liverpool and London: LDS Booksellers Depot, 1875), 52.

39. The selection appears in a copy of Anderson's handwritten manuscript in my possession, pp. 169 – 170. In the typescript version, Anderson has crossed the entire section out (see pp. 121 – 122). In the typescript version, Anderson replaces "comment on" with "dissertation on." This selection would have appeared beginning on page 134 of the first edition. See dorian.peculiarpages.com for pdfs of these originals.

Anderson is drawing on a now-forgotten element of early Mormon theology which was marginalized in part due to enthusiastic expectations that science and religious tenets would mutually reinforce each other. The idea of a "Royal Planter" bringing "choice seeds of the older Paradise" to this earth from other planets, not to mention "every species of animal life" and "a son of God, with his beloved spouse" (Adam and Eve), first appears in Parley P. Pratt's 1855 *Key to the Science of Theology*.[40] Brigham Young repeatedly invoked this apparently fantastical interplanetary scene of Creation in which Adam was "first brought here from another planet," while at the same time ridiculing literalist readings of Genesis in which Adam was "fashioned the same as we make adobies [bricks]."[41]

The view faded from Mormon discourse over the years, but even the intellectual B.H. Roberts held out for an interstellar transplant theology as a good "means of harmonizing those facts established by the researches of men and the facts of revelation."[42] Roberts's harmonization included an earth much older than 6,000 years with pre-Adamite animal and vegetable life and death—views which led to a standoff with Mormon apostle Joseph Fielding Smith a decade after *Dorian* was published.[43] But when Roberts first published them in an 1889 issue of *The Contributor* magazine, he ruffled few feathers.[44]

Ongoing speculations on these matters reached their peak just before *Dorian* was published.[45] A few months after the centennial anniversary of Charles

---

40. Parley P. Pratt, *A Key to the Science of Theology* (Liverpool: F.D. Richards, 1855), 47 – 50. A late (1877) reminiscence attributes the claim that Adam and Eve "came here from another planet" to Joseph Smith. See "Reflections of John M. Whitaker," BYU Lib. Call # Mar. M270.1 W58r, from phelpsfamilyhistory.com/branches/tolman/bio_anson_cal.asp (accessed September 4, 2013).

41. Brigham Young, "The Gospel, Etc.," JD 2:6; "Intelligence, Etc.," 7:285. These ideas formed part of Young's "Adam – God" theological matrix. See also JD 1:50; 3:319; 17:144. Heber C. Kimball also promoted transplant theology in JD 1:356; 8:243 – 244.

42. B.H. Roberts, *The Gospel. An Exposition of its First Principles* (Salt Lake City: George Q. Cannon & Sons, 1893 [revised and enlarged edition]), 333 – 336.

43. See James B. Allen, "The Story of *The Truth, The Way, The Life*," in B.H. Roberts's, *The Truth, The Way, The Life*, ed., John W. Welch, clix – cxcvii.

44. B.H. Roberts, "Man's Relationship to Deity," *The Contributor* 10, no. 7 (May, 1889): 263 – 268. Interestingly, Roberts quotes a section of W.W. Phelps's hymn, "If You Could Hie to Kolob," just like Uncle Zed does for Dorian (100 – 102).

45. For more detail, see Gary James Bergera, "The 1911 Evolution Controversy at Brigham Young University," in *The Search for Harmony: Essays on Science and Mormonism*, ed. Gene A. Sessions and Craig J. Oberg (Salt Lake City: Signature Books, 1993), 23 – 43.

Darwin's birth was celebrated at BYU, the First Presidency of the Church sanctioned an official statement called "The Origin of Man" regarding evolution controversies. The statement didn't pronounce specifically on the age of the earth, or the mutability of various species, or other hot-button claims. The statement opened a wide space for various interpretations by describing Adam simply as "the primal parent of the race" without referring to the transplant theology, and the controversy continued.[46] The Church's 1910 Priest Quorum manual affirmed that human "descent has not been from a lower form of life, but from the highest Form of Life." Citing Brigham Young and Parley P. Pratt's transplant theology, the manual hedges that Adam was "probably not the first mortal man in the universe, but he was likely the first for this earth."[47] This sparked another round of questions resulting in the final public Church statement on the controversy of the era. The piece lists all of the scriptures referring to the creation of Eve and Adam and concludes by once again leaving the matter open to various opinions:

> These are the authentic statements of the scriptures, ancient and modern, and it is best to rest with these, until the Lord shall see fit to give more light on the subject. Whether the mortal bodies of man evolved in natural processes to present perfection, through the direction and power of God; whether the first parents of our generations, Adam and Eve, were transplanted from another sphere, with immortal tabernacles, which became corrupted through sin and the partaking of natural foods, in the process of time; whether they were born here in mortality, as other mortals have been, are questions not fully answered in the revealed word of God.[48]

Returning to *Dorian*, Zed could have drawn the transplant theology from Brigham Young or *The Contributor*, as he cites these as important sources. But for some reason, Anderson thought better of including it even though the Church's 1910 statement left the possibility on the table, resulting in further

---

46. "The Origin of Man," *Improvement Era* 13, no. 13 (November, 1909): 75 – 81. The article has since been reprinted several times in Church magazines, most recently in the February 2002 issue of the *Ensign*. See lds.org/ensign/2002/02/the-origin-of-man (accessed September 5, 2013).

47. n.a., Divine Mission of the Savior, Course of Study for the Priests (2d Year), Prepared and Issued under the Direction of the General Authorities of the Church (Salt Lake City: Church of Jesus Christ of Latter-day Saints, 1910), 35.

48. "Priesthood Quorums' Table," *Improvement Era* 13, no. 6 (April, 1910): 570.

discussions and private First Presidency statements directed at leaders of the Church. Transplant theology was one of the biggest sticking points between B.H. Roberts and Joseph Fielding Smith, both of whom appealed to transplant theology in different ways.[49] Roberts's version died with Roberts in 1933, and despite instructions from the First Presidency otherwise, Joseph Fielding Smith continued to promote his anti-evolutionary version for the next several decades.[50] Even so, transplant theology has faded entirely from the current Mormon theological lexicon.

It isn't immediately clear why Anderson removed transplant theology from *Dorian,* but the deletion is illustrative of the way Mormon leaders have tended to allow certain aspects of theology to quietly disappear rather than to openly confront and replace them. Armand Mauss describes a "myth of history as time-filtered" which developed in tandem with Mormonism's affirmation of continuing revelation from God. According to this myth, "Obsolete ideas and practices simply do not count any more, even if they originated as divine revelations" to past Church prophets like Brigham Young. For various reasons ("organizational morale," the "influx of new members," felt allegiance to past leaders and anxiety to maintain confidence in present leaders), Mormon leaders have been more likely to let the past melt away than to directly confront no-longer-usable theological claims.[51]

This seems to be the case with the transplant theology, illustrating the perils of threading theological threads through scientific needles. In a faith tradition which affirms the presence of living prophets, the discoveries of science can challenge their authority. Anderson recognizes that Young's sermons and the likelihood that the "doctrinal articles of these first elders were no better than those of more recent writers, but their plain bluntness and their very age seemed to give them charm" (143).

This unstated tension permeates *Dorian,* as Anderson repeatedly cites Brigham Young's optimism about the powers of human reason and science to

---

49. Roberts held that Adam was not yet immortal when he was transplanted while Smith affirmed there could be no death—not even the potential for death—before the Fall of Adam. See Roberts, *The Truth, The Way, The Life,* ed. John W. Welch, 324 – 327.

50. Joseph Fielding Smith, *Man, His Origin and Destiny* (Salt Lake City: Deseret Book, 1954), 276 – 277; *Doctrines of Salvation* (Salt Lake City: Bookcraft, 1954) 1:139 – 140.

51. Armand L. Mauss, *All Abraham's Children: Changing Mormon Conceptions of Race and Lineage* (Urbana: University of Illinois Press, 2003), 263.

discover the things of God, but ultimately removes Young's increasingly science-fiction-like teachings about transplanted life forms from the final draft. At the same time, many Mormon leaders didn't hesitate to cash in on the cultural prestige attending new scientific theories. Brigham Young, George Q. Cannon, and others turned Darwinian evolution to their advantage by baptizing it in their theology of eternal progression—the ultimate evolution from humanity to godhood.

CONCLUSION

The harmonization of the natural sciences and Mormonism was a project that ultimately sidelined many faithful Mormons. B.H. Roberts, perhaps the most Dorian-like general authority the Church ever produced, described experiencing "the severest mental and spiritual strain of my life" while seeking hierarchical approval to publish his personal harmonization attempt.[52] "I am trying to summarize and reconcile all truth—all truth. But it is so hard."[53] Roberts, like Anderson, felt the weight of the New Testament query, "When the Son of man cometh, shall he find faith on the earth?" (Luke 18:8). Zed, Dorian, and Roberts each believed an affirmative answer to this scriptural question would depend on their efforts to reconcile their religious beliefs with a scientific worldview (75, 221).[54]

Uncle Zed and B.H. Roberts died before their masterworks could be completed, while Dorian's story ends on a pretentiously optimistic—though ambiguous—note. Dorian warns Carlia that she'll be a "poor man's wife," given his academic aspirations. Carlia "silently worshipped" as Dorian quaintly exclaims he must strive to become "greater than" scientific giants like Lord Kelvin and Sir Oliver Lodge (221 – 222). But first—reminiscent of the opening scene—Dorian must attend to Carlia, who asks if they can read *David Copperfield* together first:

> "Why, yes, of course," he said.
> Then they went on again, hand in hand, down into the valley of sunshine and shadow (223).

---

52. Roberts, *The Truth, The Way, The Life*, ed. Welch, cxci.

53. Ibid., cxcii.

54. B.H. Roberts, "Higher Criticism and the Book of Mormon," *Improvement Era* 14, no. 9 (July 1911): 786.

Perhaps Anderson sensed that there is enough shadow in this life to ultimately prevent the sort of "maximized" harmonization Dorian envisions.[55] Looking back over almost one hundred years of scientific and technological developments makes the harmonization project seem amazingly quaint; no single person could ever hope to encompass all truth. Anderson's optimism regarding the possibilities for faithful and scientific inquiry throws light on a particularly progressive strain of turn-of-the-century Mormonism, although the specific suggestions his characters make regarding how a Mormon might reconcile their religion with the natural sciences were already beginning to fade from wider Mormon thought. By presenting a character like Dorian, Anderson also seemed to anticipate the decline of LDS general authority involvement in harmonization projects. Once Joseph Fielding Smith and Bruce R. McConkie passed from the scene, discussions about evolutionary theory and the origin of humans have taken place almost exclusively among lay Mormons.[56]

Nephi Anderson's *Dorian* offers much material that can shed light on the theological horizons and cultural considerations of early twentieth-century Mormonism. While other literary characters like Robert Elsmere and Theron Ware encountered severe crises of faith as the nineteenth century edged into the twentieth, Dorian Trent encountered a certain confidence of faith as he aspired to create the ultimate harmonization between his belief in a personal God and his faith in the power of human reason—a harmonization that eludes us still, here in the valley of sunshine and shadow.

---

55. Michael Welker provides a useful schema of different models of scientific and religious discourse in "Science and Theology: Their Relation at the Beginning of the Third Millenium [sic]," in *The Oxford Handbook of Religion and Science*, ed. Philip Clayton and Zachary Simpson (New York: Oxford University Press, 2006), 551 – 561.

56. BYU evolutionary biologist Duane Jeffrey's contributions shouldn't be overlooked, but see also Howard C. Stutz, *Let the Earth Bring Forth: Evolution and Scripture* (Draper, UT: Greg Kofford Books, 2011) and Steven L. Peck, "Crawling Out of the Primordial Soup: A Step Toward the Emergence of an LDS Theology Compatible with Organic Evolution," *Dialogue: a Journal of Mormon Thought* 43, no. 1 (Spring 2010): 1 – 36.

A PLEA FOR FICTION

ORIGINALLY PUBLISHED IN *THE IMPROVEMENT ERA*
VOLUME I, NUMBER 3, JANUARY 1898

NEPHI ANDERSON

The statement made by critics that fiction reigns supreme in the literature of the day is no doubt true. In the list of published books, the novel takes the lead. Fiction comes in a continuous stream from the press of the country, and it reaches all classes of society.

Is the Latter-day Saint justified in reading fiction? I think I hear a mighty chorus of "No" from the spectacled fathers and mothers as they pause in their reading the latest tabernacle sermon, and a faint hearted "Yes" comes from our boys and girls as they timidly half conceal the story with the proverbial yellow back.

Both may be right, both may be wrong, for this reason: There are good novels and there are bad novels, as well as good and bad in all classes of books. This fact every reader, every parent, and every provider of reading matter should know.

I enter a plea for fiction, the good, pure, elevating kind. You, good soul, who claim that everything that is not a fact, or that does not literally happen is bad, have no scruples in hanging on your walls a beautiful oil painting, whose majestic hills, green foliage, and blue waters have no existence save in the imagination of the painter. The incidents of a story are just as existent as the scenes of your picture. You distinguish between drawings, praising the beautiful and condemning and shunning the evil. Consistency claims that you should do the same with the products of the pen.

Again, some, who strictly exclude every work of fiction from the home, admit any newspaper. The latter may be and often is filled with accounts of base deeds and revolting crimes put into readable form and which are eagerly "devoured" by the young. As such reading matter is supposed to be true and deals with facts, it is all commendable or at least, permissible; but the story wherein characters are drawn that beautify honor and virtue and nobleness, is shunned and condemned. Facts may be debasing, fiction may be elevating. Jesse James was a reality, Adam Bede was not.

The Great Teacher recognized the value of fiction in presenting truths to the understanding. Of him it is said: "But without a parable spake he not unto them." Many eminent writers have recognized this. The dreariest description or argument may have vitality and interest brought into it by bringing it in contact with human life and action. Vivid life pictures of any time or any place may be portrayed by the story. What historian has so correctly colored historical characters as Shakespeare? What can be better than Hugo's pictures of Parisian society? If you would know English life read Dickens.

Now then, if reading novels is not a sin, what will help us to choose the right kind? Among the vast amount of advice given on this subject, perhaps none is of more importance than this: Know the authors, learn something of the writers. "Doth a fountain send forth at the same place sweet water and bitter?" A writer consciously or unconsciously weaves within his work his own emotions, sentiments, conceptions of right and wrong, of duty, or morality. Then first, even above the literary qualifications of a writer, see to it that he or she views the virtues from the proper standpoint. Too few people know nothing about the authors of the books they read.

We should know that many names do stand for something. What a help it would be, for instance, if we always remembered that Scott and Lytton wrote historical romances, and that Cooper's were mostly of Indian adventure; that George Eliot's works are always deep, but the Duchess' are shallow; that Crawford is a romancist and Howells a realist; that Mary D. Ward writes of English life, religion and social problems, and Mrs. Herbert D. Ward describes New England scenes; that Mrs. Holmes writes solely of love, Mayne Reid of adventure, and Antony Hope of love and adventure, mixed; that no father or mother need fear to place in their children's hands stories written by Mrs. Alcott.

"The prose story," says a recent writer, "comes close to the heart of the world, gets into the pulses of the people, lounges in the slippered ease of the drawing room, swings in the summer hammock, circulates in the brain of the day, airs its opinions, its theories and philosophies through human lips in a hundred lands, and is read, read, read!"

Yes, the world reads fiction. If one has a message to deliver, he puts it in a novel, into a living, breathing thing. The Latter-day Saints have a great message to the world. What a field is here for the pen of the novelist. As Tennyson says:

> "Truth in closest words shall fail,
> When truth embodied in a tale,
> Shall enter in at lowly doors"

Transcription of this essay by Clare Wang.
Inclusion of original errata intentional.

PURPOSE IN FICTION

ORIGINALLY PUBLISHED IN *THE IMPROVEMENT ERA*
VOLUME I, NUMBER 4, FEBRUARY 1898

NEPHI ANDERSON

In his preface to the sixth edition of "Tom Brown's School Days," Thomas Hughes says:

"Several persons, for whose judgment I have the highest respect, while saying very kind things about this book, have added that the great fault of it is, 'too much preaching;' but they hope I shall amend in this matter should I ever write again. Now this I most distinctly decline to do. Why, my whole object in writing at all was to get the chance of preaching!

My sole object in writing was to preach to boys; if ever I write again it will be to some other age. I can't see that a man has any business to write at all unless he has something which he thoroughly believes and wants to preach about. If he has this and the chance of delivering himself of it, let him by all means put it in the shape in which it will be most likely to get a hearing; but never let him be so carried away as to forget that preaching is his object."

In contrast to this view, the more modern novelist, F. Marion Crawford, says:

"Probably no one denies that the first object of the novel is to amuse and interest the reader. The purpose-novel constitutes a violation of the unwritten contract tacitly existing between writer and reader. A man buys what purports to be a work of fiction, a romance, a story of adventure, pays his money, takes his book home, prepares to enjoy it at his ease, and discovers that he has paid a dollar for somebody's views on socialism, religion, or the divorce laws. In ordinary cases the purpose-novel is a simple fraud, besides being a failure in nine hundred and ninety-nine cases out of a thousand."

Here are two radically different views on the province of fiction. Dr. Hughes claims that the story could be a means by which to teach nobler principles, Mr. Crawford says that amusement and interest is its main object. It might here be said that Mr. Crawford is mistaken in one thing: Often a man buys a novel because of the "purpose" that sticks so prominently from it.

Many present day critics and reviewers agree with the latter writer. Their cry is "Art for art's sake," whatever that means. They denounce as inartistic any novel written for the definite purpose of presenting a principle, expressing a truth, or holding up an ideal.

It is hard to see the philosophy of this last proposition. Perhaps a work of fiction wholly purposeless may conform to this strict "law of art;" but surely a story full of purpose, a high, noble purpose may also be in harmony with that art which lifts the soul into the realm of the beautiful. Art deals with beauty, and the highest beauty centers in God. Art deals with love, and God is love. Art deals with truth, and God is the source of all truth. All of the Creator's laws are full of meaning, full of purpose. By all means let us have in literature, as in all else, "Art for Art's sake;" only let us understand what art is.

Dr. Hughes' little story with all its preaching, has become a classic. Will Mr. Crawford's Italian romances ever attain to that rank?

Have the world's greatest novelists given us purposeless stories? George Eliot was somewhat addicted to this "preaching." It is claimed that Dickens' novels have been great factors in bringing about the abolition of the unjust poor laws of England, of bettering the common schools, and correcting many other abuses. Undoubtedly, the motive that moved Dickens to write was a noble purpose. "Les Miserables," surely, was not written merely to please or amuse some idle reader. Hawthorne's "Scarlet Letter" is a mighty sermon against sin. "Uncle Tom's Cabin" was written for a purpose. It created more anti-slavery sentiment in the North than all other pamphlets and treatises combined. Bellamy has hung a score of socialistic sermons on a frail thread of romance. Not even Mr. Crawford can say that "Looking Backward" is a failure. Even that delight of boyhood, "Robinson Crusoe," is not without its sermons, as Taine in his "History of English Literature" says:

"Robinson Crusoe is quite a man of his race, and might instruct it even in the present day. He has the force of will power, etc., which formerly produced sea-kings, and now produces emigrants and squatters.

Even now we hear their mighty hatchets and pickaxes sounding in the claims of Melbourne and in the log houses of Salt Lake."

And so on down the list.

The Latter-day Saint understands that this world is not altogether a play ground, and that the main object of life is not to be amused. He who reaches the people, and the story writer does that, should not lose the opportunity of "preaching," as the author of "Tom Brown's School Days" puts it. A good story is artistic preaching. A novel which depicts high ideals and gives to us representations of men and women as they should and can be, exerts an influence for good that is not easily computed.

Transcription of this essay by Clare Wang.
Inclusion of original errata intentional.

APPENDIX

CURATED BY SCOTT HALES

Manuscript and typescript drafts of Nephi Anderson's novels are archived in the Nephi Anderson Collection, 1855 – 1939 (MS 5619) at the Church History Library of The Church of Jesus Christ of Latter-day Saints in Salt Lake City. Anderson wrote the first drafts of his novels in longhand, revised them, then typed them out using what he called his "two-finger exercise." These typescripts were also revised and, at times, extensively rewritten.

Anderson began writing *Dorian* some time around 23 May 1919, the date he first mentions the "new story" in his journal, and finished the manuscript in February 1920. The typescript was then completed one year later.

Following are transcripts of five significant deletions from the typescript archived in the Church History Library. They reveal more information about Uncle Zed's views on evolution, the intensity of Dorian's animosity for Jack Lamont, local views on gender and chastity, and Carlia's time away from Greenstreet. With the incorporation of passages from Louisa May Alcott's *Little Women* (1868) and John Townsend Trowbridge's "Midsummer" (1887), they also reveal an even more intertextual novel than what was finally published.

While some of the deletions are unfortunate, they suggest, as a whole, a desire on Anderson's part to make the novel more subtle and less didactic in its treatment of gospel themes. Moreover, they provide insight into Anderson's struggle to create characters who are at once realistic and models of good behavior for Latter-day Saint youths in the early twentieth century.

In transcribing the following material, I have tried to retain as much of Anderson's typescript errors and idiosyncrasies—deletions, insertions, etc.—as possible without sacrificing coherence. In some cases, I have corrected minor typographical errors and standardized the punctuation.

Full scans of both the manuscript and typescript
are available for download at
dorian.peculiarpages.com.

DELETION A

FROM TS CHAPTER TWELVE, PP. 121 – 122

The very first paper was in the old man's own hand, and was a comment on the evolutionist's theory that life originated on this earth some millions of years ago and developed from that ~~theme~~ <time> to this by these long ages of growth. Uncle Zed wrote:

"Life, in its various stages of progress has always existed in some place or other; therefore, life, in its so-called perfected state exists now as it always has existed. Worlds are and always have been created and endowed with life. What a waste of time and energy to have life begin on each separate world from a protoplasmic form and then have to evolve through ages of time to its present earth-stage condition! How much more reasonable to think that the germs or seeds of life in a form perfected for its environment is transplanted from a world where it exists to one ready for the planting. A gardener, having a number of plots of land would be foolish to begin with the wild rose or the crab apple from which to develop ~~by~~ perfect flower and fruit by long and slow process of cultivation, if that gardener already had these perfected products in one of his gardens from which he could transplant. Surely God is as wise as any earthly husbandman."

DELETION B

One evening when the feeling of spring was in the air, Dorian was going to call on Carlia, when he heard the approach of an automobile. As it turned into the bystreet, leading to the Duke home, Dorian saw the driver to be Mr. Jack Lamont. Dorian kept in the road, and presently the machine was close upon him, then slowed down with a signal to clear the way. ~~Honk, honk~~ <As the walker> paid no heed to the warning, and as the roadway was narrow, the automobile had to come to a full stop.

"Hi, there, can't you get out of the way?" shouted the driver.

Dorian turned. His face was pale, his jaw set. "Oh, is that you, Mr. Lamont?" he asked.

"Yes; let me get by, won't you?"

"Where are you going?"

"Well—I—I don't thank [sic] that's anybody's business, is it?"

"Yes, it's mine." He stepped from the front of the car to the side, close to the driver.

Mr. Lamont appeared as if he were going to resent this, but he seemed to think better of it as he said: "Well, I don't mind saying, seeing that you want to know so badly that I have a little business with Mr. Duke."

"Mr. Duke doesn't want to see you."

"Your knowledge is most profound."

"Yes, it is <in this respect.">

"Then, perhaps, someone else will want to see me?"

"No one at that house wants to see you."

"Indeed<!>"

"Yes—and look here, Mr. Jack Lamont, you drive right on—right on to town will be better; don't you stop at the Duke house."

"Well, who are you?"

"You know who I am."

Anger flashed from both men's eyes as they scowled into each other's faces. ~~Donald~~ <Dorian> stepped in front of the machine again.

"Get out o[f] my way, or I'll run over you", shouted the man in the ~~machine~~ <automobile>, as he started the machine.

Dorian gave way, saying as he did so: "It's all I can do to keep from drag<g>ing you from that machine; but go on. I'll be at the house in a few minutes, and if I find you there,—if I don't kill you, I'll thrash you within an inch of your life."

"The automobile speeded on, the driver casting back a derisive laugh; but ~~it~~ <he> did not stop at the Duke gate; ~~it~~ <he> went right on and soon disappeared in the distance. Dorian turned in at the gate. When Carlia saw him, she exclaimed:

"Dorian, what's the matter?"

DELETION C

FROM TS CHAPTER NINETEEN, PP. 185 – 186

The conversation ~~in such company~~ was such which should be expected of Bishop's counselors, presidents of Elder's quorums, and class leaders in the Mutual <which these men were.> On this occasion some of the always-present moral problems were discussed. The village school teacher, who that year was also trying to become a dry-farmer, was taking part in the discussion, and was claiming that the girls could do a lot in keeping the boys straight. "Here, that reminds me," he said, "of something I read i[n] my book."

The conversation ceased until the teacher had pulled his book from ~~its~~ <a> tight-fitting pocket. He held it up so that all could see what it was. "<u>Little Women</u>"

"Yes," he commented, "you are perhaps surprised that I should be taking 'Little Women' to my boys; but I have found in my experience that the boys are just as interested in the story as the girls, and it certainly carries with it a high moral tone, which is not lost on the boys. Here is the quotation I mentioned: 'Women work a good many miricles [sic], and I have a persuasion that they may perform even that of raising the standard of ~~of~~ manhood ... Let the boys be boys, the longer the better, let the young men sow their wild oats if they must; but mothers, sisters, and friends may help to make the crop a small one, and keep many tares from spoiling the harvest by believing and showing ~~and showing~~ that they believe in the possibility of loyalty to the virtues which make men manliest in good women's eyes.'"

"All very beautiful and true," said the Bishop's counselor; "but the greater responsibility rests with the boys. They should be the girl's protectors rather than their destroyers; and the boys should not only be taught this, but ~~they~~ the fact should be trained into their very being. ~~Eh,~~ Dorian, what do you have to say? You're so quiet today."

DELETION D

FROM TS CHAPTER TWENTY-ONE, PP. 200 – 204

Dorian lay at full length on the grass, looking over the valley to the distant mountains. Carlia sat near him. The red glowed in her lips again, and the roses in her cheeks. The careworn look was gone from her face. Peace had come into her heart, peace with herself, with the man she loved, and with her God.

"I wonder who's preaching at home in the meeting-house, this afternoon," said Dorian.

"You're not," she laughed.

"No; Carlia, I must confess my sins. The Bishop said he might call on me to talk today, and here I am twenty miles from the meeting-house."

"Why, Dorian, I'm surprised at you." She tapped him lightly on his uncovered head with a branch of choke-cherry blossoms which he had broken off for her.

"Oh, it was no<t> definite; ~~appointment;~~ but I'm in for an early appointment, I can see."

"Well, you're equal to it."

"Thank you. But really, I don't very often remain on the farm over Sunday. There is something about the ordained time and place for worship, and especially the sacrament which cannot be obtained in any other way."

"The sacrament. Yes, I shall miss that today."

"We'll try to make up our neglect in some other way. Where's our Bible? We'll read a chapter or two. You know, there's something about the time and place <in> which one reads which leaves its imprint for good or for evil. I always try to read the Scriptures when the environment is right for sacred thoughts."

He opened the book and read the seventh chapter of St. John. After the reading he closed the book and said:

"If Jesus needed to go to the Father for strength, how much more do we[?] That's one of the most beautiful chapters in the Bible." Then he turned to the thirteenth chapter of First Corinthians and read Paul's exposition of charity. Carlia, during the reading, looked out over the distant hills, saying nothing, only softly repeating the closing sentence, "'The greatest of these is charity'".

They both were silent for a time, then he asked, "What do you see?"

"I can't describe it."

"Let me try:
'Around this lovely valley rise
The purple hills of Paradise.
O, softly on yon banks of haze
Her rosy face the Summer lays,
Becalmed along the azure sky
The Argosies of Cloudland lie,
Whose shores with many a shining rift
Far off their pearl-white peaks uplift.'
That's from Trowbridge, one of my <boyhood> favorites.["]

"It's pretty."

"Carlia, look closely at these green bushes at which you seem to be gazing, just under the ridge. Well, there's a fine patch of service-berries there, and this year, there's a big harvest. Do you like service berries?"

"Not very much."

"They're rather sickly sweet; but there's a way to remedy that. Up that hollow to the right there is a small spring, ~~and there is~~ <where> a patch of wild goose-berries ~~there~~ <may be found.> When ripe the berries are small, but full of tart flavor. Mixed with service-berries, they make a fine preserves. I ought to know for I made some myself last summer."

The girl made no comment. She doubted not that this young man could do this successfully, if he set his hand to ~~do~~ it.

"And wild strawberries! O, girl, did you ever taste wild strawberries? This year there ~~are~~ <is> going to be a lot down in the meadow-land by the creek. It's too much of a job to pick them for preserving, but just for eating, Mm,mm. You get down on all fours, follow your nose to where the sweet smell guides you, push aside the grass where the berries hide, and then, Oh, my!"

"Is there any fish in the creek?"

"Not many. Only a few small trout. I'll catch you some for breakfast. But the stream down there serves other purposes. Many a time I listen to it when I am alone. It is about all I can hear then. When I sing or feel like singing it sings with me; when I laugh, I think it echoes me; sometimes it roars, and at times in the silence of the night, our of my half sleep, I hear it sobbing as if it had a heart which could break ... Let's go up the hill a little further," said Dorian, springing to his feet. "Here's a beautiful spot up near that quaking-asp grove, a sacred spot to me."

<"Your> Mother will not think us lost, will she?"

"No; there are no bears."

As they climbed slowly upward, Carlia gathered a bouquet of wild flowers which she stuck in the girdle of her dress. They stopped to watch the busy ants about the tiny-pebbled mound.

"Do you know," said he, "I'm always sorry when I have to plow up an ant bed. It seems cruel to destroy at one sweep what these interesting little creatures have so long and so patiently been building."

"I've often wanted to see inside one of their homes," she said, "if it could be done without ruining it. I've heard that bees and ants are wonderful creatures."

"Yes; all life is wonderful; and the wonder increases when one learns that life in one form or another is everywhere on the earth. There seems to be no spot ~~on the earth~~ so isolated or barren as not to contain life. The earth teems with life regardless of what or where man is. In that ant-bed there is a world all by itself, independent of an away from all other animal life. If I ascend to the tops of the highest mountain I can find some ~~living~~ creatures living and moving and having their being; and I suppose if I should descend to the lowest depths of the ocean, I would find the same there. The world is full of mystery, which sometimes I desperately long to solve."

~~They reached the grove and found a comfortable seat.~~ <They> were silent for ~~some~~ <a> time, letting the contentment of their love suffice.

DELETION E

FROM TS CHAPTER TWENTY-ONE, PP. 205 – 206

And so Dorian Trent and Carlia Duke, being of the pure in heart, saw much of God and His glory that afternoon.

"Dorian, what are your thoughts just now?"

"Of you, of course."

"Fibber. You are looking up in the sky."

"Well, I can see you there, can't I. I don't have to always look at your person to see you. When you were away I saw you every day; and I dreamed of you at night; one night I dreamed you came home, but you went away before I could wake up and detain you."

"That was a true dream. I did come home, and go away again."

"You have never told me that."

"I'll tell you now. About six weeks after I had left, the longing for home became so intense that I came back. I walked from the city to Greenstreet at night. It was cold, but I did not seem to feel it. There was a light in the window of our house as if it had been placed there for someone, but when I thought of what father and mother <and you> would say—and you I dared not go in. I turned and walked back to the city under the cold stars. Then—"

"That will do, Carlia. Don't tell any more. Let us try to forget the ugly past. We are living in the forgiven present, and that is worthy of all our attention. My dear girl," and he put his arms about her and drew her head <protectingly> close, and then he seemed to lack words for further expression.

"Now, what are you thinking about?" he asked at last.

"Of Mildred Brown."

"And what about her?"

"I was wondering, if she had lived, she—she would have been—a great artist."

"I don't know that, of course; but she taught me all I know about art. If she were here with us, now, she would point out to us all the colors of the rainbow in the distant mountains. She would surely want to paint this scene."

"How I did envy Mildred, what she was and what she could do and what she had—and especially what she had."

"What did she have?"

"You."

"Well, I don't deny it; but you have me now," which remark his arm made emphatic.

Then they spoke of Uncle Zed and what he had done for them, and their talked t ranged to their neighbors down in Greenstreet; and so the conversation came around <again> to their own immediate affairs.

CONTEMPORANEOUS
NOTICES OF *DORIAN*

DORIAN WAS REVIEWED IN THE MORMON PRESS.

The notices give a sense of what about Anderson's writing appealed to the general Mormon readership of the time.

FROM THE *IMPROVEMENT ERA*, FEBRUARY 1922

Dorian, a new story by Nephi Anderson, is a neatly printed volume of 223 pages. Dorian Trent, the hero, is introduced in the first chapter, as a young man who starts out to buy himself a pair of shoes. The son of a widowed mother the incidents of his ordinary life are traced through a number of years until he finally discovers his life companion. Various temptations, sorrows, and ups and down, in his career, are related in a way to hold the interest throughout. As in all of Nephi Anderson's stories, there is a splendid underlying current of religious sentiment in the pages the book. "Mormon" philosophy of earth-life and the hereafter is set forth in the teachings of a venerable character whom they call Uncle Zed. The girl heroine is Carlia and her rescue, and final setting straight, is one of the attractive themes of the story. The lives of both Dorian and Carlia teem with exciting, youthful episodes and sentiment that will attract young people. The book, as a whole, is of special interest to boys and girls, and furnishes a class of reading which aims to teach the way of righteousness in attractive story form.

FROM THE *YOUNG WOMAN'S JOURNAL*, JANUARY 1922

"Dorian" by Nephi Anderson, is an interesting story with a big major message and several minor messages. It shows the lives of simple village folk, their hardships and joys, their yearnings and achievements. It leaves the reader better for having read it. Price $1.

FROM THE *RELIEF SOCIETY MAGAZINE*, JANUARY 1922

NEW STORY BY NEPHI ANDERSON, "DORIEN." One of the best and most interesting stories written by the popular home author, Nephi Anderson, has just been printed, and the story should be in every home. It breathes a pure devotion to the best in life, it holds within its pages inspirational truth on many vital subjects, and above all, it shows that the gospel of hope lingers in the spirit and genius of "Mormonism." Make it a Christmas present to your dearest and best.

PECULIAR EDITIONS

FUTURE PECULIAR EDITIONS ARE BEING PLANNED.

TO CONTACT PECULIAR PAGES WITH QUESTIONS, PROPOSALS, ETC,
PLEASE WRITE TO PECULIAREDITIONS@PECULIARPAGES.COM.

SIMILARLY, ANY COMMENTS, SUGGESTIONS, OR CORRECTIONS
RELATED TO *Dorian* ARE EQUALLY WELCOME AT THE SAME ADDRESS.

OTHER TITLES FROM
PECULIAR PAGES

THE FOB BIBLE
edited by eric w jepson, et al.

The authors have put together an amazingly amusing work of biblical storytelling that brings new life to a tired old book. Am I being irreligious by calling the Bible tired and old? Not really. It's been around a long time. The stories have been told and retold from one generation to another. It's had its defenders and its detractors. But, in the end, breathing new life into the biblical canon can be a wonderful exercise in creative devotion ... There's pity and pathos, humor and hubris ... and will surely find a welcome place in your home.

—Jeffrey Needle,
Association for Mormon Letters

Though many of these stories have strong elements of entertainment and humor, seemingly done with ironic glee, they also present challenging experiments that remind the reader of what makes the Bible unique. While much religious fiction based on biblical stories tries to water down the inherent strangeness of the Old Testament for the sake of a commercial audience, *The Fob Bible* foregrounds the strangeness. By juxtaposing the strangeness with various literary forms and contemporary approaches, it creates a type of meta-scripture, in which literary truth is exalted over doctrinal correctness.

—Dallas Robbins,
for *Dialogue: A Journal of Mormon Thought*

None of the chapters present particularly LDS readings, but each chapter offers an opportunity for extended pondering on an oft-neglected portion of the LDS canon. If the Bible itself can be represented by a dot on a page, the Fob version is a bunch of lines running through its center, racing off in various directions ... [with] enough humor, eroticism, tragedy, and creativity to justify my strong recommendation. This one's for literature lovers.

—Blair Dee Hodges
for *By Common Consent*

OUT OF THE MOUNT:
19 FROM NEW PLAY PROJECT
edited by davey morrison dillard

Out of the Mount delivers comedy and tragedy and social commentary, allegory, politics, and healthy doses of armchair philosophy and theology in plays that mainly focus on (as most good plays do) relationships that unfold via crackling dialogue. Whether it's Clark Kent and Lois Lane applying for a marriage license or Adam and Eve feeling their way toward some sort of post-fall rapprochement or young couples falling in and out of love, these playwrights are writing for these Latter-days, even when there's nothing particularly LDS about their characters and settings. That said, what I love most about this anthology is that we get—especially with the fantastic concluding trio of "Gaia," "Prodigal Son," and "Little Happy Secrets"—works that artfully and poignantly explore key aspects of the grand drama that is the Mormon experience.

—William Morris
for *A Motley Vision*

The scripture says that through small and simple means great works will come to pass … maybe this will be part of a process that people can look back on someday and call a Mormon Renaissance.

—James Goldberg,
author of *The Five Books of Jesus*

New Play Project is a respected and vibrant force within the Mormon theatrical community. Vision is becoming reality, a prophetic fulfillment … New Play Project could still be a power player in the Mormon Arts scene for years to come.

—Mahonri Stewart
for *A Motley Vision*

FIRE IN THE PASTURE:
21ST-CENTURY MORMON POETS
edited by tyler chadwick

If I have any credibility with you regarding Mormon art, I encourage you to purchase a copy of *Fire in the Pasture* and to consume this book whole. You will be quoting from it. Lines of its poetry will invade your waking and sleeping thoughts.

—Glen Nelson,
Mormon Artists Group

With eighty-two representative poets, Chadwick provides an exhaustive look at the previous decade in Mormon poetry. For the obvious time and energy required both to assess available materials and to administer the project, Chadwick deserves high praise.

—Brent Corcoran
for *Dialogue: A Journal of Mormon Thought*

Reading this book was a thoroughly enjoyable experience. I think I have dog-eared more pages than I haven't. I highly recommend it to anyone interested in contemporary poetry.

—Dayna Patterson,
editor of *Psaltery & Lyre*

For those who erroneously believe that LDS poetry is primarily comprised of sentimental rhymed verses or charming couplets, this anthology is proof that the complexity and beauty of Mormon life can, and should, be rendered in powerful, sophisticated poetic expression.

—Angela Hallstrom,
author of *Bound on Earth*
for *BYU Studies*

Everywhere in *Fire* readers will find evidence of artistry, of control and discipline, of structure wedded to content ... of *poetry* ... *Fire in the Pasture* is not a volume to be read in a day, or a week, or perhaps in a month or longer. Page after page reveals fruits to be tasted, savored, lingered over, and transmuted into ideas and images that may change lives. Each reader will discover favorites that speak directly to the individual's mind and heart—and for that reason I have hesitated to point to particular titles that pleased me, since what I look for in poetry may not be consonant with what others seek. Instead, at one point or another, with one poem or another, the anthology is likely to feed any hunger, resonate with any need. Highly recommended.

—Michael R. Collings,
poet-in-residence emeritus
of Pepperdine University

MONSTERS & MORMONS

edited by wm morris and theric jepson

Isn't it incredible that existence even exists? So much is taken for granted, right? For anyone that ever wanted to crack open their consciousness to what might be beyond the beyond, *Monsters & Mormons* could be the read for you.

—Michael Allred,
creator of *Madman*

Perhaps the most intriguing thing that comes to mind upon reading *Monsters & Mormons* is the extraordinary range of ideas, themes, images, and tales that fit underneath the general umbrella of "Mormon" … Most of the tales could stand on their own in any anthology of horror or science fiction, regardless of their Mormon content; many are first-rate, truly exceptional examples of contemporary storytelling.

—Michael R. Collings,
author of *The Annotated Guide to Stephen King*

This anthology has discovered a bizarre yet wonderful seam of material far richer than any of the participants may have realized when they started last year.

—Dan Wells,
author of *I Am Not a Serial Killer* and *Partials*

The selections range from the cosmic and light-hearted to the poignant and provocative.

—Terryl Givens,
James Bostwick Chair of English at
University of Richmond

It's a great book with fantastic reads. Bishops battling demons, live wives meeting dead wives, aliens rescuing missionaries, vampires, and of course George A. Romero-type zombies … and a lot more, find their way into Mormon-themed plots.

—Doug Gibson
in *The Standard-Examiner*